Labor Mobility and Population in Agriculture

Labor Mobility and Population in Agriculture

Assembled and published under the sponsorship of the

IOWA STATE UNIVERSITY CENTER FOR AGRICULTURAL AND ECONOMIC ADJUSTMENT

GREENWOOD PRESS, PUBLISHERS
WESTPORT, CONNECTICUT

Library of Congress Cataloging in Publication Data
Main entry under title:

Labor mobility and population in agriculture.

Reprint of the 1961 ed. published by Iowa State University Press, Ames.
Includes bibliographies and index.
1. Agricultural laborers--United States--Congresses. 2. United States--Rural conditions--Congresses. 3. Labor mobility--United States--Congresses. 4. Rural-urban migration--United States--Congresses. I. Iowa. State University of Science and Technology, Ames. Center for Agricultural and Economic Development.
[HD1525.L25 1976] 331.7'63'0973 74-7535
ISBN 0-8371-7584-4

Originally published in 1961 by Iowa State University Press, Ames

Reprinted with the permission of Iowa State University Press

Reprinted from a copy in the collections of the Brooklyn Public Library

Reprinted in 1976 by Greenwood Press, Inc.

Library of Congress Catalog Card Number 74-7535

ISBN 0-8371-7584-4

Printed in the United States of America

Preface

ONE CHARACTERISTIC of economic growth is lag of returns to labor in farming behind that of other national sectors. This tendency has held true in the United States, just as it has for other major nations over the world. It is a long-run phenomenon. While labor returns in agriculture have pushed near the nonfarm level during periods of international wars and market developments, the long-run and world-wide persistency has been for lower returns in agriculture. This situation holds true for U. S. agriculture in the 1960's as it did three decades before.

Labor is surplus in agriculture for several reasons. One is new mechanical and biological techniques which replace it and allow remaining labor to produce more. Another is the trend in resource prices under economic growth – causing labor to become higher in price relative to capital with substitution taking place accordingly. As labor becomes surplus in agriculture, returns to labor decline, and it is encouraged to migrate to other industries where the embodiment of this resource into products and services has greater premium under economic growth.

A remarkable amount of labor has transferred from agriculture in the last several decades. The labor force of the industry has been approximately halved since 1920. It has declined by nearly 40 percent since 1940. Yet returns of the industry still are depressed relative to major nonfarm sectors. Agriculture was an extremely important element of national economic growth in early decades. It performed this role in providing a capital surplus which was drawn off with the transfer of people, taking with them the capital invested in their person and their inherited share of farm assets. Now, however, agriculture has become increasingly dependent on national economic growth and the prevention of depression to allow surplus labor to be drained from the industry.

This conference, November 8-10, 1960, was called to analyze the problem of labor supply in, and its transfer from, the agricultural industry. How much additional reduction would have to be made in the farm labor force if this avenue of adjustment is continued as a means of drawing farm income up to the level of nonfarm income? What are the characteristics of migrants, and how do they fare in nonfarm jobs? What are the impacts of migration on the rural areas from which they come and the urban areas which receive them? How well is the labor market working, in providing promising opportunity and reflection of individual capacities for persons who are faced with low returns in agriculture? What public aids and mechanisms need to be created and improved to facilitate mobility for those who thus are given greater opportunity than in agriculture? What compensation mechanisms are needed for those who cannot and should not use migration as escape from low returns? What alternatives to migration exist for solving the major problems of commercial agriculture?

The conference attempted to provide answers and hypotheses to these and other questions. It was a successful means for summarizing and interpreting current knowledge and in suggesting some areas of needed research. As with other conferences sponsored by the Center for Agricultural and Economic Adjustment, the conference was possible only by the contribution of persons from other colleges, universities and research organizations.

Earl O. Heady, Director
Center for Agricultural and
Economic Adjustment

Table of Contents

Chapter 1

D. G. MARSHALL
University of Wisconsin

Nature and Role of Mobility in Modern Society

SOCIAL MOBILITY is one factor that determines the type of social stratification to be found in any society at any particular time. Individual differences often determine the relative rank (stratification) of an individual within a particular society. A person has a certain status rank depending on his contribution to the culture. Individual variations account for ranks within certain sub-groups. The type of culture or social order determines the relative mobility of a person within and between these status groups. Social mobility is a relative term; no society is completely mobile or completely rigid. The role and/or status of an individual in a society is based on specified rules, and his anticipatory status is related to such things as his power, his abilities, his contributions to society.

Lowry Nelson in his book entitled Rural Sociology indicates that there are two types of mobility — horizontal and vertical.[1] Usually migration or geographical movement is considered horizontal mobility, while vertical mobility is movement of persons or groups from one class or status group to another; this can be either upward or downward. It is conceivable that one could have vertical mobility without horizontal mobility, although the chances are that a relationship exists.

In an article entitled "The Concept of Social Mobility," Charles F. Westoff, Marvin Bressler, and Philip C. Sagi have this to say:

> Sociologists exhibit a gratifyingly high degree of consensus in their conception of the most general meaning of the term social mobility. In his recent text, Barber offers a definition which in substance is similar to formulations appearing in nearly all treatises devoted to this topic: "We have been using the term social mobility to mean movement, either

[1] Lowry Nelson, Rural Sociology, Chap. 12, "Social mobility," American Book Company, Chicago, 1952.

upward or downward, between higher and lower social classes; (underlying rural) or more precisely, movement between one relatively full-time, functionally significant social role and another that is evaluated as either higher or lower."[2]

The term social mobility thus becomes a "sensitizing concept," useful in codifying our research, yet using broad principles.

A considerable volume of literature exists on the subject of social mobility. Taking only the American Sociological Review for the years 1959-61, this writer found that roughly one-third of the articles written in that journal dealt with social mobility. Hence, an attempt will be made to limit this paper to certain aspects of social mobility. The limits will be as follows: (a) Emphasis will be on social mobility in a contemporary society with special reference to rural United States. (b) Emphasis will be given to migration data or horizontal mobility. This does not mean that vertical mobility will be ignored, but rather that emphasis will be placed on horizontal mobility and the impact of this type of mobility. The impact of social mobility on some selected rural communities will be indicated by review of some current Wisconsin research.

THE IMPACT OF SOCIAL MOBILITY ON CONTEMPORARY AMERICAN SOCIETY

The major function of social mobility is to give less stratification within a particular culture. Because mobility is a vehicle by which social movement can be brought about, both horizontally and vertically, within a particular culture, it lessens the possibilities of developing a closed type of society.

In the United States, social mobility is probably the most important single type of social process to be found and is emphasized throughout the culture. American culture is continually dramatizing the lives of people who rose from the ranks. One of the basic premises in the American scene has been the ability of people to move from one status to another. It is assumed, for example, that people in agriculture would want to move from the farm laborer category to farm owners, or more generally they might want to move from agriculture into the nonagricultural

[2] C. F. Westoff, M. Bressler, and P. C. Sagi, "The concept of social mobility," Amer. Soc. Rev., Vol. 25, No. 3, June, 1960. The reference to Barber is from Bernard Barber, Social Stratification, Harcourt Brace, 1957.

occupations such as skilled workers, professionals, or proprietors.

Table 1.1 indicates the changes in the major occupational groupings between 1910 and 1950. The detailed analysis is found in Kurt B. Mayer, Class and Society.[3] This indicates the obvious fact that farmers have been declining from a high of 16.5 percent in 1910 to a low of 7.3 percent in 1950, and that farm laborers have been declining even more precipitously from 14.5 percent to 4.3 percent. The total farm category has declined rapidly from a high of 31 percent in 1910 to a low of 11.6 percent in 1950. There has been a shift occupationally from agriculture to nonagricultural pursuits. The growth of the white-collar category, and particularly the professional sector, has been important. In contrast, the total group in the manual category has remained stable.

Table 1.1. Distribution of the Working Population of the United States by Major Occupation Groups 1910-50

Occupation	Percent of working population				
	1910	1920	1930	1940	1950
Total	100.0	100.0	100.0	100.0	100.0*
Farmers (owners and tenants)	16.5	15.5	12.4	10.1	7.3
Farm laborers	14.5	9.4	8.6	7.1	4.3
	31.0	24.9	21.0	17.2	11.6
Professional persons	4.4	5.0	6.1	6.5	8.5
Proprietors, managers, and officials	6.5	6.8	7.5	7.7	8.6
Clerks and kindred workers	10.2	13.8	16.3	17.2	18.9
Total white-collar	21.1	25.6	29.9	31.4	36.0
Skilled workers and foremen	11.7	13.5	12.9	11.7	13.8
Semiskilled workers	14.7	16.1	16.4	21.0	19.8
Unskilled workers	21.5	20.0	19.8	18.8	16.5
Total manual	47.9	49.6	49.1	51.5	50.1

*Includes 2.3 percent "occupation not reported."
Source: Stat. Abst. of U.S., 1951, Table 220, p. 188; and U.S. Census of Population, 1950, Vol. II, Part 1, Table 53, p. 1-101.

Paul Landis in his book entitled Population Problems also describes changes in occupational patterns in the United States.[4] He shows the occupational groupings for 1820, 1840, 1870, 1900,

[3] Kurt B. Mayer, Class and Society, Doubleday and Company, Garden City, N. Y., 1955, especially p. 74, Table 5.

[4] Paul H. Landis, Population Problems, American Book Company, Chicago, 1948, especially p. 327.

and 1930. Agriculture, fishing, and forestry accounted for 72.3 percent of all the gainfully employed in the United States in 1820 and only 21.3 percent in 1930. Gainful workers employed in physical production in the United States changed from 84.7 percent in 1820 to only 51.9 percent in 1930. In contrast, professional services went from a low of 2.8 percent in 1820 to a high of 6.5 percent in 1930.

These data indicate the direction in which occupational groupings are shifting in the United States. There is no doubt the 1960 figures will confirm the pattern of development. But even though, in theory, one has the possibility of moving from one category to another in the United States, there are certain restrictions. For example, at any particular time only a certain number of people can be accommodated occupationally within a particular group. More generally, the level of development of culture determines to a large part the proportion of people it can replace in any given type of occupation at any given time.[5]

If mobility is analyzed in terms of economic shifts in the United States, the same patterns emerge since occupation is obviously related to income. Mayer employs a chart which plots the shifts in personal income between 1929 and 1952 in the United States.[6] In 1929 only 4 percent of the families and individuals in the United States made over $7,000 in personal income. In 1952 this increased to nearly 11 percent. The greatest increase, however, has been in the median income category, $3,000 to $7,000. In 1929 just over 14 percent of families and individuals in the United States had an income of $3,000 to $7,000; by 1952 nearly half of the families in the United States had incomes in this range. In 1929 nearly two-thirds of the families in the United States made less than $2,000. Even with no corrections for the difference in purchasing value of the dollar, there has been a real shift in personal income patterns in the United States. This would be consistent with the occupational shifts indicated earlier. These shifts demonstrate a gradual upward trend in occupation and economic status within the United States. Many other kinds of data could be presented such as educational patterns, professional groupings, etc., which would indicate similar movements among status categories. All the data indicate a gradual shifting upwards or a leveling off, depending on how one analyzes the status groups in our current culture.

---

[5] Landis, op. cit., p. 329.

[6] Mayer, op. cit., p. 78.

TABLE 4.4 Planned Studies of MSC Therapy for PVD

NCT number	Cell	Sponsor	Phase	N	Last updated	Outcome measures
NCT01216865	Umbilical cord MSCs	Qingdao University	I/II	50	Oct. 2010	Angiographic evaluation of angiogenesis at ischemic limb, pain, ABI, wound healing (wound size, wound stage), walking distance, rate and extent of amputations
NCT00922389	Mobilized PB MNCs	Beike Biotech India Pvt Ltd	I/II	36	Jun. 2009	$TcPO_2$
NCT01558908	Endometrial MSCs	Medistem Inc	I/II	15	Mar. 2012	
NCT01686139	ABMD-MSCs	Sheba Medical Center	I/II	10	Jan. 2014	Healing of all wounds in the target limb
NCT01903044	BM MNCs	5 institutions in Brazil and Cuba	I/II	60	Jun. 2014	Wound healing (wound size, wound stage), pain and analgesics use, QOL, improvement of the coronary and collateral circulation, amputation-free survival

ABI, ankle brachial index; *ABMD*, allogenic bone marrow derived; *BM*, bone marrow; *MNC*, mononuclear cell; *MSC*, mesenchymal stem cell; *NCT*, national clinical trial; *PB*, peripheral blood.

STUDIES ILLUSTRATING MOBILITY TRENDS

Many mobility studies could be selected, but the decision was made to take two studies centered in the North Central region; these will be considered in detail, with reference to other studies. We have first a study in an area which has heavy out-migration, low industrial development, and low income. In the North Central regional research scheme this is commonly labeled an out-low-low area. At the other end of the scale is an area labeled in-high-high or high in-migration, high industrialization, and high urbanization. A third area, not studied in Wisconsin, would be a predominantly agricultural area with modest out-migration and low industrialization. The Greene County, Iowa, study is an example of this third type. The study has been carried out by the North Central regional technical committee. Only the two types studied to date in Wisconsin will be discussed here. It is assumed that some generalizations for the United States can be made from the studies in Wisconsin.

The first study is Price County, Wisconsin — an out-low-low area. The present situation in Price County is summarized in a research bulletin.[7] Findings that have special reference to mobility are:

1. Occupational diversity. Few open-country people were found to be exclusively engaged in a single occupation. Over a fourth of the families combined farm and nonfarm work. This indicates a mobile situation, occupationally speaking, within the population. In this case mobility acts as a positive force, allowing persons to have more than one job to supplement their relatively low income.

2. Low incomes. Most of the open-country people with low incomes, that is, making less than $2,000 in 1956, were found to be mainly in farm or farm with part time nonfarm work, and in retired groups. Income is again related to status and age groupings within the society. As Lowry Nelson indicated, mobility is a function of aging and of the aged categories.[8] It was found that the small size of the farm enterprise was particularly associated with low incomes. In Price County, lack of mobility has been in many ways a deterrent to higher income. This is consistent with Mayer's comment that it is possible to have a

---

[7]Jon A. Doerflinger and D. G. Marshall, "The story of Price County, Wisconsin: population research in a rural development county," AES Res. Bul. 220, University of Wisconsin, Madison, June, 1960.

[8]Nelson, op. cit., p. 220.

coexistence of flexibility and rigidity within a society, both having their effect on status.[9]

3. Abnormal age distribution. The population has many older people and few working age persons compared with the state as a whole. Age is found to be related to disability. The aged population also contributes materially to the low income situation. The open-country family heads doing nonfarm work tend to be younger than farmers. Age was also related to educational attainment, with older groups having less education. A number of mobility relationships are suggested here. If any one thing stands out, it is the definite relationship of the age factor to mobility within the society. Older people tend to be less mobile, primarily because of lack of education, lack of income, etc. They are unable to move in many cases from a community, even though they may wish to do so. In this case, lack of mobility is a major factor bringing about an abnormality in the age distribution in a particular area. The results, for the most part, have a negative impact on the communities.

4. High out-migration of youth. The evidence suggests that youth have left the county in large numbers in the past and are continuing to leave at present. Through mobility, the youth are being drained from many of the low-income agricultural communities into urban communities. This has many implications for a community. Many communities are losing their young educated potential leaders. On the other hand, this high out-migration acts as a positive factor in taking excess population from an agricultural community, allowing those who leave the opportunity to move occupationally and status-wise into other classes in society.

Mobility, at least geographical mobility, does not in itself solve the adjustment problem. In many cases, the movement has been so great in so short a time that the adjustment of both communities and individuals has been very difficult. In fact, in many areas, including Price County, Wisconsin, population losses have been so great in some communities that adjustment of the people to the institutions has been very difficult, if not impossible.

Migration (horizontal mobility) in Price County has been very selective. This in turn has had both a positive and a negative impact on both the people staying in the communities as well as on those leaving. For the most part, the young people complete high school before they leave the community, with the result they have been able to make a more satisfactory adjustment in the urban setting than earlier generations. On the other hand, many middle

---

[9] Mayer, op. cit.

aged and older age groups are unable to leave even though they might wish to do so. This acts as a negative force in many communities.

The situation is quite different in an area of high in-migration, high industrialization, and high urbanization. A study in Kenosha County, Wisconsin,[10] is under way. Although the data at this point are tentative, many different situations are being found. For one thing, there are more high income patterns; there are only about half as many reported incomes of less than $2,000 in Kenosha County as in Price County. In contrast to the abnormally heavy old age distribution in Price County, Kenosha County tends to have a more normal age pattern with fewer, proportionally, in the age group 65 and over. Kenosha County also retains a much higher proportion of its youth; many of them stay within the county but move from rural to urban areas. This also implies an occupational shift, which tends to confirm the Landis thesis that in many cases people make a geographical move (horizontal mobility) to achieve a vertical move or to better their status.[11] For the most part, it seems that the adjustments of individuals and communities are made more easily in an area of heavy in-migration, high industrialization, and high urbanization. This does not mean there are no problems of adjustment. There are, for example, still a large number of farmers even in a good land area, such as Kenosha County, who are employed off the farm to supplement their income. In fact, Kenosha County has an even higher proportion of farmers than Price County not farming 100 days or more per year. This indicates that many are making economic adjustments. This adjustment is being made throughout all of rural America regardless of whether it is a low income or high income area.

All in all, the research cited here in the two opposite types of rural situations indicates that social mobility is a basic social process that allows people and communities to make the adjustments necessary to accommodate the changing scene in agriculture and rural life in America.

---

[10] Jon A. Doerflinger, "Kenosha County, Wisconsin, study: an overview of the social effects of population change, Report Number One," Department of Rural Sociology, University of Wisconsin, Mar., 1961.

[11] Landis, op. cit. Chap. 23.

Chapter 2

LARRY SJAASTAD

University of Minnesota

Occupational Structure and Migration Patterns

THIS CHAPTER is concerned with migration behavior and the occupational structure of the American economy. The pattern of broad geographic movements over time will be observed first. Next off-farm migration from 1930 to 1960 will be reviewed to determine trends as well as any relation to aggregate economic variables. Finally it will be shown whether the characteristics of the migrant population, primarily with respect to age and occupation, are favorable for continued high levels of migration.

MIGRATION

Geographic

Geographic migration in the United States strongly reflects two related features of our growing economy: decline of agriculture and rapid development in the West. Streams of migration out of the old South, the Great Plains, and northern New England, coming largely at the expense of agriculture, have been sufficient to occasionally offset natural increase, leaving static populations in their wake. The major industrial states of the East and Middle West, occupying fairly neutral positions, have experienced but few sharp changes in population due to migration in recent decades. At the other extreme, however, are the rapidly growing areas of the West and Southwest (and Florida). Since 1930, several of these states have grown fully as much or more from in-migration as from their natural increase. Since the farm-nonfarm migration aspect is so clearly evident in these geographic patterns, special attention is given to it later.

This regional redistribution of population is growing. During the decade of the 1940's, North Dakota lost the largest percentage —

approximately 20 percent — of its population through net out-migration. Migration supplemented California's average population in excess of 30 percent.[1] These magnitudes, larger than anything experienced in the previous decade, are in turn surpassed by estimates for the 1950's. Migration rates by state for the three decades, 1930-60 are presented in Table 2.1.[2]

One of the more striking impressions conveyed by these data is the strong correlation between the three sets of estimates. The population flows, in and out, have tended to be in the same directions from 1930 to 1960. It is also worth noting that there has been a substantial increase in magnitudes of migration (rates) since the 1930's. By the "bracketing rule" we estimate that overall migration rates increased between 36 percent and 98 percent from the 1930's to the 1940's, and between 8 percent and 53 percent from the 1940's to the 1950's.

This increase in mobility has taken place in spite of the fact that there has been little or no increase in income inequality since 1930. It is true that absolute differentials have widened somewhat, but the percentage differences have fallen sharply.[3] Moreover, it is argued that the reduction in relative interstate dispersion arises from "wage equalizing shifts within industries" rather than from increased industrial homogeneity of the several states.[4] Interstate migration without change of industrial affiliation apparently has become relatively less attractive from the income incentive viewpoint. Thus the United States population is

---

[1] These estimates are made employing the census survival rate technique. For each census of population we know the number of people by race and sex for several age categories. We also know the percent of those people expected to survive the ten years to the next census (based upon national averages). By comparing the expected numbers with the actual numbers one can estimate to what extent the population has been augmented or depleted by migration. These estimates have been prepared in detail for age, sex, and race categories for each of the states, 1870-1950. See Ann R. Miller, et al., Population Redistribution and Economic Growth, United States, 1870-1950, Vol. I; Methodological Considerations and Reference Tables; American Philosophical Society (Philadelphia: 1957); directed by Simon Kuznets and Dorothy Thomas.

[2] Estimates of population change due to migration for the 1950-60 decade are not available in the Kuznets-Thomas Study. However, crude estimates for that period can be made by applying the national growth rate (17.5 percent) to the 1950 population as reported by the 1960 Census of Population. These estimates were made and are recorded in Table 2.1 as a percent of the average population, by state, for the 1950-60 decade. This procedure is essentially an approximation and assumes, among other things, that (1) immigrants from abroad settled in each state in proportion to the population of that state, and (2) birth rates and death rates were identical by state.

[3] The coefficient of variation of relative interstate differentials in per capita personal income has fallen from 37 to 41 percent during 1929-32 to a level of 21 to 24 percent since 1945. See Frank A. Hanna, State Income Differentials, 1929-54, Duke University Press, Durham, North Carolina, 1959, p. 6.

[4] Ibid., pp. 145-50.

Table 2.1. Population Change Due to Migration, As a Percent of Average Population, by State, for Three Decades

State	1930-40	1940-50	1950-60
Maine	-0.2	-4.6	-12.4
New Hampshire	2.1	-2.0	-5.0
Vermont	-5.7	-7.2	-15.3
Massachusetts	-1.7	-0.7	-8.6
Rhode Island	-0.4	0.4	-11.3
Connecticut	2.5	5.4	6.6
New York	3.3	0.7	-5.3
New Jersey	-0.7	4.9	6.1
Pennsylvania	-3.3	-4.8	-10.6
Ohio	-0.9	2.3	3.1
Indiana	0.4	1.7	-0.2
Illinois	-0.8	-0.3	-2.9
Michigan	0.4	4.9	3.7
Wisconsin	-0.4	-3.2	-3.3
Minnesota	1.5	-6.3	-4.0
Iowa	-3.2	-7.7	-13.1
Missouri	-0.6	-4.8	-9.1
North Dakota	-17.9	-19.8	-15.8
South Dakota	-17.2	-12.8	-14.1
Nebraska	-11.3	-10.4	-11.7
Kansas	-9.6	-5.2	-3.4
Delaware	6.9	5.5	17.7
Maryland	5.5	11.6	11.5
Virginia	*	5.8	-0.3
West Virginia	-4.5	-12.2	-26.9
North Carolina	-2.9	-6.1	-6.1
South Carolina	-6.4	-9.9	-6.2
Georgia	-5.0	-7.8	-4.2
Florida	18.3	24.8	42.2
Kentucky	-3.8	-12.4	-15.4
Tennessee	-0.6	-3.7	-10.2
Alabama	-6.8	-10.5	-11.6
Mississippi	-4.9	-18.3	-18.7
Arkansas	-7.6	-18.7	-26.2
Louisiana	0.3	-5.1	2.3
Oklahoma	-13.0	-17.8	-14.6
Texas	-1.3	2.1	4.5
Montana	-4.0	-8.5	-4.4
Idaho	4.8	-6.1	-5.0
Wyoming	-0.1	-1.9	-5.0
Colorado	0.1	3.0	11.7
New Mexico	4.8	2.0	17.3
Arizona	-0.9	24.2	39.6
Utah	-6.5	1.2	9.4
Nevada	14.4	25.1	42.2
Washington	7.3	19.6	0.9
Oregon	10.1	21.3	-2.3
California	17.2	31.7	23.1
Simple Average	-0.82	-0.64	-1.28

*Not available.

clearly becoming more mobile in an absolute sense, and, more importantly, more mobile with reference to relative income incentives.

Farm — Nonfarm

One of the most significant single aspects of human migration in the twentieth century United States has been the unrelenting movement of labor out of agriculture. In a 25 year period following 1929, over 18 million farm people (three million short of our current farm population) migrated to cities and towns. Even with rural farm birth rates historically exceeding nonfarm rates, this out-migration produced a 28 percent decline in the farm population while the total population of the United States expanded 32 percent. Since immigration accounted for roughly 10 percent of the natural increase in U. S. population, it follows that since 1929, off-farm migration reduced the farm population by about 28 percent. In its absence that population would have experienced about an equal amount of growth (assuming the same rate of natural increase as in the nonfarm sector).

If anything, the number of off-farm migrants increased since 1940, in spite of the decimated population base. During 1935-39, the average annual migration as estimated by the U.S. D.A., amounted to about 570,000 individuals, while for 1950-58, it averaged some 900,000. The earlier figure represents a loss of less than 2 percent of the farm population annually; the latter about 4 percent per year for the first nine years of the 1950-60 decade.

The U.S.D.A. data have several undesirable qualities.[5] First they are largely for changes in residence — a change from a farm to a nonfarm residence (and vice versa) in any given year. Such a move does not necessarily imply a shift from a farm to a nonfarm job. As will be apparent later, a substantial number of farm-nonfarm movers do in fact retain agricultural jobs. Secondly, the data are subject to a relatively large sampling error.[6] This source of variation seriously reduces the usefulness of the single year migration estimates for quantitative analysis. In

[5] USDA, AMS, "Farm population ... migration to and from farms, 1929-54," AMS-10, and "Farm Population Estimates," AMS-80 (annual series).

[6] Between April, 1955, and April, 1956, the farm population estimates indicated an increase of 100,000, which is well within the range of frequent sampling error. With no change in farm population, the probability is 0.45 that the survey would show an increase greater than 100,000. USDA, AMS-80 (1956), op. cit., p. 1.

addition, the estimates are on an April 1 to March 31 basis, which makes them not comparable with most other series of economic variables.

A crude adjustment on the data to partially correct sampling error as well as render the series more comparable with other annual data is a two-year moving average. The observation for 1950, for example, becomes the average from April 1, 1949, to March 31, 1951. While the adjusted migration series is a slightly leading series by definition, the lead is offset, and even reversed in some cases, by the nature of the migration swings. A comparison of peaks and troughs in Table 2.2 shows that the averaged series frequently lags the raw series but never leads it.[7]

Inspection of the series in Table 2.2 suggests immediately that the rate of off-farm migration is related to the business cycle. The three post-World War II recessions are reflected, and in 1957 the unadjusted series actually indicates a (temporary) reversal of the net off-farm trend.[8] Percentage unemployment rates are perhaps the best single index to reflect the manner in which swings of the cycle are likely to affect off-farm opportunities for potential migrants and hence the rate at which they abandon agriculture. For any given income differential between farm and nonfarm employments, the flow rate should respond to the ease or difficulty of obtaining a nonfarm job after migration. High levels of unemployment in the nonfarm sector can seriously reduce the immediate income gain the potential off-farm migrant

[7] In Table 2.2, the years 1941-46 are omitted. These are years of heavy net migration to and from the military, which should not be ignored in looking at civilian migration. Military migration can surely be a substitute for civilian migration. Had migration from farms to the armed forces been less in the years 1941-43, one would expect that civilian off-farm migration may have been even larger, the reverse being true for 1945 and 1946. However, it would be in error to assume that all off-farm migration, both civilian and military, would have taken place without the war (apart from its stimulation of the economy).

Adjusted estimates for the war period were made by assuming that half of the gross migrants to the military would have left the farms in any case. For the years 1940-44, net migration is estimated as civilian minus returns from the military plus one-half of the gross flow to the military. This leaves 1,027,000 persons having left the farms but which have not been counted as migrants during these years. These were allocated as off-farm migrants during the 1945-47 period in direct proportion to the gross returns to the farm of persons from the military. Essentially it was assumed that these people left the farm during the 1940-45 duration but migrated from the farms by taking nonfarm jobs upon discharge from the military. In most of the analysis of this data, the years 1941-46 are omitted, but the adjusted observations for 1940 and 1947 were used, as was 1946 in computing the moving average.

[8] This reversal does not appear in revised estimates recently published by the USDA, which unfortunately were not found until the analysis was complete.

Table 2.2. Migration From Farms to Cities, Towns, Villages, and Armed Forces As a Percent of Beginning-of-Year Farm Population

Year	USDA annual estimate	Two-year moving average of USDA annual estimate
1929	1.56	----
1930	1.00	1.28
1	-0.26	0.37
2	-1.04	-0.65
3	1.49	0.23
4	1.28	1.38
5	2.00	1.64
6	2.17	2.09
7	1.69	1.93
8	1.36	1.53
9	1.89	1.63
1940	1.95	1.92
....	....	....
1947	6.48	3.75
8	1.43	3.96
9	5.06	3.25
1950	5.20	5.13
1	1.12	3.16
2	8.22	4.67
3	5.16	6.69
4	0.42	2.79
5	1.16	0.79
6	10.05	5.61
7	-0.46	4.80

can reasonably expect.[9] If a reduction in unemployment is current, he can easily defer his move to a future date.

Several migration series for various time periods were correlated with the percent unemployment of the civilian labor force. The aggregate unemployment rates are intended as proxies for the unemployment levels prevailing in the occupations which

[9] D. Gale Johnson estimates that off-farm migrants have a labor capacity approximately 90 percent of that of nonfarm people of the same age and sex. See "Comparability of labor capacities of farm and nonfarm labor," Amer. Econ. Rev., June, 1953. By weighting the 1950 median income of the 10 broad occupation groups by the distribution of all employed males, 14 years and over, their average 1950 income is estimated at $2699. The occupational distribution of male off-farm migrants, 14 and over, yields an estimate of $2348, only 87 percent of the income for all males. Similarly, an age correction alone yields an estimate of off-farm migrants which is 88.6 percent of that for all males (over 14). By using Johnson's adjustment, the male off-farm migrants could, in 1950, expect an income between 80 and 87 percent of the average in the total employed male labor force. Note that these estimates are based upon medians rather than means.

off-farm migrants move into in large numbers. The latter "effective" rates would be more relevant but cannot be constructed for a sufficiently long period.[10]

The correlations shown in Table 2.3 are all negative, and some are surprisingly high — particularly in view of the level of aggregation. The regional concentration of agriculture as well as the "proxy" nature of the unemployment rates would lead one to expect that aggregate United States data may not be well correlated. Nevertheless, there can be no doubt that employment conditions in the nonfarm labor market are a crucial variable for off-farm migration. Furthermore, it is much more plausible that off-farm migration is suppressed by rises in unemployment (in the nonfarm sector) rather than unemployment being affected appreciably by that migration. The sign of the correlation coefficient is negative. If off-farm migration were causing the higher levels of unemployment, a positive correlation should result. While off-farm migration may contribute to unemployment during down swings, it cannot be the dominant factor. In addition the net off-farm migration in the years preceding rises in unemployment is relatively small compared to those rises. Even if all off-farm migrants became unemployed upon migrating, they can account for only a portion of the increased unemployment. Thus one can reasonably interpret the correlations in Table 2.3 as implying that farm-nonfarm migration is seriously impeded by surplus labor in the nonfarm sector.[11]

While unemployment measures are strongly related to the rate of off-farm migration, only a weaker correlation is found for measures of (relative) farm income. Here there exists a serious aggregation problem. One can plausibly argue that labor leaving agriculture is essentially facing a national market, and hence a national unemployment rate is somewhat relevant. Such is not the case for farm income measures. Because of the variability in crops and prices in space, national farm income need not reflect the income position of any one region. The South, for example, has about one-half of the total farm population in the United States, yet this is precisely the area most insulated from the effects of farm price changes over time. If off-farm migration was purely an income maximizing choice, a change in farm

[10]Some implications of using the aggregate unemployment rates are discussed later in this section.

[11]The fact that the squared correlation coefficient between unemployment and the two-year moving average of migration rates is more than twice as large as the one using the single year estimates of migration is consistent. It is assumed that averaging does remove errors in measurement of the migration series, especially since the unemployment variable explains a greater amount of absolute variance in the averaged case than when actual estimates are used.

Table 2.3. Correlation of Unemployment Rate of Civilian Labor Force and Net Off-farm Migration Rates – United States, 1930-57 Inclusive

Time period	N	USDA annual[a] migration est.	Two-year[a] moving av.	Three-year[b] moving av.	r^2
1930-40, 1947-57	22	X			(-) 0.23*
1930-40, 1947-57	22		X		(-) 0.60**
1930-40, 1947-57	21			X	(-) 0.45**
1934-57[c]	24		X		(-) 0.22**
1934-40, 1947-57	18		X		(-) 0.62**
1934-40, 1947-58[d]	19		X		(-) 0.48**

[a] Table 2.2. Moving average for year t is simple average of USDA estimate for year t and t-1.
[b] Computed from Table 2.2. Observation for year t is simple average of USDA estimate for years t-1, t, and t + 1.
[c] War year observations (1940-47) are adjusted as described in footnote 7.
[d] Migrating observations for 1953 through 1958 based upon revised USDA data.
*Significantly negative at the 5 percent level.
**Significantly negative at the 1 percent level.

prices and income at the national level will not necessarily be accompanied by a commensurate change in off-farm migration. While one expects a strong link between (relative) farm income and the rate at which people leave agriculture, aggregation weakens this link – perhaps more so than in the case of the unemployment hypothesis.[12]

The partial regression coefficients for the relative farm income variables in Table 2.4 are negative in the instances when most significant. They generally contribute very little to the explanation of off-farm migration rates.[13] Additional statistical

[12] The obvious solution, disaggregation, is restrained by data limitations, the main problem being that readily available regional income data do not reflect the amount of off-farm income earned by farm people. That income is of growing importance, and is obviously a good substitute for farm income.

[13] The simple correlations between the income ratio and off-farm migration are quite strongly positive, particularly for the years excluding World War II. The squared correlation coefficient between the revised migration series and single year income ratios for the 19 years (1934-40 and 1947-58) is (+) 0.33; when the moving average income series is used, it goes to (+) 0.36. This positive correlation between the rate at which people leave agriculture and the income level of agriculture, represented by parity ratios, has been noted by at least one investigator. See G. A. Mumey, "The parity ratio and agricultural out-migration," Southern Econ. Jour., July, 1959. Of course, there is no real reason to expect that parity ratios are even a good proxy for agricultural income levels relative to nonagricultural alternatives since they ignore the latter, and furthermore the changing technology in agriculture places the entire parity concept in deep suspicion. In any case, Mumey's conclusions might have been different had he run a multiple regression with unemployment as one of the independent variables.

Table 2.4. Regression Coefficients, Standard Errors, and t-Ratios for Regression of Net Off-farm Migration[a] (U.S.) in Relative Farm Income and National Unemployment Rates, United States

Reg. Eq.	Period	X_1	X_1	X_2	N	R^2
1.	1934-1957[b]		-12.99†	-0.25**	24	0.31
			(7.77)	(0.06)		
			-1.67[d]	-3.98		
2.	1934-1958[c]	-6.94		-0.18**	25	0.23
		(7.05)		(0.07)		
		-0.98		-2.73		
3.	1934-1958[c]		-8.58	-0.20*	25	0.24
			(7.52)	(0.08)		
			-1.14	-2.41		
4.	1934-40, 1947-57[b]		-7.57	-0.25**	18	0.67
			(5.77)	(0.06)		
			-1.31	-4.07		
5.	1934-40, 1947-58[c]	2.86		-0.12*	19	0.49
		(5.15)		(0.05)		
		0.56		-2.27		
6.	1934-40, 1947-58[c]		2.79	-0.12†	19	0.32
			(6.57)	(0.07)		
			0.42	-1.72		

Variable Identification:

X_1 = Single year farm-nonfarm per capita income ratio.

X_1' = Two-year moving average of X_1.

X_2 = Percentage unemployment of civilian labor force.

[a] Dependent variable is always two-year moving average of USDA estimate of net off-farm migration rate.

[b] Dependent variable not revised by most recent estimates.

[c] Dependent variable computed from revised USDA estimates for 1953-58.

[d] Regression coefficients and standard errors were rounded to two-decimal places after computation of t-ratios.

† Significantly different from zero at the 10 percent one-tail level.

* Significantly different from zero at the 5 percent one-tail level.

** Significantly different from zero at the 1 percent one-tail level.

investigation of these migration rates was made using Department of Commerce farm and nonfarm income estimates. Unfortunately, these estimates do not include income of farm people from nonfarm sources. While the results were similar to those presented in Table 2.4, the income variables were even less significant.

Similar regression analyses were made of the out-migration rates for two regions, the North Central and the South. Together they contain over 80 percent of the United States farm population.[14]

[14] In 1958, it was estimated that 48.8 percent of the United States farm population resided in the South, with 32.9 percent in the North Central; AMS-80, 1958, op. cit.

The independent variables were the national unemployment rate and the ratio of regional per capita farm to nonfarm income for that region as well as for the United States as a whole.[15] For both regions, the relative farm income variable failed to be significantly negative, but unemployment rates were again very important, more so in the South than the North Central region. However, the unemployment regression coefficient was significantly less negative for the North Central region than for the United States; but this difference between the two regions does not reflect different behavior, as it is largely explained by the occupational mix of the migrants within these regions. Since the unemployment rate is generally not the same for all occupations (at a given point in the business cycle), the "effective" level of unemployment as well as the variance of that level over the cycle need not be identical over all occupational mixes. In the regional regressions, the unemployment rate of the civilian labor force is essentially a proxy for the effective unemployment rate facing off-farm migrants; and its variance is substantially less than that of the effective rate. Adjusting for this difference in variance accounts for most of the gap between the regional coefficients.[16]

It would be an error, I think, to conclude that income differences are not a relevant force influencing off-farm migration. The income variables employed are crude and the level of aggregation is high. The migration series is subject to considerable sampling error, and the equations fitted are certainly less than perfectly specified. Even with these limitations, some evidence was found of a negative relationship between off-farm migration and relative levels of farm income. I might suggest that improvement of the income measures to take into account factors such as skill and educational levels, further disaggregation, a development of a more sophisticated "permanent income" concept may be

---

[15] The income measure is the ratio of per capita (wage and salary plus proprietor's) farm income to per capita (wage and salary plus other labor plus proprietor's) nonfarm income. Property income was excluded as that income can easily be independent of place of residence.

[16] The occupational mix of off-farm migrants in 1950 and national unemployment rate for each of the occupations since 1950 are known. By assuming that the occupational mix of off-farm migrants is unchanged since 1950 and that the incidence of unemployment, by occupation, is identical by region, we define "effective" unemployment rates facing off-farm migrants as national rates weighted by the occupational mix for the respective region, for each year, 1950-58. The ratio of the variance of the unemployment series used to the variance of the effective unemployment rate yields the adjustment factor for the coefficients. The adjusted coefficients are those estimated if in effect unemployment rates were used rather than the rate for the civilian labor force. In addition to the assumptions above, this last step assumes that the variance relationship as measured also prevailed during the period prior to 1950 for which the necessary data are not available.

productive areas of research for understanding off-farm migration more fully.[17]

The implications of the strong relationship between labor market conditions, as reflected by unemployment, and the rate at which people leave the farm for nonfarm occupations are obvious. The regression coefficients obtained suggest that a rise in national unemployment from three to seven percent is associated with a drop in the percent of farm people that leave agriculture annually by up to one percentage point. If past trends in agricultural supply conditions continue into the future, necessitating further reductions in the absolute size of the farm labor force, maintenance of full employment conditions outside agriculture should substantially facilitate that out-movement. To date, the reasons advanced for a full employment policy generally do not include reference to the "farm problem," but well they might. It is becoming increasingly clear that the solution to that problem lies in the factor and not the product markets, and the evidence presented above makes a strong case for stimulation of factor markets by maintenance of full employment.

OCCUPATIONAL DIFFERENCES AND TRENDS

The Age Effect

The occupational distribution of the migrant population is quite different from that of the population as a whole, part of which stems from the very strong tendency for migrants, particularly off-farm, to be a relatively young population. In this section we determine the effect of this age selectivity on the types of occupations favored by migrants. In particular, we shall see to what extent age structure alone can explain the occupational differences between migrants and nonmigrants. If migrants within age groups tend to distribute themselves among occupations much like the rest of the population, the implications are clearly different than if they concentrate themselves in a few occupations to the exclusion of others.

[17] In particular, it is to be noted that ratios of farm to nonfarm per capita income were consistently employed. The implicit assumption in using ratios is of course that the "equilibrium" differential between farm and nonfarm income, resulting from cost-of-living differences, tastes, etc., is a constant percentage over time. The validity of this assumption has not been tested, although some tentative investigation was done with absolute differences first deflated by the Consumer Price Index and secondly by per capita farm income. Neither of these appeared more promising than the ratios actually used, but the evidence was admittedly scanty. Efforts to estimate this "equilibrium" differential, if any, should be a first step to any further time-series or cross-sectional analysis of off-farm migration.

Table 2.5 presents the 1950 age distributions for the total population of the United States and for individuals migrating during the year preceding the census.[18] The youth of the migrant group is immediately evident, that of farm-nonfarm migrants particularly so. Nearly 60 percent of the farm-nonfarm migrants and about 50 percent of all migrants were under 25 years of age, with only slightly more than 40 percent of the total population in this category. This is roughly true for both sexes. It is also worth noting that farm-nonfarm migrants are exceptionally concentrated in the 14-19 age bracket. This is about the time they are entering the labor force, while the nonfarm migrants are not substantially more frequent in that group than the total population. Off-farm migrants are thus likely to be less experienced workers than either the nonfarm migrants or the population as a whole.

Table 2.5. 1950 Age Distribution of Total U.S. Population and of Migrants by Type of Residence[a]

Total population		Migrants		
Age group	(percent)	Total (percent)	Farm to nonfarm (percent)	Nonfarm to nonfarm (percent)
1-13	24.0	23.4	25.4	22.2
14-19	8.7	10.7	18.0	9.9
20-24	7.8	15.6	14.8	16.2
25-29	8.3	13.6	9.8	14.7
30-34	7.8	9.3	6.8	9.8
35-44	14.4	12.0	9.9	12.3
45-64	20.6	11.2	11.1	11.0
65+	8.3	3.8	4.3	3.8
Total	99.9	99.9	100.1	100.2
		MALES ONLY		
1-13	24.8	23.1	25.3	21.9
14-19	8.8	10.4	16.6	9.7
20-24	7.7	15.2	14.9	15.7
25-29	8.1	14.2	10.1	15.2
30-34	7.7	9.8	7.0	10.3
35-44	14.3	12.7	10.4	12.9
45-64	20.7	11.4	11.4	11.1
65+	7.9	3.3	4.2	3.1
Total	100.0	100.1	99.9	99.9

[a]Computed from 1950 Census of Population, Special Report PE No. 4D, Tables 1-4.

[18] A migrant is defined as an intercounty mover during a period no longer than one year preceding the census.

Table 2.6 compares the 1950 occupational distributions of employed males (14 years old and over) for the total and migrant populations. Since the 10 occupations are arranged in descending order by median income received in 1949, it is clear that nonfarm migrants, in spite of their youth, have a superior occupational distribution. The off-farm group is of a decidedly inferior allocation, income-wise, when compared to employed males in the total population. Off-farm migrants are apparently quite a different group than the migrants as a whole, even after taking account of age, the reason for which is fairly obvious. Migrants whose residential classification changed from farm to nonfarm are more likely to have simultaneously changed occupations than are the nonfarm migrants. While the one distribution reveals largely how off-farm migrants allocate themselves among occupations, the other is probably more indicative of the relative mobilities of individuals already in given occupations.

By a simple device one can ascertain to what extent the differing frequencies of the various groups in occupational categories can be explained by age. Assume that within each age group, the farm-nonfarm migrants are distributed among the occupations in the same manner as the population as a whole. By so allocating the migrants among the age groups and summing across them

Table 2.6. 1950 Occupational Distribution of Employed Males, 14 Years and Over, for Total Population and Migrants, by Type of Residence, United States[a]

Occupation	Total population	Migrants[b]		
		Total	Farm to nonfarm	Nonfarm to nonfarm
Managers, officials, and proprietors	10.7	9.6	4.4	11.4
Professional and technical	7.3	13.1	3.3	15.8
Craftsmen and foremen	18.6	17.2	15.1	19.3
Sales	6.4	8.0	4.2	9.4
Clerical	6.4	5.6	3.1	6.6
Operatives	20.1	17.9	25.7	18.9
Service workers	6.0	5.2	6.1	5.9
Laborers (except farm and mine)	8.1	8.3	16.6	8.2
Farmers and farm managers	10.3	6.2	5.3	0.8
Farm laborers and foremen	4.8	7.5	15.0	2.6
Occupation not reported	1.1	1.2	1.3	1.2
Total	99.8	99.8	100.1	100.1

[a] Computed from 1950 Census of Population, Special Report PE No. 4D, Tables 1, 2, and 4.

[b] Nonfarm-farm migrants are omitted, hence percentages in total column need not appear as a weighted average of other two.

within the 10 occupations, one obtains "expected" frequencies. These would prevail if the farm-nonfarm migrants do not differ from the total population in their occupational choice. This has been done for several groups of employed males, 14 years or older, and the results are tabulated in Table 2.7.

In the total population, 10.7 percent of the employed males are in the managerial, official, and proprietor classification. Only 4.4 percent of the farm-nonfarm migrants are in that group. After correcting for age, the expected frequency is 8.1 percent. Thus, age could explain 2.6 of the total deviation of 6.3 points. The expected distribution minus the actual distribution gives the residual not explained by age alone. This residual is expressed in the last column of Table 2.7 as a percent of the expected value. The frequency of off-farm migrants in the managerial category for example, is about 46 percent less than expected if off-farm migrants were distributed identically as the total population. This residual can only be explained by occupational selectivity peculiar to male off-farm migrants.

For the distribution of male farm-nonfarm migrants, the sum of the absolute deviations from that of employed males, 14 years and over, is 48.7 points. In some cases, age explains none of the deviation, but in others it can explain a total 12.7 points, over one quarter of the total deviations. The remaining three-quarters are necessarily due to other factors. Looking at the nonfarm migrants, age is quite unsuccessful in explaining the deviations. Only about 10 percent are accounted for. This is consistent with the previous judgment that the differential rates for the nonfarm migrants reflect, if anything, the mobility rates among the occupations, rather than occupational selectivity of the migrants.

The remaining computations summarized in Table 2.7 largely speak for themselves. Among the higher income occupations, the male off-farm migrants are much less frequent than their age distribution would suggest. The nonfarm migrants are more frequent. Just the reverse is true in the lower income categories, with minor exceptions. Farmers and farm managers are less numerous than expected among farm migrants (but farm laborers and foremen more than twice as frequent). The service workers are more frequent among the nonfarm migrants.

Two facts emerge clearly from Table 2.7. In an absolute sense, off-farm migrants in 1950 were highly concentrated in three occupations: craftsmen and foremen, operatives, and laborers. These three accounted for over 70 percent of their total nonfarm employment. Relative to their age, they are more highly concentrated among laborers and operatives than the total population, indicating some relative advantage for these occupations.

Shifts in the composition of the labor force increasing the share of these two occupations will be especially advantageous to off-farm migration, the converse being true as well.

Regional computations of the expected occupational frequencies reveal much the same thing.[19] In each of the four regions, the greatest relative concentration of off-farm migrants is in the category of operatives and laborers. Likewise, the absolute frequencies favor the craftsmen and foremen category. Only minor regional differences in actual frequencies exist, with migrants in the South and West being more concentrated in the laborer category and the latter being substantially weaker in the operative group.

The sum of the positive (or negative) differences between actual and expected distributions estimates the percent of the migrants required to shift occupations in order that they fit the occupational structure of the respective employed male labor forces. The results of this computation are shown below for several groups and several regions:

Migrant Group	Region	Sum of positive residuals
Nonfarm-nonfarm	United States	15.0
Farm-nonfarm	United States	18.9
	Northeast	19.4
	North Central	15.3
	South	19.2
	West	23.5

Clearly the off-farm migrants within the North Central region are best adapted to the occupational structure of their region in the sense that they fit it more closely than is the case for other regions or for the United States as a whole. The next best fit is for the South; the poorest is for the West where almost a quarter of the migrants lie outside the total occupational structure. This might be interpreted as encouraging, as the overwhelming majority of the farm population are currently living in the North Central and South.[20]

[19] The regional computations could be made only for migrants within the respective regions; no data were available for the composition of all migrants by region. However, most migrations are within regional limits; for 1949, the ratios of migrants (14 years and over) within regions to total migrants by regions ranged from a low of 0.707 for the West to a high 0.790 for the South. The source of the regional data is 1950 Census of Population, Special Report PE No. 4D, Tables 6 and 10.

[20] The interpretation is not unambiguous; the "good fit" of off-farm migrants for the regions where they are most plentiful may be a result of their large numbers and not an indication of superior adaptability or a favorable labor force composition. Small numbers of migrants, relative to the size of the labor force they are moving into, may well concentrate themselves into a few of the most advantageous occupations, while areas experiencing a relatively large influx may absorb them only through a broader distribution among occupations.

Table 2.7. Actual and Expected Occupational Distribution of Employed Male Migrants 14 Years and Over, United States, 1950

Occupation	Total population: Employed males 14 yrs. and over (percent)	Farm-nonfarm migrants: Actual (percent)	Deviation from male population	Expected (percent)	Amt. of dev. explained by age	Residual as a percent of expected
Managers, officials, and proprietors	10.7	4.4	6.3	8.1	2.6	-46
Professional and technical	7.3	3.3	4.0	6.8	0.5	-51
Craftsmen and foremen	18.6	15.1	3.5	16.8	1.8	-10
Sales	6.4	4.2	2.2	7.1	----	-31
Clerical	6.4	3.1	3.3	7.1	----	-46
Operatives	20.1	25.7	-5.6	22.2	2.1	16
Service workers	6.0	6.1	-0.1	5.6	----	2
Laborers (except farm and mine)	8.1	16.6	-8.5	9.1	1.0	82
Farmers and farm managers	10.3	5.3	5.0	8.2	2.1	-35
Farm laborers and foremen	4.8	15.0	-10.2	7.4	2.6	103
Occupation not reported	1.1	1.3	----	----	----	---
Total	99.8	100.1	48.7[a]		12.7	
			Nonfarm—nonfarm migrants			
Managers, officials, and proprietors	10.7	11.4	-0.7	9.0	----	27
Professional and technical	7.3	15.8	-8.5	7.6	0.3	108
Craftsmen and foremen	18.6	19.3	-0.7	18.3	----	5
Sales	6.4	9.4	-3.0	6.7	0.3	40
Clerical	6.4	6.6	-0.2	7.1	0.2[b]	-7
Operatives	20.1	18.9	1.2	21.4	----	-16
Service workers	6.0	5.9	0.1	5.3	0.1[b]	11
Laborers (except farm and mine)	8.1	8.2	-0.1	8.6	0.1[b]	-5
Farmers and farm managers	10.3	0.8	9.5	8.7	1.6	-91
Farm laborers and foremen	4.8	2.6	2.2	5.3	----	-51
Occupation not reported	1.1	1.2	----	----	----	---
Total	99.8	100.1	26.2[a]		2.6	

[a] Sum of absolute values.

[b] Age over-explains deviation from total population value.

The off-farm male migrant, presumably due to his youth and farm background, undoubtedly is more narrowly confined in his occupational choice than the nonfarm migrant or even that part of the population of nonfarm birth. Because of the regional divergency in occupational composition in the United States, some areas obviously will be more favorable for future off-farm migrations than others. This question is considered in the section that follows.

Occupational Trends Over Time and by Region

Above it was found that male off-farm migrants, for both the United States as a whole and by regions, tend to concentrate in three occupations: craftsmen and foremen, operatives, and laborers. Further, they avoid, both relatively and absolutely, the professions, managerial, clerical, and sales occupations. One cannot assert that the fortunes of off-farm migrants will be completely tied to the relative expansion or contraction of these occupations, but there surely is some connection. This connection is stronger the greater the extent to which previous training of off-farm migrants limits their range of opportunities in the nonfarm sector. In particular, the level of education of off-farm migrants is inferior to that of the population as a whole, for ages 14 years or better. This low level of education attainment will certainly restrict many off-farm migrants from entering some occupations. For this reason, the impact on these migrants of changes in the relative earnings of skilled versus unskilled occupations expected to accompany any wholesale upgrading of the occupational distribution would probably be minor, at least in the short run. One can with reasonable validity, then, assume that the elasticity of substitution of the supply of off-farm migrants between skilled and nonskilled jobs is small. It is necessary to assume, in addition, that changes in the structure of the labor force are exogenous with respect to the supply of off-farm migrants, which seems quite reasonable since currently less than 10 percent of our population lives on farms.

Table 2.8 shows the occupational distribution of employed males, 14 years or over, in the nonfarm sector for three years (1940, 1950, and 1958). It reveals that each of the categories where off-farm migrants are especially abundant are relatively declining, with the possible exception of craftsmen and foremen. On the other hand, the professional and the managerial categories have made substantial gains, the former having increased its share by 60 percent from 1940 to 1958. However, while two of

Table 2.8. Nonfarm Occupational Distribution of Employed Males, 14 Years and Over – United States, 1940, 1950, and 1958

Occupation	1940[a] (percent)	1950[b] (percent)	1958[c] (percent)
Managers, officials, and proprietors	12.8	12.8	15.0
Professional and technical	7.2	8.7	11.5
Craftsmen and foremen	19.0	22.2	21.4
Clerical and sales	16.7	15.3	14.3
Operatives	23.8	24.1	21.5
Service workers	9.0	7.2	7.3
Laborers (except farm)	11.4	9.7	9.1
Total[d]	99.9	100.0	100.1
Total[d] (numbers)	----	33,911,607	38,456,000

[a] Computed from 1940 Census of Population, Vol. II, "Labor force," Part 1, Table V.
[b] Computed from 1950 Census of Population, Special Report PE No. 4D, Table 2.
[c] Computed from Bureau of Census, Current Population Reports, Series P-50, No. 89, Table 14.
[d] Excludes those in "Occupation Not Reported" category.

the three occupations especially favored by farm out-migrants have failed to maintain their relative positions, they have made absolute gains. As this expansion continues, they should readily absorb off-farm migrants. If these occupations should begin declining in absolute terms – begin releasing workers – off-farm migration will be hurt; this prospect seems unlikely.

A brighter picture prevails at the regional level. Table 2.9 shows the shift in occupation shares for the four regions from 1940 to 1950. In both the North Central and the South, which contain over 80 percent of the farm population and have recently furnished even a larger percentage of annual out-migration, the operative category shows a rise in relative share over the decade, while in the West and the Northeast it declined. Since 1950 the operative share of the United States labor force has fallen, but judging from the 1940-50 experience, one would expect that this would move more at the expense of other regions than the South and the North Central. In addition, there is rapid growth of the craftsmen and foremen group, which, although it attracts fewer off-farm migrants than one would expect, is important in the migrant distribution. The universal decline in the laborer category is, on the other hand, detrimental.

The conclusion emerging from available data on occupational distribution is not strongly unfavorable for off-farm migrants. The occupational distribution is not depreciating rapidly, especially

Table 2.9. Nonfarm Occupational Distribution of Employed Males 14 Years and Over, for Regions 1940 and 1950

Occupation	Northeast 1940[a]	Northeast 1950[b]	North Central 1940	North Central 1950	South 1940	South 1950	West 1940	West 1950
Managers, officials, and proprietors	11.8	12.7	13.1	12.2	12.7	12.6	14.6	14.6
Professional and technical	7.3	9.2	7.2	8.4	6.6	7.9	8.3	10.2
Craftsmen and foremen	19.1	21.7	20.4	23.2	17.1	21.3	19.1	23.0
Clerical and sales	17.6	15.9	17.2	15.4	15.0	14.2	17.1	15.6
Operatives	25.1	24.3	24.2	25.3	23.7	24.7	19.9	18.9
Service workers	9.2	7.9	7.7	6.7	9.8	6.8	10.2	7.5
Laborers (except farm)	10.0	8.2	10.1	8.7	15.1	12.3	10.8	10.1
Total[c]	100.1	99.9	99.9	99.9	100.0	99.8	100.0	99.9

[a]All regions computed from 1940 Census of Population, Vol. II, Labor Force, Part I, Table 64.
[b]All regions computed from 1950 Census of Population, Special Report PE 4D, Table 6.
[c]Excludes those in "Occupation Not Reported" category.

in those areas where those migrants are most plentiful. In addition, those occupations favored by off-farm migrants continue to grow in absolute terms. Further it must be remembered that the farm population is declining rather rapidly. Past migration out of agriculture has been sufficient to reduce the farm population by almost a third since 1930, while the nonfarm sector grows. An additional shift of one million workers from agriculture should have more far-reaching effects on agricultural income but, at the same time, be more readily absorbed by the nonfarm sector simply because that number is an ever-decreasing portion of the total nonfarm labor force. Even with some further deterioration of the relative number of jobs best suited to off-farm migrants, growth in the absolute number of such jobs is likely to continue in the face of an almost certain decline in the number of off-farm migrants. For if this migration were to continue at an average of about one million per year, the farm population would completely disappear within another three decades. While it would be hazardous to suggest the extent of future diminution of the farm population, the important fact is that any conceivable reduction can be realized within at most a couple of decades at current out-migration rates (assuming no sudden increase in farm birth rates). Viewed in this fashion, a fairly optimistic outlook is justified; the long run aspects of our farm income problem appear less formidable.

SUMMARY AND QUALIFICATIONS

The trend in the United States is toward greater mobility of labor, both geographically and occupationally. The direction of broad geographic movements reveals a high degree of stability over the past three decades and have been largely at the expense of agricultural states and advantageous to industrial states. Migration levels into and out of the several states have clearly increased, this increase coming in spite of declining relative income differentials. Some evidence was found that geographic migration is reaching an ever-faster pace with respect to absolute income gaps as well.

Off-farm migration, found to be highly volatile over time, is also increasing (both absolutely and as a percent of the parent population) such that since 1950 an average of about 4 percent of the total farm population left agriculture each year. That such a high pace of evacuation can continue for an extended period of time is remarkable in itself, and cannot conceivably continue indefinitely if for no other reason than complete exhaustion of farm labor. Unemployment in the total labor force is the key variable explaining fluctuations in the rate of out-movement from agriculture, this being true regionally as well as nationally. Both the level and the variation of unemployment in those occupations most favored by off-farm migrants is substantially higher than is the case for the total labor force, which presumably accounts for the volatile nature of off-farm migration over the post-war business cycles.

The structural changes in the nonfarm labor force are not viewed as unduly adverse to continued high mobility of the male farm population. While those nonfarm occupations most frequently chosen by these migrants during their first year represent a slightly declining share of the total labor force, the rapid growth of the nonfarm sector relative to the number of potential migrants from agriculture is an off-setting development.[21] The immediate threat to continued high rates of off-farm migration suggested by past trends in the nonfarm occupational structure appears far less serious than that of rising levels of unemployment.

The conclusion I would venture is that long-run prospects of American agriculture are improving with each passing year. As the relative size of the farm sector diminishes, a greater ease of adjustment to even further revolutions of supply should result. It is conceivable that with a conscientious maintenance of full employment and no blunders in government farm policy, an alleviation of the farm income problem may reasonably be anticipated. This is not to be construed as meaning, however, that additional policies aimed at facilitating the adjustment are neither necessary nor desirable, especially at a regional level.

[21] The occupational analysis, it is to be noted, was limited to males, but the implications of the declining farm sector hold for females as well.

Chapter 3

VARDEN FULLER
University of California

Factors Influencing Farm Labor Mobility

MOVEMENT OF FARMERS from their farms and out of agriculture is only one of many possible forms of farm labor mobility; however, it is the one that seems to be of central interest to agricultural economists. The farmer who stays behind and absorbs the land of the migrating farmer has mobility. The farmer who supplements his farm work with outside employment has mobility. A farm tenant who becomes an owner has mobility. The person who newly enters or returns to farming has mobility. Adjustments and changes that must fall within the general category of mobility can and do take many forms. Those involving hired farm labor cannot be omitted in the full analysis, notwithstanding the propensity of most persons to do so.

In the broadest form of the concept, mobility embraces all forms of fluidity, of adaptability and capacity to respond to stimuli. But such an inclusive concept is not operational for those who seek to measure the magnitude of mobility or to identify its determinants. The analyst then must restrict himself to selected fragments of mobility that are definable and measurable. Thus, industrial labor market analysts have come to depend upon movements among employers, occupations, industries, and localities for concept and measurement of something they – sometimes cautiously – call mobility. Similarly, agricultural economists take up the ready image of movement off farms as concept and measurement of farm labor mobility, even though they have been warned by Bishop and others of its insufficiency.[1]

Mobility is elusive in both concept and measurement. In industrial labor markets, there is, for example, the problem of distinguishing between labor turnover and the maximizing behavior that economists recognize as mobility. In agriculture there are counterpart problems of distinguishing movement and mobility.

[1] U.S. Congress, Joint Economic Committee, Policy for Commercial Agriculture, 85th Cong., 1st Sess., 1958, p. 437.

For example, if migratory workers settle out of migratory work patterns and diversify their occupational base in one location, has their mobility increased or declined?

Ultimately, the significance of any concept of mobility lies not in the identification and measurement of mobility acts in the past but in the assessment of capacities and propensities to be mobile that may apply in the days to come. If our main interest is to know how many farmers will leave their farms in this decade under various possible combinations of circumstances, fundamental knowledge of human motivation and behavior would be more useful than detailed statistics of past movements. This includes even the details of the attributes of those who moved and the circumstances surrounding their movements. One need only think about farm population projection for the 1950's based on the evidence of 1920-40 to clinch this point. Nevertheless, the much more cosmic hypotheses about rural commitments, creeds, and values which undertake to get at the question of why seem even less useful in projecting what people are likely to do. Consequently, the estimates of prospective behavior and the types of policies and programs that may influence it in desirable ways must rest mainly on knowing what we can of the characteristics of those who have been mobile in some defined sense and the combinations of circumstances under which this mobility has occurred.

In this chapter I shall: (1) attempt to integrate some of the research findings concerning mobility behavior from the literature of industrial labor markets; (2) project that movements out of agriculture are likely to be substantially smaller in the 1960's than in the 1950's; and (3) argue that acceleration of mobility is not, as such, a proper objective of public policy.

GENERALIZATIONS FROM MOBILITY RESEARCH IN INDUSTRIAL LABOR MARKETS

The literature of industrial labor market research contains much that is instructive to those who would understand the influences underlying mobility of farm people. Had this literature been more utilized, those who have written complainingly about the apparent nonmaximizing behavior of farm people would possibly have done more sophisticated work. The same goes for those who have claimed that the principal missing ingredient to enhanced movement is information on job opportunities, such as public employment services are presumed to provide. Industrial jobholders do not contrast sharply with farm people in their resistances to being wage maximizers within the premises of the classical model.

From this literature, I draw three main conclusions which I believe are relevant to the subject at hand:

1. The maximization goal of workers is a considerably more complex bundle than is assumed in the classical equilibrium theory.
2. Voluntary decisions of workers to change their employment are restrained and conditioned by a generally prevailing anxiety about change, which is to say that certainty in the immediate present has more value than most model builders are inclined to give it.
3. Private and personal information, although it may be subjective and not reliable, plays a greater role than does public and official information in the job decisions of industrial workers.

On the matter of maximization, Charles A. Myers of the Massachusetts Institute of Technology offers a conclusion that other investigators have corroborated and accepted:

> ... These findings, taken together with the material here presented, suggest the fallacy of attempting any universal generalizations on 'what workers want in a job.' The answer will depend on what they already enjoy in their work, which is, in part, a function of the time dimension. In short, we can expect that changing business conditions (among other variables) will affect the relative importance that workers attach to various job satisfactions, and hence will affect their willingness to move from one job to another.[2]

Based on her own investigations in Philadelphia and upon the findings of others, Gladys L. Palmer concludes that the rationale of job changing does not clearly emerge from the series of transactions within a given period of time. She says systematic behavior patterns may be observed over the span of work careers. Miss Palmer generalizes that:

> ... Over time, a process of 'accommodation' appears to take place in which the worker's initial vocational aspirations are adjusted to the economic realities of the job market in his community and are increasingly restricted to a consideration of opportunities in the occupation or industry in which he finds that he has some proficiency and to which he considers himself attached. The work record over time may therefore reflect more consistent and purposeful movement than the activities at any particular point in time. Even a high degree of immobility represented in a lifetime of experience in a single plant is not necessarily the result of ignorance or irrational behavior.[3]

---

[2] "Labor mobility in two communities" in Labor Mobility and Economic Opportunity, The M.I.T. Press, Cambridge, Massachusetts, 1954, pp. 75-76. Note also the concurring comment of Gladys L. Palmer in her article in this volume, "Interpreting patterns of labor mobility," p. 63.

[3] Ibid., p. 62.

Perhaps, job seeking by those who are unemployed or are newly entering the labor market is a closer counterpart to the situation faced by farm people than is job changing by those already situated within a labor market. Assuming this, the work of Adams and Aronson of the New York State School of Industrial and Labor Relations, Cornell University, is of immediate interest.[4] They studied the adjustments that followed the preannounced shutdown of the major employing plant in Auburn, New York, with the aim of gaining knowledge of the capacity of workers to meet the problems of industrial change. Among many important conclusions are these:

> The findings of this study do not contradict the theory that differential net advantage produces movement, but they qualify it severely. It was only when there were job openings, and this is perhaps the most important qualification, that workers did voluntarily change jobs in order to improve wages and working conditions or other aspects of work. Voluntary movement of this kind accounted for a majority of the changes recorded in the work histories and observed in the experience in Auburn during the expansion of employment resulting from the Korean War.[5]
>
> Changes of industry and occupations in the case of the displaced workers were not a matter of choice but of sheer availability of jobs. A small proportion of these workers found new jobs with higher pay or better conditions, but this outcome was mostly the accidental result of the opportunities available at the time. Most of the workers who found employment after the shutdown took jobs with lower pay or less satisfactory working conditions than they had enjoyed at Harvester. This was because such openings were the only ones available in the local labor market at the time.[6]

I shall leave this brief glimpse of industrial labor mobility with two germane impressions. First, the complex of needs and desires that a person attempts to maximize in his job and career experience is multifaceted and subject to variation by many influences. Even in periods of full employment, workers feel so uncertain about their chances of obtaining work that eliminating uncertainty by taking something that may be had assumes a high value as compared with extended shopping around for a possible better choice. Since workers are generally apprehensive about exposing themselves to unemployment and since the economy offers very little assurance against it, it follows that high-level employment is a necessary, but not in itself sufficient, condition to induce voluntary mobility. This applies whether one is thinking about either intra- or intermarket mobility. Considering that

---

[4] Leonard P. Adams and Robert L. Aronson, Workers and Industrial Change, Cornell University Press, Ithaca, 1957, p. 209.

[5] Ibid., p. 161.

[6] Ibid., p. 162.

off-farm mobility involves complex intermarket and interregional transfers, as well as the reshaping of the work satisfaction complex, the amount of movement from farms that has occurred in the past two decades is quite astonishing. The nation is fortunate that the pockets of rural poverty left by the two decades of intense and unplanned economic change are not worse than they are.

DIMINISHED PROSPECTS FOR OFF-FARM MIGRATION IN THE SIXTIES

I argue that the prospective economic environment of the '60's will be less favorable to continued large-scale off-farm migration. This proposition rests essentially on three major points: (1) The economy will have the burden of absorbing the extraordinarily large number of new labor force entries resulting from the sharp upturn in birth rates after 1940; (2) at the same time, automation and new technology will put a premium on young persons with good high school and college training, to the disadvantage of those whose age, education, and other attributes do not make them readily adaptable to specialized job training; and (3) the large ex-farm population will be a massive and influential source of opinion, information, and rumor bearing upon the decisions of those still on farms.

The research of Luebke and Hart in the Southern Appalachian area demonstrates the great value placed upon environments and associations that are familiar and comparatively certain as against an inevitably uncertain "pot of gold somewhere else."[7] These investigators also determined that decisions on whether to migrate rested heavily upon informal channels of information reflecting the reported experiences of those who had migrated or had unsuccessfully attempted to do so. Martin's work in Weakley County, Tennessee, confirms these findings and also demonstrates that only in periods of sustained high employment does the comparative disadvantage facing the less well-educated potential migrant tend to disappear.[8]

The general dimensions of the manpower issues in prospect have been projected by the U.S. Department of Labor. Its popular brochure, Manpower: Challenge of the 1960's, is a convenient source. It shows that the number of persons reaching eighteen

[7] B. H. Luebke and John Fraser Hart, "Migration from a southern Appalachian community," Land Econ., Vol. 34, No. 1, Feb., 1958, pp. 44-53.

[8] Joe A. Martin, "Off-farm migration: some of its characteristics and effects upon agriculture in Weakley County, Tennessee," Tenn. Agr. Exp. Sta. Bul. 290, Knoxville, Aug., 1958.

will jump from 2.6 million in 1960 to 3.8 million in 1965 and for the next five years will exceed the 1955-60 rate by nearly 50 percent. Similarly, the number of new workers entering the labor force through the 1960's is projected to be 50 percent above the new entries of the 1950's.

Two papers given at the 1960 annual meeting of the American Statistical Association further emphasized the sharply different manpower prospects for the '60's. They presented the difficulties that will be confronted in providing needed work and in effectively utilizing the national manpower resources. I refer to the papers of Robert J. Meyers, deputy commissioner of labor statistics, and Louis Levine, deputy director of the Bureau of Employment Security.[9]

Officially and formally in many other ways, the employment question has become a major concern. Nevertheless, in the September 29, 1960, issue of The Reporter, Sar A. Leviton, under the title "Our Creeping Unemployment," pays his respects to the perceptiveness of economists, social scientists, and politicians by saying:

> Economists have been slow in grasping and appraising the impact of this trend. Absorbed in the problem of full employment and inflation and busy creating myths about the middle-class suburbanite American worker, social scientists have paid little attention in the postwar period to problems created by unemployment. Even more surprising in this particular year, politicians have been more or less indifferent too.

The persistence of unemployment rates in the range of 5 to 6 percent, coupled with the inevitable changes in labor supply and demand, does not add up to a favorable picture for the absorption of low-income farm people in large magnitudes. And, if this complex or a similar variant is the reality of the next several years, one can expect that the news passed back by those who have left farms will be sufficient to restrain voluntary farm leavings, regardless of what the policies and programs to accelerate migrating may be.

THE BASIC QUESTION IS PRODUCTIVE CAPACITY, NOT MOBILITY

These prospects impel me to another line of argument which I have held passively for several years and which now seems

[9] Robert J. Meyers, The Labor Force and Unemployment in Mid-1960, 29pp. Mimeographed. Louis Levine, Characteristics of the Insured Unemployed: A Tool for Economic Analysis, 21pp. Mimeographed.

more urgent. This is whether the widely made appeals for accelerated off-farm migration are addressed to the proper question. It has been commonly recommended that proper therapy for several of the pathologic conditions in agriculture required some people to move somewhere else. Various notions of income disadvantage have been the principal element of the syndrome. For some writers, the prescriptive image has been that people should not persist in agriculture if they can do better elsewhere. For others, the image has been that somebody should get out of agriculture so that those who remain can do better. Although the validity of these propositions (especially the latter one) is suspect, I will press on to my own allegation that both fail to address basic pathology. If the prescription is right, it is by chance.

The essence of democratic society is not maximum or equal income but equal and unrestrained opportunity to be productive. Identifiable pockets of poverty may be attributable to disabilities in an area economy or to disabilities in the population or to a combination of the two. Out-migration from such a pocket may relieve the burden upon an under-par local economy, but it is likely only to transfer elsewhere the disabilities of its migrating populace. Disabilities associated with poor education, poor physical or mental health, or discrimination should presumably be as solvable in place as elsewhere. Such problems are not actually solved by getting them out of sight or through attenuation elsewhere, regardless of whatever asepsis that may occur in the income statistics of the places of evacuation.

Under the circumstances in prospect, it is important that a distinction be recognized between the development of capacity to be productive and therefore to be mobile as against the more superficial notion of motivating the movement of disadvantaged people to some place where it is assumed they will be better off. If primary emphasis is placed on developing capacity, it may be found that preferred solutions can be found for many within the locale of their present domiciles. Proposing better education, of course, is not unusual. Moreover, it is usual to imply that the immediate purpose of better education is to enhance mobility. For example, D. Gale Johnson in his December, 1959, paper to the American Economic Association[10] emphasized primary and secondary education in farm areas. He also clearly regards this education as being valuable because it will better prepare people to move somewhere else. What I am attempting to say is let us have the educational, health, and manpower policies that will

[10] D. Gale Johnson, "Policies to improve the labor transfer process," Amer. Econ. Rev., Vol. 50, No. 2, May, 1960, pp. 403-12.

result in capable, self-dependent people and leave the question of where and at what they will work to them.

Direct attack upon disabilities and incapacities of people who are poor is mainly appropriate to the general agencies concerned with health, education, and welfare at the several levels of government. There are additionally some specific ways in which agricultural economists might be useful. If my analysis is in the right direction, part-time farming and off-farm employment will both increase in this decade. Accordingly, agricultural economics research could redirect its emphasis from farm income to family income from all sources. It could be concerned more fully with effective complementary relations between agricultural and nonagricultural occupations.

My analysis also implies that farm consolidations will not be as rapid in this decade. If so, agricultural economics research could fruitfully be concerned with external as well as internal economies of scale and with alternative ways of attaining both types of economy independent of actual changes in scale of individual firms.

Finally, there are the questions of central or regional location of industry. These issues are complex. Yet, it would seem that the grim realities of huge cities and their chaotic suburban sprawls ought to motivate industry leadership and planners to constructive thinking about possible ways to overcome the forces to centralization. The papers of Perloff and Welch[11] and the work of Nicholls and Tang in the Tennessee Valley and Piedmont are good examples of what economists can do in aid of such constructive thinking.

[11] Harvey S. Perloff, "Lagging sectors and regions of the American economy," Amer. Econ. Rev., Vol. 50, No. 2, May, 1960, pp. 223-30. Frank J. Welch, "The evolving low-income problems in agriculture," Amer. Econ. Rev., Vol. 50, No. 2, May, 1960, pp. 231-42.

Chapter 4

C. E. BISHOP[1]
North Carolina
State College

Economic Aspects of Changes in Farm Labor Force

SINCE 1920 there has been a net migration of approximately 27 million people from farms to nonfarm areas in the United States.[2] During this period about 68 million people actually migrated from farm to nonfarm areas, but about 41 million migrated in the opposite direction. This leaves a net migration of 27 million. Continued net migration from farms to nonfarm areas is taken as evidence that farm people achieve higher levels of living by migrating. Our interest in migration is primarily from the standpoint of the apparent increase in efficiency of labor use associated with the transfer of farm people to nonfarm areas and with the apparent inefficiency associated with people who return to farms.

In a highly dynamic economy, labor mobility is essential for most efficient use of resources. Economic and technological conditions change at different rates in different segments of the United States economy. In this process opportunities are created for increasing the productivity of labor by transfer of labor among uses.

The demand for labor on farms is derived from the demand for farm products. The demand for labor on farms also is affected by the rate at which other resources can be substituted for labor in the production of farm commodities.

From 1940 to 1960 the technical rate of substitution of labor and other resources in farming in the United States changed radically. The development of machinery and equipment increased the marginal productivity of capital relative to that of labor. Consequently, it has been profitable to substitute machinery and other forms of capital for labor in farm production.

Productivity of labor in farm uses also has increased rapidly.

---

[1] The author is indebted to T. D. Wallace and J. C. Williamson, Jr., of North Carolina State College, for their helpful suggestions.

[2] Source: Farm Population Estimates for 1950-59, USDA, AMS-80, Feb., 1960.

The rate of increase in productivity of farm labor has exceeded the rate of increase in demand for farm products. It now is profitable, therefore, to produce the volume of farm products needed with less labor than was previously the case.

It may be seen in Figure 4.1 that, on balance, labor has migrated from farm to nonfarm areas in all but four years since 1920. The number of persons who migrated, however, has varied substantially from year to year. It is the purpose of this chapter to appraise the migration of labor from farm to nonfarm areas with respect to the behavior that would be expected under conditions of underemployment of labor in agriculture. It shall be my task, therefore, to indicate first the patterns of labor migration that would be expected to occur under conditions of underemployment of labor in agriculture and, second, to confront these hypotheses with empirical data to see whether farm people are in fact transferring labor in accordance with the postulates of economic theory.

THE CONCEPT OF UNDEREMPLOYMENT

Farm labor is underemployed when the marginal real return received for labor services in farming is less than the marginal real return received for comparable labor in other uses.[3] Underemployment may be considered from the standpoint of the individual owners of resources or from the standpoint of society. From the standpoint of society, underemployment implies that there would be a social gain from the transfer of labor from one use to another even though the individuals concerned might not necessarily regard the transfer as profitable. In other words, there may be a conflict of interests between society at large and the individuals owning labor resources. Such a situation may arise when farm people place a high value on nonpecuniary returns. In such cases, compensation to resource owners for damages incurred in migration may be necessary to encourage migration in line with social interests. Here, however, I shall comment primarily on those aspects of underemployment pertaining to individual owners of resources and shall consider social and individual interests as compatible.[4]

From the standpoint of individual resource owners, a

[3] C. E. Bishop, "Underemployment of labor in agriculture," Jour. Farm Econ., Vol. 36, May, 1954, pp. 258-72.

[4] For a discussion of the preference problem and underemployment, see C. E. Bishop, "Public policy and the low-income problem," Farm Policy Forum, Spring, 1955.

meaningful definition of underemployment must give due weight to nonpecuniary as well as to pecuniary considerations. The definition of underemployment in terms of real income as used here, therefore, implies that there is labor in agriculture which is willing to move to other employment at prevailing rates of return for labor. Under these conditions, labor of a specified quality is underemployed for one of three reasons: (1) capital is not available to finance the transfer of labor among uses; (2) people in agriculture do not know of opportunities for employment of labor in higher paying uses; or (3) alternative jobs simply are not available at the prevailing wage, i.e., there is rationing of jobs which prohibits labor from transferring freely among industries.

The effective supply of nonfarm labor may well be limited by the amount of capital available for transfer of labor from farm to nonfarm employment. It is the opinion of this author, however, that this particular impediment to labor mobility is not of sufficient importance to explain the differential in returns for labor services in farm and nonfarm employment. Studies have illustrated that costs involved in transferring labor from farm to nonfarm residences even for long distances in the United States are rather trivial.[5] Furthermore, the rate of migration from farms in the United States is highest in low income areas. The rate of migration from farms in low income areas is about 20 percent greater than the rate of migration from agriculture as a whole.[6] It is expected that the rate of migration is greatest from low income areas. This causes us to question the importance of lack of capital as an impediment to labor mobility.

A second type of underemployment may result from lack of information by farm people of the availability of nonfarm jobs. In this case nonfarm employers are likely to view underemployment as resulting from failure of the supply of labor for nonfarm employment to increase in line with increases in demand. Underemployed laborers, on the other hand, are likely to view the problem as one of insufficient increase in demand for nonfarm labor. From the viewpoint of potential migrants, obtaining information relative to additional employment opportunities in effect shifts the demand curve for labor to the right; that is, it increases the number of people who transfer from farm to nonfarm employment without altering their willingness to respond to differences in returns for labor services.

---

[5] J. G. Maddox, "The private and social costs of migration of people out of agriculture," Amer. Econ. Rev., Proceedings Issue, L, No. 2, May, 1960, pp. 392-402.

[6] Gladys K. Bowles, "Farm population net migration from the rural farm population," 1940-1950. Stat. Bul. No. 176, USDA, AMS, Washington, D.C., June, 1956.

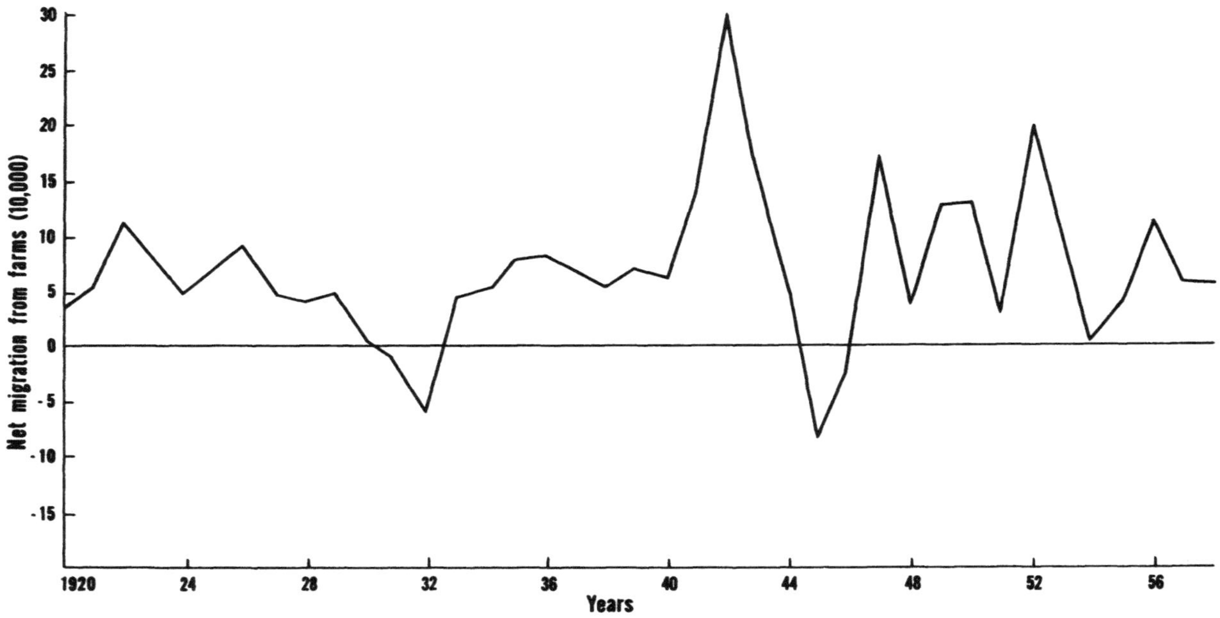

Fig. 4.1. Net migration from farms, United States, 1920-58.

Although lack of knowledge of job opportunities undoubtedly was important as an impediment to migration at an earlier time, I suspect that its importance has decreased. Large numbers of people do migrate, and patterns of migration are fairly well established. It is reasonable to assume that those who migrate communicate fairly accurate information about conditions in the communities to which they migrate. During the last four decades over 41 million people migrated from nonfarm areas to farms. Admittedly, these people may have given biased views of conditions in nonfarm employment, but they also must have communicated much information that was accurate.

As the farm population continues to decline relative to the nonfarm population, the information that farm people have with respect to living conditions and earning opportunities in urban areas is likely to become more accurate. It seems reasonable, therefore, to expect lack of knowledge of economic and social conditions in nonfarm areas to become less of an impediment to migration of farm people.

A third type of underemployment exists when more labor is willing to transfer to nonfarm jobs at prevailing rates of return than jobs are available.[7] In this case, job rationing limits migration. The supply of labor to nonfarm firms is essentially infinitely elastic in the relevant range. Labor stands ready and willing to transfer from farm to nonfarm employment at prevailing farm and nonfarm rates of return for labor. Under these conditions the actual rate of migration is determined by shifts in demand for labor in nonfarm employment.

New technology in the United States is largely labor saving both in agriculture and in nonagricultural industries. In their efforts to reduce costs, firms adopt this new technology as rapidly as is feasible. Faced with organized labor and relatively high and rigid wage rates, nonfarm firms concentrate on labor-saving invention and innovation and on plant relocation as means of decreasing costs rather than on recruitment of labor from areas characterized by underemployment and on wage reductions.[8] Since growth in the market for farm products is limited by low price and income elasticities of demand, growth in aggregate

---

[7]W. E. Hendrix, "Income improvement prospects in low-income areas," Jour. Farm Econ., Vol. 41, Dec., 1959, p. 1070. See also C. E. Bishop, "The mobility of farm labor," Policy for Commercial Agriculture, Hearings before the Joint Economic Committee, Washington, 1957, pp. 437-47.

[8]The price of labor in the United States has been increasing relative to the price of other factors. Under these conditions there is an incentive to focus research upon labor-saving inventions. See J. R. Hicks, Theory of Wages, Macmillan Company, 1932, Chap. 6.

levels of employment is determined in large part by the rate of growth in the nonfarm sectors of the economy. This rate of growth has not been sufficient to absorb the labor released from agriculture as rapidly as farmers are able to free this labor. Hence, labor that is willing to transfer to nonfarm positions at current relative rates of remuneration for labor is dammed up in agriculture. This is the third type of underemployment.

AN ECONOMIC ANALYSIS OF MIGRATION

If underemployment of farm labor developed in a perfectly functioning economy, one would expect that labor would transfer from farm to nonfarm areas until the real return for labor at the margin was again equalized in all sectors. The very existence of underemployment, therefore, is prima facie evidence of a departure from competitive equilibrium. Persistence of underemployment raises serious questions about the competitive character of the economy.

We see from Figure 4.1 that labor has been responsive to nonfarm employment opportunities and that large numbers of people have moved from farm to nonfarm areas. Furthermore, there has been an increase in average annual migration since 1940. Another noticeable feature of Figure 4.1 is the low rate of migration from farms during periods of recession. There was a sharp dip in net migration in the early 1930's, followed by another dip in the 1937-38 recession. After World War II many people who had accepted jobs in defense industries and many people who were released from the armed services returned to farms, resulting in net migration to farms for the period 1945-46. Large scale net migration from farms resumed in 1947 only to be halted by a recession in 1948. Following that recession migration increased again until 1951 when the United States was called upon to assume abnormal obligations in providing food and fiber for the people of Korea. The high rate of out migration resumed in 1952 but was reduced during the recession of 1954. Migration recovered in 1955-56 but was reduced again during the recession of 1957-58.

The data presented in Figure 4.1 suggest that the level of economic activity in the economy is an important factor in determining the rate of migration from farms. Certainly it seems reasonable to believe that the expectations of farm people with regard to earnings in nonfarm employment are affected by the rate of growth in demand for labor in nonfarm sectors of the economy as well as by the level and percent of the labor force that is unemployed at any given time.

This view is contrary to that developed by Dr. Karl Fox in his paper presented at the Agricultural Adjustment Center in 1958.[9] Fox argued that mobility of labor in the United States remains high even during recessions. He noted that 42 percent of the males aged 20-24 changed industries during one year in the recession of 1947-48. Fox suggested that this high degree of mobility is indicative that the economy operates "as a vast game of musical chairs in which almost anyone can find a seat most of the time." This may be a correct appraisal of the operation of the economy, but this author does not believe a high level of unemployment is conducive to decisions to migrate from farms to nonfarm areas. Furthermore, the behavior of farmers suggests that they are not prone to migrate during periods of large unemployment.

How effective has migration been in narrowing the gap in returns for labor services on farms and in nonfarm sectors of the economy? The terms of trade worsened against agriculture in the early 1920's (Figure 4.2). Some recovery was made in the late 1920's only to be followed by a worsening of the situation in the early 1930's. Recovery set in again in the late 1930's, and the terms of trade moved in favor of farm workers until 1947. In spite of the large out-migration of labor from farms, the terms of trade have moved sharply against agriculture since 1947. Consequently, 1959 incomes of farm workers were lower relative to the incomes of factory workers than at any time since 1940. In 1959, per capita real income of the nonfarm population was 56 percent greater than per capita income of the farm population compared with only a 9 percent difference in 1948.[10] It can be concluded, therefore, that in spite of large out-migration of labor from farms from 1940 to 1960, migration has failed to equalize returns for labor in farm and nonfarm sectors of the economy.

Why has migration failed to close the gap in earnings of farm and nonfarm people? We know that the productivity of labor in agriculture has been increasing very rapidly and that this has complicated the job for migration. We cannot ignore the fact, however, that a large number of farm people have migrated to nonfarm areas. Neither can we ignore the fact that in general the rate of migration is highest from low income areas. I submit

---

[9] For an opposite view, see Karl A. Fox, Problems and Policies of American Agriculture, Iowa State University Press, Ames, 1959, pp. 114-58.

[10] Adjusted for differences in age, sex composition, dependency ratios, purchasing power of income, labor capacity, relative share of labor earnings, and income tax incidence. See D. Gale Johnson, "Labor mobility and agricultural adjustment," in Agricultural Adjustment Problems in a Growing Economy, Iowa State University Press, Ames, 1956, pp. 163-72.

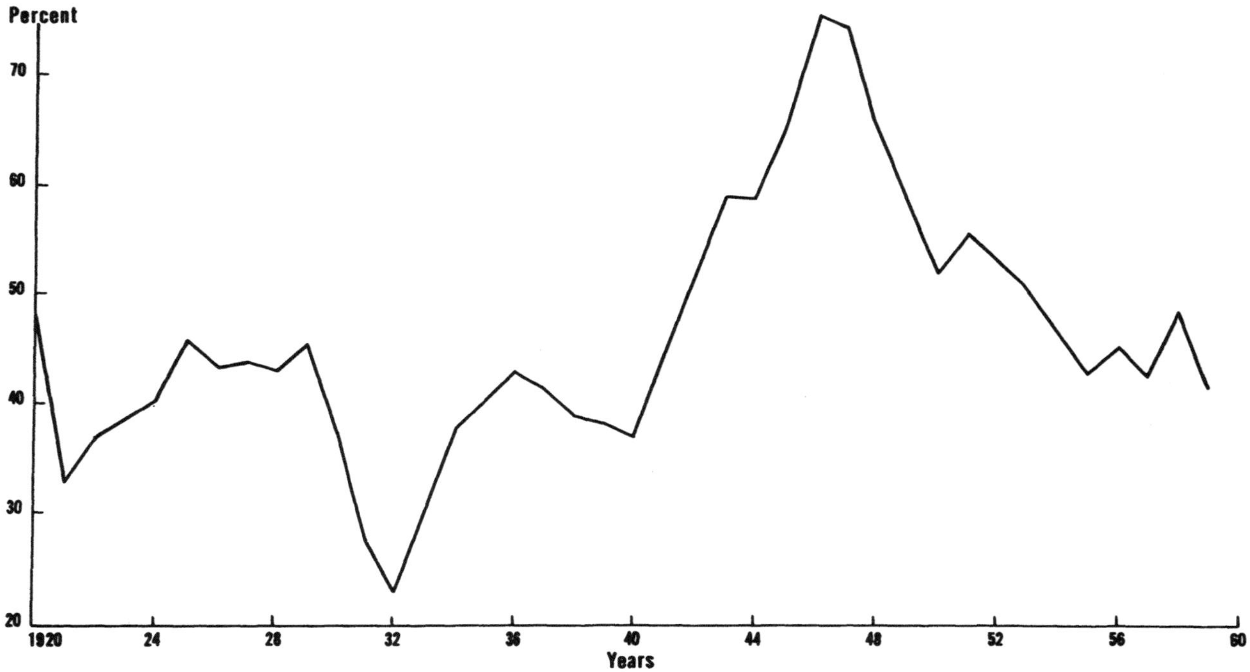

Fig. 4.2. Net income per farm worker relative to income per employed industrial worker, adjusted for changes in the consumer's price index, United States, 1920-59.

the hypothesis, therefore, that migration has failed to equalize returns for farm and nonfarm labor because the number of people who are willing to transfer to nonfarm jobs at prevailing rates of return exceeds the number of jobs that are available. I wish to test the hypothesis, as stated in the earlier section of this chapter, that the supply of labor to nonfarm firms is highly elastic in the relevant range, that labor stands ready and willing to transfer from farm to nonfarm employment at prevailing farm and nonfarm relative rates of return for labor, and that under these conditions the actual rate of migration is determined largely by shifts in the demand for labor in nonfarm employment.

If migration of labor from farm to nonfarm areas is determined largely by availability of jobs in nonfarm sectors of the economy, it would be expected that farm product prices would have little or no influence on the rate of migration. When the rate of migration is related to the index of prices received by farmers, we find that over time migration has increased as farm product prices have increased (Figure 4.3). Unless we can argue that the increase in farm product prices provided capital needed to finance the transfer of labor from farm to nonfarm areas, it is difficult to make economic sense of the relationship between migration and prices received by farmers. Rather, the observed relation suggests that factors other than farm product prices have been instrumental in determining the rate of migration from farms.

It would be expected that the decisions of farm people to migrate to nonfarm areas would be determined in large part by changes in the return for labor in farming relative to the return for labor in nonfarm employment. If the economy were in equilibrium and the return for labor in nonfarm employment increased relative to the return from the employment of labor in farm production, we could expect an increase in the flow of labor from farm to nonfarm areas. On the other hand, if the economy were out of equilibrium, we could expect an increase in the income from nonfarm employment relative to the return for farm employment to have little or no bearing upon migration decisions. It was decided, therefore, to relate migration to the relative earnings of farm and factory workers.

Since much of the migration that took place during the period 1942-47 involved drafting for military service and the release of people after cessation of hostilities, it was decided to omit these years from the analysis. Also, since migration of farm people to nonfarm areas has been so heavy during the period of study as to substantially reduce the farm population, it was decided to use the percent of farm population that migrated in a given year as the dependent variable. The following regression equation was

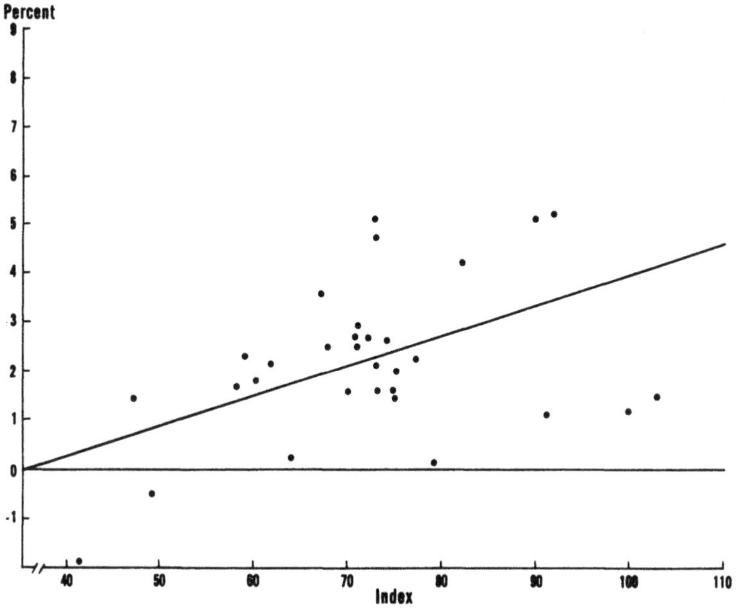

Fig. 4.3. Percent net migration of farm population and index of prices received by farmers deflated by consumer price index (1947-49 = 100).

obtained: $Y = -2.476 + .111X$. The coefficient of X is significant at the 1 percent level. The elasticity of migration with respect to changes in the income ratio is 2.07 percent.

The regression equation suggests that the rate of migration of the farm population to nonfarm areas increases when the income per farm worker increases in relation to the income of factory workers. Obviously, this relationship is not what would be expected in an economy operating near full employment. Again, there are two possible explanations. First, it is conceivable that the increase in incomes of farm people resulted in providing them with additional capital needed to finance the transfer of labor to nonfarm areas. A second condition under which this type of behavior is to be expected is that depicted in the third hypothesis presented above, i.e., that more farm people are ready to transfer from farm to nonfarm jobs at prevailing rates of return than jobs are available. Hence, migration increases when jobs become available even though during these periods the return per worker in agriculture increases relative to the return per worker in nonfarm employment.

To further test the relationship between migration and job opportunities, it was decided to regress the rate of migration on the percent of the labor force unemployed in the economy. Again, due to the unusual circumstances associated with migration during the period 1942-47, these years were excluded. The regression $Y = 3.822 - .130X$ is obtained. The coefficient of X is significant at the 5 percent level. The elasticity of migration with respect to unemployment is 0.58. Two factors are worthy of emphasis in this regression. First, the rate of migration does decrease as unemployment increases. Second, the elasticity is less than unity. Although migration is responsive to employment opportunities, therefore, the rate of response is less than the rate of change in unemployment. The pattern of behavior described in this regression is consistent with what one would expect to find under conditions of underemployment as depicted in the third hypothesis.

Next, it was decided to regress the rate of migration on the relative earnings of farm workers to nonfarm workers and the percent of the labor force unemployed in the economy. The following regression was obtained: $Y = -2.560 + .118X_1 - .014X_2$. It was expected that in the multiple regression the sign of the coefficient for X_1 would have changed to negative when the percent of unemployment was contained in the multiple regression. Under normal economic conditions approximating full employment, one would expect that the rate of migration would decrease as the percent of the labor force unemployed increased and as the ratio of earnings from farming increased relative to the earnings from nonfarm employment. The sign on the unemployment coefficient is as would be expected. The sign of the relative earnings coefficient, however, is still positive. The F value of the regression is significant at the 5 percent level. There is a substantial degree of collinearity, however, and the squared correlation of X_1 on X_2 is 0.58. This is greater than the square of the coefficient of correlation for the regression, 0.32.

Undoubtedly, some unemployment in the economy at any given time is "frictional unemployment," that is, it is unemployment which is temporary and which is to a large extent associated with transfers from one job to another. Economists frequently cite unemployment at any given time of 3 percent of the labor force as representing frictional unemployment. Examination of the data for 1930-60, however, reveals that the economy has had more than 3 percent of its labor force unemployed in all except four years — three years during World War II and one during the Korean war. It was decided, therefore, to regress the rate of migration of the farm population on the relative wages of farm and factory workers for periods when unemployment exceeded the median rate, 5.3

percent, and for periods when unemployment was less than this. For periods of high unemployment the following regression was obtained: $Y = 4.736 + .164X$. The coefficient of X is positive and it is significant at the 1 percent level. The elasticity of the rate of migration with respect to changes in the relative wages of farm and factory workers is 3.67 percent. Elasticity in this case is relatively high, and the regression indicates that during periods of unemployment farm people are willing to migrate to nonfarm areas in large numbers even though relative earnings of farm workers are increased. This, of course, is consistent with our hypothesis that availability of jobs at the prevailing rate of return for labor is the predominant factor determining the rate of migration.

Next, the rate of migration of the farm population to nonfarm areas was regressed on the relative earnings of farm and nonfarm workers during periods when unemployment was less than the median rate. The regression obtained is $Y = 7.896 - .079X$. In this case the sign of the coefficient of relative wages is negative. As was pointed out earlier, a negative sign would be expected during periods of relatively full employment. It should be noted that the coefficient is not significant at the 5 percent level. It is significant, however, that the sign of the coefficient changes to negative in this case indicating that farm people do respond to increased nonfarm wages when the economy is operating near full employment.

Although the conclusions are not as strong as one would like for policy formation, nevertheless, they are consistent with the hypothesis that labor is underemployed in agriculture in the sense that more people stand ready to transfer from farm to nonfarm areas at prevailing relative returns for farm and nonfarm employment than jobs are available. The analysis lends support to the idea that a critical level of unemployment in terms of providing motivation for nonfarm migration develops when unemployment reaches 5 percent of the labor force.

POLICY IMPLICATIONS OF UNDEREMPLOYMENT

While the results of this study are inconclusive, it is my hope that they will stimulate additional empirical research on underemployment. It is important to determine which type of underemployment characterizes the United States economy because the policy implications of the different types of underemployment are so distinct. When underemployment results from the failure of farm people to respond to economic opportunities in line with shifts in the demand for farm labor, appropriate policies obviously must increase returns from nonfarm employment relative to returns from farming to attract additional people to nonfarm areas. Appropriate policies will include travel grants to cover costs of moving to nonfarm areas, payment of subsidies to migrants, reduction in farm product prices and other policies to reduce returns from farming relative to returns from nonfarm employment. The implication is that growth in the nonfarm sectors of the economy is impeded by the failure of farm people to migrate and that additional incentives must be provided to encourage transfer of labor.

When underemployment is the result of lack of knowledge concerning nonfarm employment opportunities, underemployment results from a malfunctioning knowledge market. The appropriate policy is to provide relevant information about returns from employment in nonfarm industries. An information program to provide employers with better information concerning labor supplies and to provide farm people with better information concerning job opportunities would be sufficient to remove this type of underemployment.

The third kind of underemployment I have discussed poses the most difficult policy problems. Under these conditions it is clear that underemployment can be removed only if the number of additional nonfarm jobs created exceeds new entries to the labor force. Clearly, monetary and fiscal policies that are consistent with the high rate of growth of employment in the general economy, should constitute an important facet of an agricultural development program in the future. It is also clear that this potential growth in employment must not be sacrificed through job rationing.

Appropriate policies for solving this type of underemployment involve altering conditions of demand for nonfarm labor by shifting the demand function to the right, by making the demand more elastic, by making the demand side more competitive and other measures to remove the job rationing. Also, it may be possible to reduce this type of economic underemployment by reducing real wages of nonfarm labor to the point that differential in returns for labor in the farm and the nonfarm sectors is removed. I doubt, however, that this policy will or should be seriously considered.

The analysis presented in this paper causes one to question whether travel grants and subsidies to farm people to encourage them to migrate to nonfarm areas are necessary. Farm people migrate in large numbers and without subsidies to nonfarm areas when jobs are available. As was pointed out previously, in all but four years since 1929, migration has been sufficient to keep the level of unemployment above a reasonable frictional level. With unemployment in excess of a reasonable frictional level, it is hardly conceivable that there would be a social gain from subsidies for additional migration.

The analysis also causes one to reconsider effects of farm price supports and production controls on the mobility of farm people. I pointed out in an earlier paper that migration has been greatest from those areas receiving the highest proportion of their farm income from price supported commodities.[11] If underemployment is of the third type discussed in this paper, farm price supports have acted primarily as a means of redistributing income between farm and nonfarm sectors, and their effects on mobility of labor have been negligible. In fact, one could argue that, on balance, the effect may have been to increase migration through providing farm people with the capital needed to transfer to nonfarm areas. I am not willing to argue on the one hand that price supports impede migration and then argue on the other hand that farm people do not migrate in sufficient numbers to equalize the real returns for labor in farm and nonfarm uses because of insufficient capital to finance the transfer. Although these positions are not necessarily inconsistent, I do not find them acceptable without more evidence.

SUMMARY

In summary, the high rate of out-migration of farm people to nonfarm areas and the large number of farm families engaged in part-time farming attest to the mobility of farm people. The analysis of migration data presented in this paper is consistent with the hypothesis that farm people do not migrate in sufficient numbers to equalize the returns for farm and nonfarm labor because the number of jobs available has not increased in line with the number of people who are willing to migrate at prevailing wages. The behavioral response of farm people to economic incentives is quite consistent with economic logic. Migration response to changes in relative wages during periods when the economy is operating near full employment is especially important. The analysis emphasizes that in our efforts to solve farm problems within agriculture we must not overlook the importance to farm people of a high rate of national economic growth.

---

[11] C. E. Bishop, "The mobility of farm labor," Policy for Commercial Agriculture, Hearings before the Joint Economic Committee, Nov., 1957, pp. 437-48.

Chapter 5

DON F. HADWIGER

Southwest Missouri
State College

Political Aspects of Changes in Farm Labor Force

IT IS MY ASSIGNMENT to comment on the political significance of changes in the farm labor force. I would like to define changes in the farm labor force to include changes in the ecology and the economics of farm areas and also changes in rural attitudes and values.

At the same time, I wish to confine the discussion of political significance to the effect of these changes on farmer political power even though, as a result of these changes, more than twice as many farm-reared adults are living off the farm as are living on the farm in the United States.[1] Two hundred sixty thousand Negro farmers left the state of Mississippi during the eight year period 1950-58,[2] and two-thirds of them took residence in cities.[3] They needed a place to live, orientation, education, and work. Many of them took advantage of a new opportunity to join the electorate. The effect of farm migration upon urban politics could constitute the subject of another chapter, and will not be dealt with here.

CHANGES IN THE FARM LABOR FORCE

Reduction in Number

The changes in number of farmers mentioned earlier have obvious political significance. Farmers were a major group; they have become a fractional minority. Interest is naturally aroused as to the political consequences with reference both to the weight which is to be attached to rural values and to the strength which can be mustered in behalf of agriculture's economic demands.

[1] Ronald and Deborah Freedman, "Farm-reared elements in the nonfarm population," Rural Soc., Vol. 21, Mar., 1956, p. 50.

[2] Mississippi Farm Research, May, 1959, p. 6.

[3] Mississippi Farm Research, June, 1958, p. 2.

But it may not be taken for granted, as Galbraith has done, that "the day is not too far distant when . . . the rural vote will be too small to worry about."[4] Although we live in a majoritarian society, it is obvious that minorities are often not without great power. The case of the farmer minority appears especially worthy of investigation in view of its unique advantages within our political system.

Diversification Within Regions

The farm labor force is also changing in that, while production on individual farms is, in most cases, becoming more specialized, diversification of production is occurring in many regions which were once dominated by one or two commodities. Illustrating the inter-migration of commodities is the fact that cotton sales in Alabama have dropped, as a percentage of total cash receipts of that state's agriculture, from 72 percent in 1924 to 24 percent in 1959. In Georgia cotton sales have fallen during the period 1934-59 from 58 percent to 12 percent of total farm receipts. Broiler sales, meanwhile, rose to 21 percent of receipts, as compared with 0.1 percent in 1934. Major production shifts have also occurred in some other areas of the country.[5]

The old one-commodity economies may have perpetuated archaic social systems, exhausted the soil, and caused economic instability, but they also facilitated cooperation among farm leaders from the various regions.

Invasion by Industry

The economic life and consequently the political life of the countryside is also being affected by the decentralization of industry, underway since World War II. The meeting of factory and farm is quite evident on a statewide basis: Iowa, the corn state, received almost as much from manufacturing in 1958 as was received from farm production in 1954.[6] But this trend has also changed the landscape in many localities; 59 Iowa counties

[4] As quoted by Louis J. Ducoff, "The farm population and the agricultural labor force in 1975," Applications of Demography: the Population Situation in the U.S. in 1975, Scripps Foundation, Miami University and Population Research a Training Center, Univ. of Chicago, p. 70.

[5] "Cash receipts from major farm commodities," Stat. Bul. No. 262, USDA, AMS, Apr., 1960.

[6] 1960 Statistical Abstract of the United States, Tables 839 and 1069.

now receive over one million dollars annually from manufacturing.[7] More and more, farm views and needs must be reconciled in the local arena with views and needs of working people and industry.

Rural Attitudes Affected

Like their economic environment, many farmers are becoming less distinctively "rural." Across-the-board technological advances have so obscured rural-urban differences that some sociologists have asked themselves, perhaps with dismay, whether their constructs of model urban and rural societies are helpful any longer in discussions of the American scene.[8]

Political scientists have learned, to their chagrin, that the legislative process at the state level cannot always be described as a simple two-sided fight involving the scrappy "city slickers" and the over-weighted "country boys."[9]

To what extent does a difference exist today between rural and urban attitudes and values which is reflected in the political behavior of those two groups? And to what extent have changes in the farm labor force affected the factors responsible for rural-urban differences?

Regarding the first question, it is apparent that in all areas of the United States, rural people consistently register differently on an attitude scale relating to the degree of willingness to tolerate nonconformity than do urban people. This is evidenced in the findings of the well-known survey directed by Samuel A. Stouffer and conducted by the American Institute of Public Opinion and the National Research Center.[10]

Respondents were classified in the Stouffer study as "less tolerant," "in between," and "more tolerant." By comparing the entire cross-section of those in farm, small town, larger city, and metropolitan communities, it was found that farm people in all regions were less tolerant than those in larger city and metropolitan communities. In fact the average of the percentages of metropolitan respondents in each region who were classified as

---

[7] 1959 Rand-McNally Commercial Atlas, pp. 163, 165.

[8] For example, Alvin L. Bertrand (ed.), Rural Sociology, McGraw-Hill Book Company, Inc., New York, 1958, p. 43.

[9] David R. Derge, "Metropolitan and outstate alignments in Illinois and Missouri legislative delegations," Amer. Polit. Sci. Rev., Vol. 52, Dec., 1958, pp. 1051-65.

[10] Samuel A. Stouffer, Communism, Conformity, and Civil Liberties, Doubleday, Garden City, N. Y., 1955, pp. 118, 120.

"more tolerant" was nearly twice that of the average of the percentages of "more tolerant" farm people in each region.[11]

Is there a rural view which is manifested in politics? This has often been held to be so. The assumption that rural legislators do express a distinctive attitude on political subjects has become part of what is sometimes called the "lore of political science." Although the rural legislator's presumed attitudes are not always given explicit content, he is said to be "out of tune" with present conditions. To put it another way, he is supposedly less willing to recognize new demands made upon government as a consequence of social and economic change. He would therefore tend to be opposed to institutional reorganization, whether in the state administration, tax structure, schools, economy, or within the legislature itself. He would oppose extension of international cooperation or revisions in legislation dealing with moral problems. He is pictured, in short, as an enemy of progress.

Evidence that rural legislators as a group are in fact relatively conservative can be found in an examination of voting by members of the United States House of Representatives. The accompanying table contains the results of an effort to illustrate the differing perspectives of rural and urban Congressmen.

As a means of testing differences, a grouping was made both of those Congressmen whose district populations were classified in the 1950 U.S. Census as being more than 65 percent rural, and those whose districts were more than 65 percent urban. Votes of the two groups were compared in roll calls dealing with a number of representative subjects.

Roll calls used in the table were especially "picked" from a larger number which were studied, others being eliminated in which party or sectional loyalties predominated, or where there was evidence of abundant logrolling or of a notable lack of agreement about the matter at issue. Those presented here indicate merely that rural-urban differences are apparently manifested in congressional voting. No evidence is provided as to their impact upon voting behavior relative to other influences such as party loyalty.

In viewing the results of the first two of these roll calls, it would seem that congressmen whose districts are predominantly rural tend to respond to the call for protection of "states rights." Most of them voted in favor of the Natural Gas Act, which would have limited federal control over pricing of natural gas. Within every region of the nation, rural congressmen cast relatively more votes for passage than did congressmen from highly urban

[11] Ibid.

Table 5.1. Rural Attitudes as Revealed in Selected House Roll Calls

		North-east	South		N. Cent.		U.S.		Both parties
Favored "States Rights"		D[a]	R[b]	D	D	R	D	R	
H.R. 6645 (83rd, July 28, 1955). Natural Gas Bill passed, 209-203. Vetoed by President.	U[c]	3	29	50	0	59	15	57	33
	R[d]			51	8	60	44	74	53
H.R. 3 (85th, July 17, 1958). No act of Congress to be construed as pre-empting a field unless expressly stated. Motion to recommit, failed 236-161.	U	97	72	17	96	33	82	38	63
	R			0	92	16	22	10	20
Opposed International Cooperation									
Gross Amendment to H.R. 6871 (85th, April 17, 1957). To decrease appropriations for international agencies, failed 166-205.	U	0	36	38	13	74	12	53	32
	R			60	33	64	52	65	56
S. 1852 (85th, June 26, 1958). To create an assistant Secretary of State for Africa, passed 224-145.	U	97	82	75	96	73	89	73	82
	R			17	54	23	32	30	32
H.R. 1291 (85th, June 11, 1958). Reciprocal Trade Act Extension. Vote to recommit on which those favoring increased trade voted "nay," defeated 268-146.	U	9	42	20	0	18	7	29	17
	R			41	38	92	38	70	47
Opposed Reorganization of the Defense Department									
H.R. 12541 (85th, June 12, 1958). To reorganize the Defense Department. Vote to recommit on which those favoring returning to committee to get stronger bill voted "yea," passed, 216-187.	U	26	92	6	12	96	16	90	51
	R			0	15	85	5	87	28
Opposed Immigration									
H.R. 6481 (83d, July 28, 1953). To authorize issuance of 240,000 special quota immigrant visas, passed 221-185.	U	97	96	18	96	57	79	81	82
	R			0	73	31	16	41	24

Table 5.1. (Continued)

Favored "States Rights"		North-east		South	N. Cent.		U.S.		Both parties
Favored Vigorous Labor Reform		D[a]	R[b]	D	D	R	D	R	
S. 3974 (85th, August 18, 1958).	U	94	52	71	100	26	93	37	68
Kennedy-Ives Labor Control Bill. Passage, at which time opposition charged appeasement of labor, defeated 198-190.	R			38	54	17	46	10	36
Opposed Daylight Saving Time									
S. 3295 (84th, June 25, 1956).	U	100	100	62	100	69	84	88	87
To permit City of Washington to extend daylight saving time till October in consonance with rest of Eastern seaboard, passed, 199-120.	R			29	30	29	37	26	32

Average number of congressmen in each group in each of the three Congresses:

	Democratic		Republican	
	Rural	Urban	Rural	Urban
Northeast[e]	0	35	2	27
South	45	16	3	2
North Central	12	27	14	24
Arid West	3	2	7	1
Far West	1	10	1	15
Total	61	90	27	69

[a] "D" – Democratic.
[b] "R" – Republican.
[c] "U" – Percentage of "aye" votes out of all those cast by congressmen from districts in which the population was classified as 65 percent or more urban in the 1950 U.S. Census.
[d] "R" – Percentage of "aye" votes out of those cast by congressmen from districts in which the population was classified as 65 percent or more "rural" in the 1950 U.S. Census.
[e] For definition of regions used, see Arthur N. Holcombe, "The changing outlook for a realignment of parties," Public Opinion Quarterly, Vol. 10, 1946-47, pp. 455-69.

areas. Over half of the rural representatives voted for passage, as compared with only a third of the urban congressmen.

The other "states rights" vote was on H.R. 3. This bill sought to redefine federal and state jurisdictions by providing that federal legislation should not be construed as pre-empting a field in which the two levels of government possessed some concurrent powers, unless the intent to do so was specifically stated in a federal statute. Although rural-urban differences within the North Central region were not substantial, they were nevertheless consistent with those in other regions. On a national basis rural and urban congressmen split sharply, the percentages favoring passage being 63 for rural congressmen and 20 for urban congressmen.

Similarly distinct rural-urban differences over the desirability of international cooperation are illustrated in votes cast on proposals to extend the Reciprocal Trade Act, to create an assistant secretary of state for Africa, and to decrease appropriations for international agencies. The Republican Administration and the Democratic leadership in the House were apparently united in all three cases, supporting the proposals for trade extension and favoring the new assistant secretary, while opposing the cut in funds for international agencies. Nevertheless, a majority of rural congressmen voted in favor of the cut in funds and against the new assistant secretary, and a large minority of rural legislators opposed reciprocal trade. Urban congressmen, on the other hand, mostly supported party leaders. On a regional basis this pattern was broken only once when a larger percentage of urban than rural North Central Democrats voted to decrease funds for international agencies.

As indicated in other roll calls in the table, rural congressmen were more opposed to extending daylight saving time in Washington, to increasing immigration, and to reorganizing the Defense Department. As might have been expected, they far outdid congressmen from urban areas in their support for a more vigorous labor reform bill than the one sponsored by Senators Kennedy and Ives in 1958.

It seems fair to assume that the differential in urban-rural voting on those issues does reflect differing rural and urban political attitudes. Our interest here is in the extent to which rural political attitudes have become more or less distinctive as a result of recent changes in the farm labor force. While I feel that this question should be raised in this paper I have found it appropriate in discussing the question to rely upon an abundance of weasel words, and also to postulate that cause-and-effect relationships govern certain parallel trends.

It would seem that some of the recent changes in the labor force have been associated with a decline in distinctive rural attitudes; other changes have, at the same time, been associated with more differentiated rural-urban attitudes. Let us first note some of the influences which may have minimized differences.

It is a commonplace observation that technology has permitted farmers of modest income a level of living and the means for contact with the rest of the world similar to that available to urbanites. Today's middle-income farmer has not only the clean air and the evening calm, but also running water, a deep freeze, and a television set. But to my knowledge the efficacy of these new additions to the farm home as agents of socialization has yet to be measured. As a TV viewer, the farmer can be as finicky as the college professor. While one watches the news and then switches off the weather, the other may just as carefully watch the weather and ignore the rest.

Due in part to the work opportunities made available by the industrial decentralization, farming is becoming a part-time activity for many, and for farmers as a group, the wages received for off-the-farm work are approaching in importance the income received from agriculture. In 1958, income received by farmers from nonfarm sources was equal to 39 percent of their net income from agriculture.[12] Studies in various sections of the United States have indicated that over a third of the farmers in many areas take full-time employment off the farms during slack periods.[13]

These studies also reveal that these part-time farmers are different in some respects from those who do not seek off-the-farm jobs. They tend to be better educated, and more of them own the farms on which they live. Their views and attitudes have been conditioned by association with urban workers, and perhaps also through membership in labor unions.[14]

It may also be noted that the residences of farmers and urban dwellers are in many cases coming into closer proximity. We are aware of the "rurbanization" or movement of urban dwellers to the countryside in and around metropolitan areas.

Farmers who are in close touch with urban neighbors, either through employment, social association, or residence, may well become less distinctive in their views.

---

[12] "Farm income situation," USDA, AMS, July, 1958, p. 24.

[13] Thirty-seven percent of Ohio's farmers had off-the-farm jobs in 1956 (Ohio Farm and Home Research, May-June, 1956, p. 39). In Kentucky 38 percent of the farmers did some off-farm work in 1950 (Ky. Agr. Exper. Sta. Bul. 646, p. 5), and a survey of one Eastern Kentucky area revealed that only 27 percent of the farmers there considered farming to be their principal activity (Ky. Agr. Exp. Sta. Bul. 646, p. 15). One-third of the farm population in California have nonagricultural occupations (California Agriculture, Nov., 1954, p. 2).

The 1950 Censuses of Agriculture, Population and Housing revealed that only 38 percent of the farm operators were "wholly dependent on agriculture" (Louis J. Ducoff, "Classification of the agricultural population in the United States," Jour. Farm Econ., Vol. 37, Aug., 1955, p. 513).

[14] According to a Wisconsin Agriculturalist poll, farmers who had worked in town tended to approve of labor unions in much larger numbers than those who had not. Twenty-three percent of all the farmers in this poll had in fact belonged to a labor union. (Wisconsin Agriculturalist, Apr. 19, 1958, p. 18).

What are the influences which may tend to preserve rural-urban differences? At least two may be worth mentioning — the relatively modest educational attainments of rural people in some areas and the advancing age of the farm population.

A comparison of median ages does not fully reflect the fact that farm voters are, on the average, much older than those in the city, both because a larger portion of the rural population is under 20 years of age,[15] and because many semi-retired farm couples or farm widows have joined the rural nonfarm population, casting their ballots in the small village or town near their farm.[16]

Perhaps it is partly for this reason that the gulf between educational attainments of rural and urban people appears to be narrowing very little. As of 1950 only 37 percent of the rural population had attended high school as compared with 58 percent in urban areas.[17] The percentage of illiteracy among rural farm people actually rose slightly between 1947 and 1952.[18] Also, those leaving agriculture may have had slightly more formal education than those in the same age group who stay on the farm,[19] except in areas where Negro out-migration exceeds that of whites.[20]

The actual gap in educational attainment between urban and farm people may in fact be larger than statistics indicate because city schools have more to offer than the small, often inadequately-equipped and poorly-staffed country and small-town schools. Two rural school experts have stated that "the rural schools in most respects have remained a decade or more behind the urban schools."[21]

It is significant, in view of Stouffer's findings, that regional variations in the level of education are in some cases greater than rural-urban variations. Rural people in Connecticut are as

---

[15] A study of the 1950 population in Kentucky revealed that rural areas continue to experience very high birth rates. The fertility ratio for the nine "most rural counties" was 984, as compared with a state fertility ratio of 671. ("The changing Kentucky population," Univ. of Ky. Agr. Exper. Sta. Prog. Rep. 67, Sept., 1958, pp. 15, 27).

[16] One Illinois population study concluded, "It is obvious that rural towns and villages with less than 2,500 inhabitants are truly the 'home of the aged,'" (Illinois Farm Econ., June, 1957, p. 1647).

[17] Everett M. Rogers, Social Change in Rural Society, Appleton-Century-Crofts, New York, 1960, p. 245.

[18] Statistical Abstract of the United States, 1959, Table No. 143.

[19] Ky. Agr. Exp. Sta. Bul. 646, pp. 24-25. Kentucky Farm and Home Science, Summer, 1958, p. 8. Mississippi Farm Research, June, 1958, p. 2.

[20] Mississippi Farm Research, Oct., 1958, p. 2.

[21] Julian Butterworth and Howard A. Dawson, The Modern Rural School, McGraw-Hill, New York, 1952, p. vii.

well educated as city folks,[22] and of those surveyed by Stouffer the percentage of farmers in the Middle West who had completed high school was nearly as great as the percentage of high school graduates among metropolitan Southerners.[23] The 1950 U.S. Census Reports reveal that only 37 percent of Mississippi's farmers had completed grade school, as compared with over 80 percent of Iowa's farmers.

Table 5.2. Educational Attainment of Farmers and Others in Iowa and Mississippi (Percent who did not finish high school or grade school)

	State		Rural farm males, 1950
In Iowa	1940	1950	
Did not finish grade school	22	15.8	19.6
Less than four years or no years in high school	70.2	60	73.9
In Mississippi			
Did not finish grade school	54.3	47.5	62.8
Less than four years or no years in high school	82.5	76.3	87.1

Source: 1950 U.S. Census, Vol. II, Table 20.

Apparently both rural-urban differences in educational attainments and age and regional differences in rural education levels are highly significant. The Stouffer survey provided evidence that certain attitudes which might be considered keys to political behavior are held in common by rural people, older people, and those who have completed fewer years of formal schooling. Further, this is due to some extent to an interrelationship between these group characteristics. Both rural people and older people tend to have less schooling than other groups.[24] Stouffer found that people in all these categories seemed more authoritarian, more conforming, and more pessimistic than others, these attitudes perhaps being basic to the political position often referred to by the term "conservative."

Stouffer's findings also indicated that urban-rural differences — at least with reference to the attitudes studied — were less related to the type of community than to the lower level of formal education in rural areas. When groups were broken down on the basis of educational attainments, farm people at similar education

[22] Conn. Agr. Exp. Sta. Bul. 326, p. 18.

[23] Samuel A. Stouffer, Communism, Conformity, and Civil Liberties, Doubleday, Garden City, New York, 1955, p. 120.

[24] Ibid., pp. 89-108.

levels tended to score higher on tolerance than did residents of small cities and towns. In fact, southern farmers who had completed grade school scored slightly higher on "tolerance" than did metropolitan Southerners who had reached a similar educational level.[25]

Nevertheless, a conclusion that rural-urban attitude differences are due entirely to differences in educational attainment and associated factors does not appear to be warranted in view of other evidence such as that revealing the differing attitudes of full-time and part-time farmers. Stouffer himself concludes that the level of education does not fully account for the variance in rural-urban attitudes.

What then can be concluded about the effect upon farmer attitudes of recent changes in the farm labor force? We have seen that attitudes which are dominant in rural areas are distinguishable from attitudes dominant in urban and metropolitan areas. Furthermore rural attitudes are more conducive to what is ordinarily referred to as a "conservative" political position.

The attitudes of an increasing number of farm people have been affected by off-farm employment or by residence in a "rurbanized" environment, unlike the decreasing number of farmers whose relative isolation has minimized the effect of these influences. At the same time, the average educational attainment remains much lower among farmers due to the aging of the farm population, a factor which tends to preserve rural-urban differences in attitude. It seems likely, therefore, that recent changes in the farm labor force, rather than having influenced a mass shift away from traditional attitudes have instead been associated with a trend toward a more heterogeneous farm population.

The impact of changes in the labor force may vary by areas. In rural communities where metropolitan influences are relatively intense, the majority of farmers may be losing their attachment to those traditional attitudes which were conducive to a conservative political position. In other areas where the rural population remains relatively isolated and less well-educated, traditional attitudes may continue to be most influential.

Preference for Economic Security Values

In states outside the South, there is an old maxim purporting to govern the political expression of rural values. It is held that the farmer "votes his pocket book" when times are bad, and votes

---

[25] Ibid., p. 121.

Republican the rest of the time. As a result of technological change in agriculture, it would appear that "bad times," in terms of continually reduced opportunities for employment and income in agriculture, will be with us for some time to come.

One student of rural values, John M. Brewster, has maintained that excessive productivity has caused a sharp conflict in the values which farmers have presumably held. Excellence in individual achievement, as a goal for which farmers are said to strive, has been realized to an extent that has frustrated efforts to reach other equally important goals – opportunity to follow one's chosen profession and a just reward to the farmer for his economic contribution. The farmer is, in short, producing himself out of both job and income, but his belief in individualism in the economic sphere has made him hesitant to seek governmental assistance as other economic groups have done.[26]

Hesitant though the farmer may be, there is evidence that this goal conflict, to the extent that it exists, is being resolved in favor of the desire to stay on the farm and make a decent income, and therefore on a choice of more governmental assistance and regulation as against more economic freedom. The evidence that this choice is being made exists in studies of farmer voting during recent elections which indicate a preference for politicians who promise higher prices and protection of the family farm.

It could be argued that these expressions of opinion by a majority of farmers are merely a protest against those who are "in," skillfully promoted by the "outs." Such an interpretation fails to account for the fact that Iowa farmers did in fact turn out for President Truman in 1948. Also it would imply – it seems to me incorrectly – that farmers see no significant difference in the political philosophies of the two major political parties. President Eisenhower was certainly popular in the farm areas, but this can be explained, according to farmer polls, not by the attractiveness of the Republican Party's economic philosophy but rather by the President's personal magnetism and by farmers' preeminent desire for peace.

Farmers have already compromised themselves on the matter of dependence on government. They have formed a habit of accepting substantial governmental assistance which, whatever it may do to their self-esteem, would now be hard to break. The history of farmer acceptance of substantial governmental assistance stretches from the REA and the depression income programs to

[26] John M. Brewster, "Society values and goals in respect to agriculture," in Goals and Values in Agricultural Policy, Iowa State University Press, Ames, 1961.

"90 percent of parity" price programs following World War II, to what a discussant at an earlier Iowa State University conference called featherbedding through the soil bank, ultimately even to accepting old age and survivors' insurance benefits. There is little to indicate that the majority of farmers will, with new resolution, reject subsequent offers of assistance in favor of more individualism and hard work.

EFFECT OF RURAL POWER WITHIN CONGRESS

The "Rural" Legislative Body

It is commonly observed that farmers have a disproportionate voice within the legislative bodies of this country, at both state and national levels. Numerous authorities have in fact described Congress as the representative of rural America, while referring to the President as the spokesman for urban America. It is often explained that urban influence on the President derives from the fact that presidential candidates must seek the margin of victory within large, two-party, predominantly urban states, while rural strength in Congress has been magnified through the operation of a number of devices — the one-party district in rural areas, the gerrymander, the seniority system, and the bipartisan coalition of rural congressmen.

Loss of Rural Institutional Advantage Within Congress

One principal effect of recent changes in the labor force has been a decline of rural influence in Congress. Although agricultural groups may continue to hold disproportionate strength in Congress, that body can no longer be considered the agent of rural America.

The homogeneous one-party district is becoming uncommon. This phenomenon of rural politics, which permitted rural areas to exploit legislative practices such as seniority, logrolling, and gerrymandering, is being undermined by the intermixing of industry and agriculture across the nation, by the dispersion of commodities, and outside the South by the willingness of farmers to vote for Democratic candidates in state and national elections.

In the South the traditional politics of agriculture has made way for industrial interests. When, as in South Carolina, two-thirds as many persons are employed in the textile industry alone as are employed in agriculture,[27] one can understand why representatives of this state and other southern states similarly experiencing industrial growth should abandon their traditional low tariff position.

Southern congressmen are also finding it ever more difficult to reconcile local interests with those of rural congressmen in the Midwest and other regions, because southern agriculture, as noted earlier, is becoming competitive with that of other areas.

Similar economic changes are affecting politics in other regions. In addition, especially in the North Central states, the percentage voting Democratic in congressional and state-wide elections has increased election by election during the 1950's. Indicative of the farmers' role in weakening one-partyism outside the South is the fact that of the 26 districts held by Republicans in 1952 in which the 1950 population was classified as 65 percent or more rural, 10 are now Democratic. In these 26 districts the average percentage of votes cast for Republican candidates declined by 5 percent between 1952 and 1954, by 2 percent between the 1954 and 1956 elections and by 4 percent in 1958. This is a decline in average percentage between 1952 and 1958 from 63 percent to 52 percent. Observing the growth of Democratic congressional strength in the 1958 elections, in which 21 of the 49 new Democratic seats came from rural or small town districts, Congressional Quarterly commented: "... the growth of Democratic strength in the farm areas is unmistakable...." Congressional Quarterly cited, as dramatic evidence of this trend, the fact that of the 20 richest farm districts, all but 3 of which were held by the Republicans after the 1952 elections, a total of 13 had been captured by the Democrats in the 1954, 1956, and the 1958 elections.[28]

Another indication of the political impact of the changing farm vote together with that of the decentralization and dispersion of industrial production (discussed on p. 51) is the fact that 11 of the 14 states included in the Midwest Democratic Conference now have Democratic governors. Also, in 8 of the 17 states outside the South in which 1950 populations were 22 percent or more rural, the Republicans had lost control of the lower house of the state legislatures as a result of the 1954, 1956, and 1958 elections, while trimming Republican legislative majorities in the other 9 states.

---

[27]In 1950, the number of persons employed in the textile industry in South Carolina was 67 percent of the number employed in agriculture (1950 U.S. Census, Vol. II, Table 30, part 40).

[28]Gordon E. Baker, Rural Vs. Urban Political Power, Doubleday Short Studies in Political Science, Garden City, N. Y., 1955, p. 44.

The gerrymander no longer safeguards rural numerical strength in the House of Representatives. Notwithstanding the increasing disparity between rural and urban populations, this device is being used less empathically, and less exclusively, in behalf of rural areas.

It is true that the rural population receives proportionately more seats in the House of Representatives than does the urban population (see Table 5.3). Outlying areas will continue to be favored in the apportionment of House seats simply because the representatives from nonmetropolitan areas are in the majority in most state legislatures. The metropolitan population is still a minority in most states and, even if this were to change, representation in at least one house of the state legislature is usually on an area rather than on a population basis.

Table 5.3. 1950 Population of Existing Rural and Urban Districts

	Urban[1]	Rural[2]
Less than 200,000		2
200-250	3	13
250-300	6	25
300-350	28	40
350-400	35	8
400-450	14	10
450-500	6	1
500-600	6	
More than 600,000	2	
	100 percent	99 percent

[1] Percentage of those districts in which 65 percent or more of the population was classified as "urban" in the 1950 U.S. Census.
[2] Percentage of those districts in which 65 percent or more of the population was classified as "rural" in the 1950 U.S. Census.

But the gerrymander was used less brazenly in the last redistricting than had previously been the case,[29] and it will likely be employed even more moderately in the future. Outside the South, there will be less incentive for Republican legislatures to move congressional districts to the countryside, because the outcome of elections in many farm areas has now become a matter for speculation. Also, resistance to the gerrymander has

[29] Ibid.

strengthened through the years. Urban forces have become somewhat more influential in the process of redistricting, by having increased their representation in that house of the legislature which is fairly representative of the population, and by the steady increase in the power and prestige of the Governor's office.

Like the gerrymander, the seniority system is of declining utility as a tool for rural influence. Seniority is the coin for gaining power positions within the Congress, and except for a possible change in method for selecting members of the House Rules Committee, it appears unlikely that seniority will be replaced as the principal and ordinarily the sole criterion governing promotion to leadership positions.

During the early 1950's rural congressmen continued to have more seniority than others, as indicated in the accompanying table. It would appear that long service will continue to provide an advantage for representatives from the rural South.

Table 5.4. Tenure of U.S. Congressmen (83d, 84th, 85th Congresses). Experience Previous to Term in Which They Were Serving, Percentage of Terms Served by Congressmen From Each Area During Three Sessions

	Northeast	South		North Central		Arid West		Far West
	Urban	Urban	Rural	Urban	Rural	Urban	Rural	Urban
No experience	14	16	13	16	10	17	10	21
1 to 5 years	32	29	24	35	28	50	37	42
6 to 10 years	31	30	26	21	26	33	37	21
11 to 15 years	8	14	16	13	15	0	10	11
16 to 20 years	10	10	14	12	15	0	0	5
Over 20 years	4	0	8	3	6	0	7	0
	99	99	101	100	100	100	101	100

In rural areas elsewhere, as already noted, the political atmosphere is no longer languid. One can easily call to mind the names of a number of powerful voices for rural America which were dropped from the Republican congressional roster during the past eight years. One may argue that it may not be long before urban areas will be suffering no great disadvantage as a result of the operation of the seniority system.

The rule for selecting leadership in the Congress does not in any event guarantee power to those selected. Some long-serving southern congressmen, in complaining recently that little mileage can be gained from a committee chairmanship when the committee is stacked against them, have thereby called attention to the fact that the strength of leadership in a majoritarian setting is to a large extent determined by the size of its following. A Congress which represents a predominantly urban America may occasionally be frustrated by tactics which leadership prerogatives make possible. One cannot discount the fact that a well-situated minority in Congress may often find itself in possession of a balance of power. Experience would indicate, however, that the majority will ultimately get what they strongly desire.

It might also be noted that official or party positions within the Congress are not the only or even the main source of initiative and leadership on important public policy. The Congress is often seen to be responding to strategy moves by combinations of massive urban interest groups such as the Chamber of Commerce and the labor union federations, and particularly by the executive branch, the most successful organizer of congressional action.

Farmers themselves have had powerful interest groups like American Farm Bureau Federation which is organized in all sections of the country. For many years the Farm Bureau provided cohesion and direction for the bipartisan coalition in Congress commonly referred to as the "farm bloc." It was this combination of rural power, based on the rural one-party district which permitted maximum advantage to be gained from the gerrymander and the seniority system for selecting congressional leadership. Although the Farm Bureau now has a wider base, a larger membership, and more money than it ever had before, it can no longer rally the farm forces in the Congress.

Farm forces in the Congress are divided, as the Farm Bureau is in fact divided, basically because of changes in the farm labor force which have divided farmers themselves. Rural people and rural areas are losing their homogeneity. At the same time, they are becoming a less significant feature of the political landscape. There is no longer any basis for describing the Congress as the representative of rural America. This is because of conflicting economic interests as well as the division among farm groups. It is because of the demise of the single-interest, one party district and the loss of exclusive advantage from seniority, and it is because the decline in the number of farmers within the total population is being followed inexorably by reduced numerical representation of rural areas within the Congress.

The Congress may remain relatively conservative in tone, and in this sense give political voice to "rural" attitudes such as those noted earlier. This conservatism need not be explained primarily by the influence of a rural power bloc within it. There are other hypotheses which help explain congressional conservatism including those which point to power vested in older men, the legislative body's natural role to deliberate and to check, and individual congressmen's responsiveness to local rather than to national economic interests.

The observation that traditional bases of rural strength within the Congress have eroded does not necessarily lead to the conclusion that farmer economic interests are receiving less sympathetic treatment within the Congress than was previously the case. In fact, subsequent discussion provides evidence that changes in the farm labor force which have been dealt with here may for some situations have strengthened the farmer's bargaining power in the national lawmaking body. It can be concluded that agriculture's strategy of rural bipartisanship which exploited institutional biases is outmoded and has already been abandoned. During the past few years no serious effort has been made by the Farm Bureau to bring farm groups together. This organization has pursued a policy leading to division rather than unification of rural forces. The achievements claimed by Farm Bureau in recent Congresses have been due less to its effectiveness among farm congressmen than to its influence within the Eisenhower Administration and its ability to round up urban votes. The successes of its opposition, likewise, are attributable in part to the support extended by urban Democrats and urban political groups.

If changes in the farm labor force have been correctly assessed in this paper, no animistic explanation for the disintegration of the "farm bloc" is needed. The reasons lie much deeper than the change in Farm Bureau leadership. Neither can the blame be laid on an intransigent Agriculture Secretary, or on President Truman and subsequent Democratic candidates who, like Riordan's Plunkitt, "seen their opportunities and took 'em."

The decay in traditional sources of rural strength has been gradual and partial, and access by some commodity and processor groups may not have been seriously affected by recent changes. But for those groups whose programs have a more obvious bearing upon a broader field of public policy and who must therefore solicit a broader concensus, a new strategy has been evolved. Nonpartisanship has been replaced by partisanship. More reliance is being placed on party mechanisms than upon institutional arrangements within the legislative body.

Some farm leaders have viewed this development with misgivings, and have sought mightily to prevent it. They have wondered whether it is realistic to expect that the loss of traditional sources of rural political strength can be compensated for by the new electioneering. Can the farm vote, now so small, be influential in congressional, state-wide, and even presidential elections? Presented on the following pages is evidence supplementing that already presented (pp. 62-63) that farmers, even though fewer in number, can actually be quite potent at the polls.

ACCESS THROUGH ELECTIONS

To my knowledge, other than the 1960 campaign, there has not been any other presidential campaign during the past 30 years in which one of the candidates has directly stated that the farm issue is the most important domestic issue in the campaign. Attention given to the farm problem in the 1960 election was indicative of the fact that the farmers' vote, though relatively the smallest in history, can well be an important factor in a presidential race, just as it has been decisive in a number of state and congressional elections.

The attention given to the farm problem in the last election is not attributable, as Galbraith has facetiously remarked, to the politician's inability to count. It is due instead to his mastery of a rather complex counting system, in which a minority vote is, under certain circumstances, worth far more than its numerical value.

What are the circumstances which have made the farm vote so important? For one thing, the farm vote since 1948 has been extremely volatile. Illustrations are plentiful from recent elections that the farm vote is most erratic.

Polling Iowa farmers after three elections, Wallaces Farmer found that, while President Truman got 56 percent of the Iowa farm vote in 1948, two-thirds of the farm voters backed Mr. Eisenhower in 1952; four years later President Eisenhower barely pulled a majority of the Iowa farm vote.[30]

Similar findings by the Survey Research Center at the University of Michigan were cited by V. O. Key, who concluded that "the farm vote has become extremely volatile."[31] The post-election polls of this group showed farm operators throughout the nation voting as follows:

	1948	1952	1956
Democrat	59	36	45
Republican	41	64	55

Further evidence of farmer volatility is found in a survey of "Group Differences in Attitudes and Votes," also by the Survey Research Center of the University of Michigan (Table 5.5). Comparing various occupational groups, it was found that farmers switched much more sharply than others, and were in fact the only group the majority of whom switched parties between the

[30] Wallaces Farmer, Aug. 1, 1959, p. 46.

[31] V. O. Key, Politics, Parties, and Pressure Groups, Fourth Ed., Thomas Y. Crowell Co., New York, 1958, p. 581.

Table 5.5. Group Differences in Attitudes and Votes

Occupation	1948			1952		
	D	R	Nonvoter	D	R	Nonvoter
Professional, managerial	15%	57%	25%	27%	59%	12%
Other white collar	38	39	18	28	52	19
Skilled, semiskilled	52	15	29	29	34	26
Unskilled	33	12	49	40	19	40
Farm operators	25	13	54	24	42	33

1948 and 1952 elections. It was noted, too, that the percentage of nonvoters among farmers varied sharply in consecutive elections.

A spectacular shift occurred in the Wisconsin farm vote for Senator between 1952 and 1958. While there was only 4 percent change in the Democratic majority in the three highly populated counties (producing 35 percent of the vote in 1958), the total state vote switched from 54 percent Republican to 57 percent Democratic.

León Epstein, who compared voting behavior of Wisconsin population groups through four elections, found that "if farmers are capable in favorable circumstances of being more Republican than any other group in the state, they can also . . . be much less Republican than voters in all groups of cities except those over 50,000." He concluded that "the lavish attention which politicians of both parties give to farmers and farm issues" was not due to the size of the farm vote, which was relatively small. "Rather it is the demonstrated capacity of Wisconsin farmers for wholesale switching of party allegiance which accounts for the concern of politicians."[32]

Farm switch voting has been made decisive by the emergence of the two-party system in a number of states in which agriculture has traditionally been important. These include all of the states in the North Central area, in addition to Wyoming, Idaho, and others. In most of these states the percentage of farmers within the total population is not large, as in Ohio where in 1950 only 7 percent of the employed persons were working in agriculture. Nevertheless the farm vote can be significant in Ohio as long as the margin of the victory is small, as in 1958 when the Democrats received 50.8 percent of the Ohio congressional vote. The reason that the farm vote can carry weight in a presidential election is

[32] Leon Epstein, "Size and place and the division of the two-party vote in Wisconsin," Western Polit. Quart., Vol. 9, Mar., 1956, p. 149.

that the polling power of the parties is roughly equal in a number of states in which farmers have responded to farm economic issues.

As shown in Table 5.6, in each of these states the total vote cast for candidates for the U. S. House of Representatives in the 1958 elections was split almost equally between the two parties. Farmers constituted a significant minority within each of these 10 North Central states, and they responded sharply to farm economic issues in this as well as in previous elections, as numerous candidates for state and national office have testified.

Table 5.6. Farm Voters and Party Strength in Certain States

	Percent employed persons in agriculture[a]	Percent farm workers and managers[b]	Percent pop. rural farm[c]	Percent pop. rural farm and nonfarm[d]	Demo. percent of total vote in 1958 cong. elections[e]
Eleven North Central states:					
North Dakota	44.2	43.1	41	73.4	50.4
South Dakota	40.5	39.5	39	66.8	51.4
Nebraska	29.6	28.7	29	53.1	47
Iowa	28.5	23.6	29	52.3	50.3
Minnesota	22	21.9	25	45.5	52.7
Kansas	23	20	23	47.9	50.1
Wisconsin	18.8	18	21	42.1	53.6
Ohio	6.9	5.9	11	29.8	50.8
Michigan	6.7	5.8	11	29.3	53
Illinois	7.1	6.4	9	22.4	50.4
Other farm states:					
Idaho	26.8	25.5	28	57.1	52
Vermont	18.2	17.3	21	63.6	51.5
Wyoming	20.5	19.6	20	50.2	46.4

[a] U.S. Census of 1950, Vol. II, Table 30.
[b] U.S. Census of 1950, Vol. II, Table 28.
[c] U.S. Census of 1950, Vol. II, Table 14.
[d] U.S. Census of 1950, Vol. II, Table 1.
[e] Congressional Quarterly Weekly, Jan. 2, 1959, p. 38.

In 1960 a majority of farmers in these states and in other areas felt that the Democratic Party could fulfill their economic needs. According to a poll by Wallaces Farmer, 50 percent of Iowa's farmers thought that the Democratic Party "could do the better job of raising farm income," as compared with only 17 percent who thought the Republicans could do better. Twenty-four percent thought there was no difference between the parties and 9 percent were undecided.[33]

[33] Wallaces Farmer Poll, released September 28, 1960.

It seems that a large majority also felt that the farm problem would be the "most important" issue in the presidential campaign. A poll by the Des Moines Register indicated that about 68 percent of Iowa's farmers regarded the farm problem as the "most important" issue on which they would be voting in the election.[34] Both of these findings are similar to those noted in surveys and in studies of the election statistics in the 1954, 1956, and 1958 elections, as well as in the testimony of numerous politicians.

Certainly there have been other issues influencing the farmers' vote, but farm economic issues need not be the only ones or even the most prominent ones in order to be important. It has already been noted that in the 1952 and 1956 elections a majority of midwestern farmers voted Republican because they were attracted by President Eisenhower's personality and because of the peace issue. At the same time, however, a state-by-state survey taken by The New York Times prior to the 1956 election indicated that the farm issue was the only factor causing a substantial vote shift in the North Central states in that presidential election.[35]

Some of the polls preceding the 1960 election indicated that Senator Kennedy might receive less than a majority of the votes in many farm areas because of his religion. What should not be overlooked is that in a state-wide or national election the political relevance of the farm issue is more likely measured by the percentage of farm votes that it influences than by the percentage of farmer votes cast for a particular candidate. Also important as factors which affected the outcome of this presidential election were the congressional seats and state offices which have fallen to the Democrats by virtue of the farm protest vote.

Unless one takes the highly optimistic view that the economic difficulties of farmers in these states will shortly be alleviated, it is to be expected that the Republican Party will deem it necessary to compete for the farmer's support by offering concrete policies for improvement of farm income in future elections, as in fact the Eisenhower Administration did in supporting the soil bank and conservation reserve programs.

There has been much criticism of the high cost of agricultural programs since 1950. Although there is some dispute about the amounts actually spent in behalf of farmers, it is undeniable that a lot was spent in the interest of a relatively small group of people. It seems that, in explaining how a small minority succeeded in getting such a large appropriation, insufficient credit has been given to considerations of national party power. The

---

[34] Des Moines Register, October 2, 1960, p. 14-G.
[35] New York Times, Oct. 1-18, 1956, p. 1 in each issue.

votes of urban congressmen which supported passage of "high parity" farm legislation were cast along party lines. Urban Democrats apparently found the farm issue of indirect importance, in that it permitted the election or reelection of Democrats from the rural or mixed constituencies. The soil bank and other measures sponsored by the Eisenhower Administration similarly indicated a recognition of the importance of the farm vote; and the attention given to it in the last presidential election provides additional evidence that, in the political and economic environment which now exists and may endure, the farm vote can be highly significant within the national political context.

SUMMARY

Evidence was cited of several changes in the farm labor force, which have affected the way in which farmer economic interests seek recognition in federal policy. These changes include the following:

1. Farmers now constitute a small minority within the total working force.
2. Agricultural regions within the United States are becoming less compatible and more competitive, because of the diversification of farm production within regions.
3. The decentralization of industry has necessitated adjustment at the local level of farmer, industrial, and labor interests.
4. Many farmers are no longer heavily influenced by traditional "rural" attitudes, especially those farmers who are younger and better educated, and those who live or work in an urban or metropolitan environment.
5. Rural value conflicts are being resolved in favor of the desire for higher income levels and greater economic security.

The effect of these changes in the farm labor force has been to create divisions within and among farmers and farm groups, and to minimize the advantages which farm interests have enjoyed as a result of institutional arrangements within the Congress. There is now no farm coalition, and even if there were, it could no longer hope to write its own ticket.

Partly as a result of the changes in the farm labor force which have been described here, farmers have become influential in congressional, state-wide, and even in presidential elections. There is a farm issue and a farm vote. So long as political parties have good reason to bid for the farmers' support at the polls, the farmer may find access within both the executive branch and the Congress in a measure never before realized.

Chapter 6

J. ALLAN BEEGLE
Michigan State University

Sociological Aspects of Changes in Farm Labor Force

THE PRIMARY AIM of this chapter is to explore the sociological significance of changes in the farm labor force. Since changes in functional roles accompany the process of urbanization and industrialization, a substantial literature already exists. The general problem of changing occupational or functional roles and allied questions generated by such changes have occupied the interest of scholars from many disciplines for a number of years both in this country and abroad. While it is distinctly advantageous to have an accumulated body of literature on this subject, the price is high in that a new appraisal of the significance of changes in the farm labor force inevitably will cover well-trodden ground. In such a context, this chapter must be selective in its scope. The initial part will be limited to discussion of some relevant features of modern American society as well as a brief discussion of some sociological variables in the explanation of migration and non-migration. The final portion will consider some aspects of the sociological significance of changes in the farm labor force.

RELEVANT FEATURES OF MODERN AMERICAN SOCIETY

Before turning to the farm sector it is appropriate, it seems to me, to look at contemporary American society as an entity. Of special utility in understanding changes in the farm labor force is the ecological model of dominance and interdependence of parts.[1] Viewed in this way, modern American society is a metropolitan economy in which the large cities organize and integrate commercial, financial, and communication activities. In this view,

[1]See R. D. McKenzie, The Metropolitan Community, McGraw-Hill, New York, 1933; Donald J. Bogue, The Structure of the Metropolitan Community: A Study of Dominance and Sub-Dominance, University of Michigan Press, Ann Arbor, 1949; and Rupert B. Vance and Sara Smith, "Metropolitan dominance and integration" in P. K. Hatt and A. J. Reiss, Cities and Society, The Free Press, Glencoe, Ill., 1956.

the important unit of observation is a series of metropolitan regions, each of which includes one or more large population aggregates and a hinterland. The metropolitan center, due to its size, centralization of many functions, and power, becomes dominant in terms of organizing the economy and social structure throughout the region.

The development of the metropolitan center, according to N. S. B. Gras,[2] the economic historian, has the following four stages: first, the organization of the market; second, the development of industry; third, the organization of transportation and communication; and fourth, the development of financial organization. While these stages are overlapping and not necessarily in sequence, they describe the necessary conditions for such phenomena as massing of people, rural-to-urban migration, and centralization of power.

It may be well to attempt some assertions as to the way in which the farm sector fits into the scheme. First, while the urban and farm components have become increasingly interdependent, the center possesses the means and the power to organize the hinterland. Hence, it may be said with considerable accuracy, that the inhabitants of rural areas have lost much of their power of self-determination.

Second, with the monopolization of means of communication by the metropolitan center, increasingly the same message is received by virtually everyone. As a consequence, a single set of norms and values tends to become shared by all. Hence, differences between residents of rural and urban areas are fading and all groups are becoming part of a mass society.[3]

Third, while specialization of function is a keynote of the metropolitan region, the old distinction between "field" and "center" activities is no longer valid. While field activities have become more specialized and large-scale, the new integration has brought a mixture of field with center activities throughout the hinterland. Thus, it would be a great oversimplification and falsification to assert that even the rural-farm part of the rural population had the sole major function of producing food and fiber for urban processing and consumption. This assertion would ignore the contribution of the farmer to the urban labor force, to use only one example. Even the functions performed by the villagers are multiple and are often not at all agriculturally oriented.

---

[2] N. S. B. Gras, An Introduction to Economic History, Harper and Brothers, New York, 1922.

[3] See Walter Firey, Charles P. Loomis, and J. Allan Beegle, "The fusion of urban and rural," in Highways in Our National Life: A Symposium, edited by Jean Labatut and W. J. Lane, Princeton University Press, Princeton, 1950, pp. 154-63.

A SOCIOLOGICAL EXPLANATION OF MIGRATION

Much literature dealing with why people move is couched in economic terms.[4] While the role of economic forces in migration is admittedly great, it fails to account for many existing patterns of mobility in American agriculture. The purpose of this section is to suggest a theoretical framework for explanation of internal migration in sociological terms.[5]

Under conditions in which freedom of choice may be exercised, internal migration[6] is viewed as an on-going decision-making process. In this decision-making process satisfactions with life in the community of residence are weighed against the social costs of moving to another area. This evaluation process takes place in relation to the level of aspirations derived from the value orientation, range of knowledge, and experience of groups and individuals. Satisfaction, the first dimension mentioned, is regarded as cohesiveness resulting from identification with groups and structures. Social cost, the second dimension, is regarded as rootlessness, or perceptions of rootlessness, attending migration. Finally, aspiration is considered the desired future condition or style of life sought. Each of the three dimensions is perceived to range from low to high, and each is viewed as interacting with the others.

Identification and cohesiveness, resulting from interaction with groups as well as structures, nourish residential stability. Cohesiveness arising from interaction and membership in such

---

[4] See, for example, Carter L. Goodrich, et al., Migration and Economic Opportunity, The University of Pennsylvania Press, Philadelphia, 1936, and Julius Isaac, Economics of Migration, Kegan Paul, London, 1947.

[5] A similar statement is to be found in "Report of procedures committee of NC-18, North Central regional project concerning field studies of migration, by J. Allan Beegle (Chairman), Thomas R. Ford, Roy Francis, S. A. Hoermann, and Ward Bauder, East Lansing (mimeographed). See also J. Allan Beegle, "Social components in the decision to migrate," unpublished paper read in Section 11, The Fields of Application of Sociology: Agriculture, Fourth World Congress of Sociology, Stresa, Italy.

The author does not wish to imply that noneconomic factors in the explanation of migration have not been recognized. See, for example, C. E. Lively and Conrad Taeuber, Rural Migration in the United States, Research Monograph XIX, U.S. Government Printing Office, Washington, D.C., 1939; Robin M. Williams, "Concepts of marginality in rural population studies," Rural Soc., Vol. 5, Sept., 1940, pp. 292-302; and Peter H. Rossi, Why People Move, The Free Press, Glencoe, Ill., 1955. Furthermore, this statement of the components of the decision-making process eventuating in migration or nonmigration owes much to others. See especially Roy G. Francis, "Relation of theory to data," Rural Soc., Vol. 22, Sept., 1957, pp. 258-66.

[6] Sociologically migration is to be regarded as the voluntary movement of individuals beyond and outside their interaction systems in the community of residence. Thus, in a sociological sense, migration does not occur unless day-to-day interaction with groups in the community of origin are terminated.

groups and structures forms the basis for the level of satisfactions. Through the act of migration, group ties and probably some ties derived from structures are severed, at some social cost to the migrant. In the decision-making process, perceptions of discomfort due to leaving friends and familiar groups and of discomforts at the area of destination are considered as generally inhibiting decisions to move. If aspirations are such that they may be fulfilled in the community of residence, they will reinforce satisfactions. If they cannot be fulfilled in the community of residence, they would be expected to weaken satisfactions and to reduce perceptions of social costs attending movement.

While this brief formulation is intended as an explanation of voluntary migration in general, it seems especially applicable to the explanation of out-migration from farm areas. If economics provide the complete explanation of migration, why are the depressed farm areas still heavily populated? Why do some farmers in a given area move while others remain? An illustration may clarify the sociological variables used. Farmer X lives in the community in which he was born, is surrounded by kinfolk, is a member of and participates in numerous local groups. Except for weekly trips to the trade center, he has not often been outside his local community. He holds a negative image of the city — that is, the city is impersonal, it inhibits one's freedom, and everyone is in a perpetual rush. Farming is the only work he has ever done. He not only wishes to live out his life in the community but has similar aspirations for his children. In this deliberately overdrawn illustration, Farmer X could hardly expect to decide to migrate. Not only is he highly identified and committed to his local community (satisfactions), but he also has no desire for change (aspirations) and holds a negative image of the city (social costs).[7]

---

[7] A number of rural sociologists cooperating in the North Central Regional Project concerning field studies of migration are utilizing the variables outlined. In a low income area of Michigan's Upper Peninsula, Mrs. Eicher found that the nonmigrants remaining in this out-migration area were highly attached to the area and had aspirations that could be satisfied locally. No statistically significant differences between Finns and non-Finns could be found in level of satisfactions or aspirations. Older age was found to be significantly related to aspirations attainable in the community. In summary, Mrs. Eicher writes: "First, the overwhelming majority of nonmigrants of all age and ethnicity groups seem extremely satisfied with the community, for few seriously intend to leave. Second, even if the community maintains its status quo and no innovations occur to bring about better schools, recreation, and other improvements then this same "hard-core" of nonmigrants will still remain in Ontonagon County. Next, it follows that out-migration will drain off only a handful of the family heads of all ages and ethnicity categories, for they demonstrate a strong preference to remain because of marriage, family, and friendship ties as well as occupational ties." Joanne Bubolz Eicher, Social Factors and Social Psychological Explanations of Non-Migration, East Lansing, Michigan State University, Ph.D. dissertation, 1959.

SIGNIFICANCE OF TRENDS IN THE FARM LABOR FORCE

Among the trends in the farm labor force the following should be enumerated: First, the farm labor force has been declining rapidly, both absolutely and as a proportion of all persons employed in agriculture. Second, while the precise nature of recent trends in some instances is difficult to establish, it is sufficient to state that certain characteristics of the hired farm labor force have persisted over time. These include seasonality of work, the casual attachments to employers, intermittent employment in agriculture, multiple job holding, low wages, and youthfulness of farm workers.[8]

Significance to the Rural Areas

Since some of the changes in the farm labor force are long-time trends, the nature of the impact upon rural areas is relatively well documented.

In keeping with the ecological model of dominance outlined earlier in this paper, the large urban areas have successfully attracted high proportions of young adults. This leaves a high proportion of older farm operators who are less likely to want to make changes in farm operations or to be as responsive to needs and opportunities as younger men. The age structure of farm populations, therefore, is unbalanced, with large proportions of very young and older-aged groups. Furthermore, the dominance of urban areas has been felt in other ways. In the competition for land in most instances, nonagricultural uses take precedence over agricultural uses. Nonagricultural functions are increasingly being performed in rural areas, and the rural areas are becoming increasingly heterogeneous.

Indications of increasing numbers and proportions of wage and salary workers in agriculture have direct meaning for the character of rural social structure. For the farm sector of the economy in which per capita incomes already lag, the trend is alarming. From virtually all points of view a growing underprivileged class is highly undesirable. From the point of view of hired workers, present conditions of seasonality of work, intermittent employment in and out of agriculture, low wages, and impersonal relations with employer must spell an all but untenable

[8] Cf. Harry S. Kantor, Problems Involved in Applying a Federal Minimum Wage to Agricultural Workers, Vol. 1, U. S. Dept. of Labor, Washington, D.C., Apr., 1960, Chap. 11.

style of life. Because of the mobility demanded in the conditions mentioned, many, if not most, of the farm wage workers neither contribute to nor partake of stable community life. In the case of professional migrant workers, many of whom are Mexicans and nonwhites[9] working in predominantly white, Protestant, Anglo-Saxon communities, the problems for the migrants and for the communities are maximized. High rates of delinquency, arrests, and low educational achievement give evidence of the consequences of the life situation of migrant workers.

Significance to the Urban Areas

As suggested previously, one of the most important and, at the same time, one of the most obvious impacts of out-migration from rural areas is the contribution to urban growth and the industrial labor force. This massive movement, however, has not been without great personal cost to the migrant and his family. Furthermore, this migration has not been without problems to the nonfarm areas of destination.

Rural migrants to cities generally have lacked the educational training and social attributes enabling them to make rapidly an adequate adjustment. It is well known that farm migrants enter the urban labor market at lower levels than locally-recruited workers.[10] Lipset and Bendix, for instance, say "...that size of community of orientation is most closely related to occupational position within the ranks of industry and large-scale organization. The smaller the community of orientation, the less likely a lower-class individual is to be upwardly mobile within bureaucratic structures."[11] Since a large proportion of rural to urban migrants initially enter the urban labor market as manual workers, they often reside in the poorer housing areas. Due to the fact that these migrants possess modest resources upon migration combined with comparatively slow upward mobility, the occupancy of poor-housing areas tends to persist for considerable periods of time.

---

[9] See Report of the President's Commission on Migratory Labor, Migratory Labor in American Agriculture, Government Printing Office, Washington, D.C., 1951, and Ernesto Galarza, Strangers in Our Fields, Second ed., Joint United States - Mexico Trade Union Committee, Washington, D.C., 1956.

[10] See Seymour M. Lipset and Reinhard Bendix, Social Mobility in Industrial Society, University of California Press, Berkeley, 1959, especially Part II; and A. O. Haller, "The occupational achievement process of farm-reared youth in urban-industrial society," Rural Soc., Vol. 25, Sept., 1960, pp. 321-33.

[11] Lipset and Bendix, ibid., p. 206.

Social adjustment to urban areas may also be slow. The evidence shows that rural migrants to the city participate less than other urban groups in social and political organizations. Zimmer summarizes the situation as follows: "When migrants first enter the new community they are much less active in the formal structure than are the natives, but with time their participation rate increases. The adjustment takes at least five years, however, and in some types of behavior migrants possessing low-status characteristics never do attain the same level of participation as the natives."[12] To the degree rural migrants possess education and skills, the evidence suggests, the problems outlined above are minimized.

SUMMARY

This chapter examines changes in the rural population within the context of metropolitan dominance over the hinterland. Despite increasing interpendence of the farm and nonfarm sectors, the metropolis holds the power to order, regulate, and otherwise control the activities of the hinterland. While economic forces are admittedly very potent in the explanation of internal migration, sociological variables are suggested to account for migration and non-migration. These variables assume the form of components in a decision-making process regarding the question of moving or not moving.

The long history of net migration from rural to urban areas has contributed enormously to urban growth and the industrial labor force and at the same time has drawn off surplus rural population. However, the income position of the farm in relation to the nonfarm sector of the economy has not been solved. Outmigration from farm to nonfarm areas has not been without problems both to the sending and receiving areas. Since rural to urban migration is selective of young adults, the age structure of rural communities is unbalanced. In the urban areas of destination, these migrants generally enter the urban labor market at lower levels. The recent indications of growing numbers of underprivileged workers in agriculture have serious implications for the structure of agriculture as well as for the entire society.

---

[12] Basil G. Zimmer, "Participation of migrants in urban structures," Amer. Soc. Rev., Vol. 20, Apr., 1955, pp. 218-24.

REFERENCES

BOGUE, DONALD J., SHRYOCK, HENRY S., and HOERMANN, SIEGFRIED A. Subregional Migration in the United States, 1935-40, Vol. 1, Streams of Migration Between Subregions, Scripps Foundation, Oxford, 1957.

BOWLES, GLADYS K. Migration Patterns of the Rural-Farm Population, Thirteen Economic Regions of the United States, 1940-1950. Rural Soc., 22:1-11, 1957.

COWHIG, JAMES D., and MAITLAND, SHERIDAN T. The Hired Farm Working Force of 1958, Agr. Info. Bul. No. 219; and An Analysis of the Experienced Hired Farm Working Force 1948-1957, Agr. Info. Bul. 225, USDA, AMS, Washington, D. C., 1959, 1960.

FREEDMAN, RONALD, and FREEMAN, DEBORAH. Farm-Reared Elements in the Nonfarm Population, Rural Soc., 21:50-61, 1956.

GOLDSTEIN, SIDNEY. Patterns of Mobility 1910-1950. University of Pennsylvania Press, 1958.

HALLER, A. O. The Occupational Achievement Process of Farm-Reared Youth in Urban-Industrial Society. Rural Soc., 25:321-33, 1960.

HALLER, A. O., and SEWELL, W. H. Farm Residence and Levels of Educational and Occupational Aspiration. Amer. Jour. Soc., 62:407-11, 1957.

JEHLIK, PAUL J., and WAKELEY, RAY E. Population Change and Net Migration in the North Central States, 1940-50. North Central Regional Publ. 56. Iowa Agr. Exp. Sta. Res. Bul. 430, July, 1955.

KANTOR, HARRY S. Problems Involved in Applying a Federal Minimum Wage to Agricultural Workers. U.S. Dept. of Labor, Washington, D. C., 1960, Vols. 1 and 11.

LIPSET, SEYMOUR M., and BENDIX, REINHARD. Social Mobility in Industrial Society. University of California Press, Berkeley, 1959.

LOOMIS, CHARLES P., and BEEGLE, J. ALLAN. Rural Sociology: The Strategy of Change. Prentice-Hall, Inc., New York, 1957.

NELSON, LOWRY. Rural Life in a Mass-Industrial Society. Rural Soc., 22:20-30, 1957.

REPORT OF THE PRESIDENT'S COMMISSION ON MIGRATORY LABOR. Migratory Labor in American Agriculture. U.S. Government Printing Office, Washington, D. C., 1951.

TAEUBER, CONRAD, and TAEUBER, IRENE B. The Changing Population of the United States. John Wiley and Sons, Inc., New York, 1958.

Chapter 7

R. M. WILLIAMS, JR.
Cornell University

Discussion of Farm Labor Force Movement Analyses

THE BASIC PROCESSES involved in industrialization and urbanization are not peculiar to the United States, nor to the West, but affect all societies at a certain level of technological and economic development. Always, once beyond a critical "take-off point," the agricultural sector loses labor to the nonagricultural sector. In my own view, it is extremely rare that the shift of population is rapid enough or complete enough to equalize marginal real returns of labor of comparable type and grade as between the two sectors. It seems clear, at any rate, that the historical tendency has been for "economically adjustive" mobility to fall short of perfect competitive equilibration. To put it in oversimplified terms, the agricultural sector in industrializing societies tends to be underpaid and overmanned.

The major factors which affect the rate of population transfer between sectors come into play on both sides of the agriculture-nonagriculture line. In the preceding chapters attention has been given to the following main factors:

	In the agricultural sector	In the nonagricultural sector
1.	Real returns to labor	Real returns to labor
2.	Social costs and advantages	Social costs and advantages
	a. Preference-schedules	a. Preference-schedules
	b. Anxiety-security	b. Anxiety-security
3.	Knowledge of alternatives	Unemployment
4.	Capital for migration	Job-rationing

Actual rates of population movement result from complex interaction among these factors, and perhaps several others. With regard to studies dealing with the causes of labor mobility, the crucial questions for research concern the relative importance of each factor and combination of factors. With regard to the consequences of mobility, there are important and interesting questions having to do with at least the following:

1. Economic productivity—agricultural and nonagricultural.
2. Political attitudes and political behavior.
3. Educational organization, ideology, and practice.
4. Family systems, including child-rearing patterns and the establishment of occupational aspirations, motivations and values.
5. Religious organization, participation, beliefs, practices—and secular social consequences.
6. Local social organization, including both formal organizations and "informal" community interactions.
7. Social control and deviant behavior and problems of anomie (normlessness).

The mere listing of these two partial sets of factors relevant to studies of changes in the farm labor force is enough to suggest that detailed and rigorous research, rather than global impression, is essential for adequate understanding. This suggestion is further reinforced when the scattered suggestions as to the varieties of labor mobility itself are pulled together. First of all, there is the farm-to-farm mobility of owners, tenants and sharecroppers and of migratory agricultural laborers. The latter may be seasonal workers, operating from a fixed base to which they return, or continuously migratory; they may be family groups or detached individuals; they often are recruited from "racial" or cultural minority groupings. Second, the off-farm or rural-urban migration is highly heterogeneous, including submarginal farmers forced off the land, retired persons, students, young workers in semi-skilled and unskilled occupations, and so on. Third, the urban-rural transfers are similarly diverse, representing movements to commuter homes, rural estates and resorts, urban workers seeking rural residence, urban unemployed. Much of the interchange of rural and urban residence represents "mobility in place," as rural areas become increasingly socially and economically penetrated by urban populations and modes of life.

These considerations point to a major conclusion which the authors of all of the chapters under discussion emphasize, namely, that the aggregate data available permit analyses of only the most gross aspects of the antecedents and consequences of population mobility. The most interesting problems and findings will require much greater differentiation and precision, as well as many entirely new types of data. The ingenious and thoughtful analyses presented show how much firm and valuable knowledge can be extracted from present information, but at the same time our appetites are whetted for data sufficient to answer the more sophisticated question we can now formulate.

Running through all the foregoing chapters is a consistent picture of the enormous farm-nonfarm interchange of population which has been going on for many years in the United States. The vast movements which occur decade after decade are well-nigh incredible, if judged by the standards of traditionalized, nonindustrial societies. The volume of population movement is an index of the extraordinary responsiveness of our people to differentials and changes in economic returns and employment opportunities (especially the latter). The more specific contributions of the chapters by Bishop, Hadwiger, and Beegle warrant individual summaries and comments.

After presenting a tightly reasoned argument, supported by impressive empirical analysis, Dr. Bishop states his central thesis in the following terms:

> ...migration has failed to equalize returns for farm and nonfarm labor because the number of people who are willing to transfer to nonfarm jobs at prevailing rates of return exceeds the number of jobs that are available...job rationing limits migration.

In its main explicit contention, I regard the hypothesis as well-supported by Dr. Bishop's analysis. For example, he is able to show that off-farm migration increases sharply when urban jobs are available even though relative income in the farm sector is going up at the same time. He suggests that this peculiar behavior has two possible explanations: increased farm income provides necessary financing for off-farm migration; and job rationing reduces migration. He believes the latter factor is primary. I find his argument convincing, on the whole, but would suggest that a third factor may play a part, namely, a greater propensity of farm workers to migrate when general economic conditions are perceived as "good." The hypothesis here would be that psychological security, or low anxiety, ranks relatively high in the preference-schedules of prospective migrants and that relatively high farm incomes help to generate the confidence required to act upon a desire to enter the urban labor market.

Dr. Bishop's discussion of the possible implications of his analysis for public policy is clear and forthright. It should have a salutary effect upon a certain tendency to loose and sentimental thinking in this matter.

The chapter by Dr. Hadwiger shifts our attention to the political concomitants of recent changes in the farm labor force — a topic which he justifiably interprets broadly enough to include "changes in the ecology and the economics of farm areas and also to include changes in rural attitudes and values."

For purposes of summary and emphasis, let us juxtapose several important generalizations revealed by Professor Hadwiger's analysis.

1. Agricultural regions are becoming internally more diversified; one-commodity regions are disappearing, and with them goes the simple log-rolling possibilities once so convenient in connection with agricultural legislation in Congress.

2. Rural and urban, industry and agriculture are becoming intermingled on a large scale even in our most intensive agricultural regions. This development forces numerous new direct confrontations of farmer and urban worker, of industrial and agricultural interests.

3. Fewer and fewer farmers are exclusively engaged in farming.

4. There is pervasive exposure of farmers to mass communications and to most of the elements of an "urban" standard of living.

5. There are heavy concentrations of rural populations within the immediate vicinity of most metropolitan areas.

6. All in all, the farm-dwelling population in each geographic area is rapidly becoming more diverse in its economic, social and cultural characteristics.

This excellent analysis points to a major conclusion which is only seemingly paradoxical: in rural America homogenization of values and interests is occurring through increasing heterogeneity of overlapping groups and interests. Historically, the farm population, as compared with the urban population, has been less tolerant of nonconformity in ideas and beliefs, more inclined to favor "states rights" and localism, less internationally-minded. Although the tendencies outlined above work in the direction of "urbanization" of political attitudes, the net effect of off-farm mobility is to leave on the farms a population which tends to be elderly and of relatively low education, and whose political attitudes tend toward authoritarianism, conformism and pessimism.

The decreasing proportion of the labor force engaged in agriculture, along with the other changes reviewed by Dr. Hadwiger, points to a decline of rural influence in Congress and in many of the state legislatures. However, the accessibility of executive agencies to representatives of rural interests and the special weight given to the "farm vote" by its volatile character indicate that American farm interests will continue to play a very important part in national politics and government for the foreseeable future.

The chapter by Professor Beegle independently reinforces several of the major conclusions already summarized. He points especially to: (1) the loss of rural self-determination; (2) the increasing interdependence of farm and nonfarm sectors of the society; (3) the homogeneity of mass communication; (4) the blurring of the functions of "field" and "center"; (5) the great magnitude of rural-urban exchanges of population. More than the other chapters, this analysis concentrates upon the differential social impacts of economic changes and population transfers. For example, Beegle calls attention to the growing numbers of farm wage workers, who live under extraordinarily difficult social and economic circumstances. Or, again, he effectively points out the very different effects of population movements upon different types of rural communities. More generally, this chapter highlights the social costs of migration in such forms as low social participation, the ravages of social dis-esteem, rootlessness and disorganized family and community life.

A cursory reading of the chapters by Drs. Bishop and Beegle might leave the impression that the economist and the sociologist flatly disagree in appraising the relation between economic factors and mobility. Beegle tells us:

> While the role of economic forces in the explanation of migration is admittedly very great, it fails to account for many of the existing patterns of mobility in American agriculture.

But Bishop says:

> The behavioral response of farm people to economic incentives is quite consistent with economic logic.

A closer inspection of the two chapters will show that the two analyses are complementary rather than divergent. Dr. Bishop explicitly includes nonpecuniary considerations in his conception of economic forces; Dr. Beegle is clearly aware of the sensitivity of rural youth to urban opportunities; he knows that we have a population trained to react strongly to economic signals. The differences in language, in short, fail to conceal the essential points of convergence in the two analyses.

In this connection, however, let me emphasize an obvious point which often escapes attention in economic analysis. One sometimes detects the hidden assumption, even in otherwise quite sophisticated analysis, that social and cultural factors are important only in economically irrational or non-rational behavior.

Nothing could be more misleading or further from a correct formulation. Social and cultural factors are omnipresent in the most impeccably rational "maximizing" behavior. As long ago as Alfred Marshall's treatment of "wants adjusted to activities" this point was made abundantly clear. In this day of major advances in systematic sociological and psychological theory and research the articulation of "economy" and "social system" can be made rather specific. Unfortunately, this possibility is still forgotten on occasion, under the influence of an unduly constricted conception of the theoretical framework necessary for empirical analysis of "economic" phenomena.

One final point emerges from a consideration of the three chapters under review, in conjunction with the presentations of Drs. Sjaastad and Fuller. It is generally agreed that:

1. Mobility does not equalize marginal real returns to labor in the farm and nonfarm sectors.

2. Future demands for labor in nonagricultural occupations will be primarily for relatively well-educated and skilled workers.

3. A persisting level of unemployment in the nonagricultural sector well above the "frictional" rate does not bode well for the easy assimilation into urban occupations of poorly educated and unskilled rural people.

4. Local rural communities, in the absence of urban-industrial developments, usually cannot solve their economic problems by out-migration alone.

5. Heavy out-migration is likely to leave on the farms in low-income rural areas a population with low achievement-motivation and achievement-values.

On the basis of these considerations, I would like to pose a possibly crucial question: Are we, as a nation, on the way of creating a kind of "sub-proletariat" of uneducated and unskilled and poorly motivated workers — in rural communities and among rural migrants to cities — who are becoming frozen in self-perpetuating enclaves within our generally affluent middle-class society? The preceding analyses would strongly suggest that this is the case. So far as I can see, an outcome of this kind is inevitable unless imaginative and decisive public action to prevent it is taken in the near future.

Chapter 8

HOWARD ROSEN
U.S. Dept. of Labor

Projected Occupational Structure and Population Distribution

ALTHOUGH MUCH of the work done in the Bureau of Labor Statistics is concerned with urban labor, an examination of the over-all labor force has brought to our attention some of the manpower problems which are developing in the field of agriculture.

Basically, the problem is the movement of workers from rural to urban areas. In many instances, the figures of the movement of workers are not cold statistics – but represent sons and daughters who have grown up in a rural society and in order to make a living are forced to move to the city.

Present estimates show that 68 out of 168 (about 40 percent) of the male children of farm families who reached the age of 20 during the 1950's had to find employment outside agriculture – even though the number of job opportunities in farming remained constant.[1] This net out-migration problem is expected to continue during the 1960's.

In our consideration of the problem of farm to nonfarm adjustment we must try to picture what the nonfarm world of work will be like in the next 10 to 15 years. This brings us to the projections of population, labor force, and occupational trends developed by the United States Department of Labor.[2] Our outlook for the 1960's is based on three assumptions:

1. A continuation of the relatively high levels of economic activity and employment which have prevailed in the United States for the past 15 years, consistent with the goals expressed in the Employment Act of 1946.
2. A continuation of scientific and technological advance, affecting our industrial methods of production; medical, health, and educational services; and consumption patterns.

[1] "The tenure status of farm workers in the United States," Tech. Bul. 1217, p. 45, USDA, ARS and AMS.
[2] "Manpower: challenge of the 1960's," U.S. Dept. of Labor, Washington, D.C.

3. The absence of war or any other cataclysmic event which would substantially alter the rate of our economic growth.

We believe that the United States has the manpower resources for a much higher standard of living during the 1960's. We think that the gross national product, which represents the total amount of goods and services produced in the United States, will rise from $500 billion in 1960 to about $750 billion by 1970. On the population side, the Census Bureau of the United States Department of Commerce estimates that the number of people in this country will increase from 180 million to about 208 million by 1970 -- about a 15 percent increase.

The important point about this population increase is that it will be especially rapid among young people reaching working age. In 1960, about 2.6 million young people reached age 18 and were ready to enter the labor force or go on to college (see Table 8.1). In 1965 there will be a still greater rise in the number of people becoming 18 years old — close to 4 million will attain that age.

Table 8.1. Young Persons Reaching Age 18 Annually 1950, 1955, and Projected 1960 to 1970 (in Millions)

Year (July 1)	Number
1950	2.2
1955	2.2
1960	2.6
1961	2.9
1962	2.8
1963	2.8
1964	2.8
1965	3.8
1966	3.6
1967	3.6
1968	3.6
1969	3.7
1970	3.8

Source: Bureau of the Census, U.S. Dept. of Commerce.

This means that rural youth seeking urban jobs will face a highly competitive situation in the 1960's. The biggest ten-year jump in the size of the labor force in our history will take place between 1960 and 1970. By far the greatest increase and, in fact, accounting for about half of the total net growth (46 percent increase), will be among the new workers under 25 years of age.

At the same time, another very large increase — 20 percent — will take place in the number of workers above the age of 45.

During the 1960's, the number of women workers will increase at nearly twice the rate for men (see Table 8.2). It is estimated that by 1970 there will be 30 million women workers in the United States, 6 million more than in 1960.

Table 8.2. Women in Labor Force, 1960 and Projected 1970, by Age Group (in Millions)

Age	1960	1970
Total women	23.6	29.6
14-19 years	2.3	3.2
20-24	2.5	3.9
25-34	4.4	4.9
35-44	5.3	5.5
45-54	5.1	6.5
55-64	3.0	4.3
65 years and over	1.0	1.3

Source: Bureau of Labor Statistics, U.S. Dept. of Labor.

Let us now turn to the kind of changes we expect in industry employment in the 1960-70 decade. This is important because if we are going to give our young people sound vocational advice and guidance, we should be alert to those employment areas which will have the greatest number of job opportunities.

In all, we expect total employment to rise by about 20 percent in the 1960's (see Table 8.3). Employment in the construction industry is expected to rise much faster than the average for total employment because of the growing number of households, increasing expenditures for schools and highways, rising volume of business activity, and higher levels of personal and corporate income.

The number of jobs in finance, insurance, and real estate is also expected to expand rapidly, owing to increasing complexity and growth of our financial activities, rising levels of income, and expansion of our industrial and urban society. Trade employment will rise as our rapidly growing population reaches higher standards of living. Although government employment is expected to increase faster than the average, the growth will primarily occur in state and local activities because of the need for increased education, public health, sanitation, welfare, and similar services. New products and processes and the need of newly married couples for consumer products will contribute to the growth of employment in manufacturing.

Table 8.3. Employment by Industry Group, 1960 and Projected 1970 (in Millions)

Industry	1960	1970
Total employment	60.6	72.9
Agriculture	5.9	5.1
Nonagricultural industries	54.7	67.8
Contract construction	3.2	4.3
Mining	.8	.9
Manufacturing	17.2	20.8
Transportation, communication and public utilities	4.0	4.5
Wholesale and retail trade	12.0	15.1
Finance, insurance and real estate	2.6	3.5
Service and miscellaneous	6.7	8.5
Government	8.2	10.2

Source: Bureau of Labor Statistics, U.S. Dept. of Labor.

Total employment in transportation and public utilities will rise more slowly than the average for all employment. The rise in trucking and warehousing and in air transportation will offset a decline in railroad employment. Gas and electric utility employment will increase about as fast as the labor force in the 1960-70 decade. In spite of employment increases in crude petroleum and gas production which will offset somewhat the decline in bituminous coal mining employment, total employment in mining will rise much more slowly than average employment. To complete the picture, employment in agriculture will continue to decline as output per farm worker increases.

When we reverse the coin and look at the occupational changes expected in the 1960's, we get close to home — because it is in relation to changes in the occupational structure that we must advise our young rural population about the important question of career choice. Parents and teachers must grapple with the problems related to making capital investments in young people who may very well leave the areas where they received their education. They must also think about the kind of education which will best prepare young people growing up in rural areas for jobs in our urban society. Above all, they must think seriously about helping rural youth overcome the handicap of educational deficiencies which puts them at a disadvantage in obtaining nonfarm employment. [3]

First, let us start with an overview of changes in the occupational structure in the past 15 years and think about the trend we expect in the next decade. In general, the shift has been, and will

[3] "Economic policies for agriculture in the 1960's," op. cit., p. 6.

continue to be, toward occupations requiring more education, training, and experience. Our occupational structure has changed because of the changing industrial pattern, improved technology, the growing complexity of business organizations, and the rising demand for services.

We expect a continuation of the rapid growth of the so-called white-collar group of occupations (professional and technical, managerial, clerical, and sales), a smaller growth in the blue-collar occupations (craftsmen, operatives, and laborers), a faster-than-average growth among service workers, and a further decline among farmers and farm laborers (see Table 8.4).

The greater increase in white-collar jobs reflects our continuing technological advances, especially the greater application of scientific findings to industry, a growing need for educational and medical services, the increase in complexity of occupations, and a growing tendency in all types of enterprise for more record-keeping and research. Although blue-collar workers, as a group, will increase at a much slower pace than white-collar workers, the number of craftsmen will grow at about the same rate as the labor force as a whole.

Table 8.4. Employment by Occupational Groups, 1960 and Projected 1970 (in Millions)

Occupational group	1960	1970
Professional and technical	7.4	10.4
Proprietors and managers	7.1	8.8
Clerical and sales	13.9	17.6
Craftsmen (skilled)	8.7	10.8
Operatives (semiskilled)	12.5	14.8
Laborers, industrial	3.8	3.8
Service occupations	8.1	10.1
Farm occupations	5.9	4.9

Source: Bureau of Labor Statistics, U.S. Dept. of Labor.

The professional, technical, and kindred workers have been by far the fastest growing occupational group in the postwar period. It is expected that the number of persons employed in this occupational group will grow substantially during the 1960-70 period. Within the professional worker group, employment in scientific and engineering fields is expected to increase at a much faster pace than in the traditional fields of medicine, law, and the ministry. The mounting expenditures for research and development programs in business and educational institutions, and the increasingly important role of scientists and engineers in the planning and production of our rapidly changing and increasingly complex military equipment are among the factors making for more demanding requirements for these technical workers. Accompanying the expanded employment of engineers and scientists will be the rapid rise in employment of technicians such as engineering aids and electronic specialists.

Changes in the size, scope, and methods of business operation are among the more important factors influencing employment trends in the manager, official, and proprietor occupational groups. The continuing rise in recordkeeping and communication required to meet the greater complexity of modern business organizations and expanded tax and other reports are expected to more than offset the labor-saving effects of improved office equipment and methods, and, as a result, it is expected that the clerical worker group will show a relatively large increase during the 1960's.

The rising population and per capita income are among the factors that will continue to support the expected employment growth among sales workers. Moreover, the increasing number of part-time workers in sales jobs (as well as in clerical and service occupations) is expected to result in an increase in the total number employed in this occupational group.

Among the blue-collar occupations, by far the largest relative growth is expected in the skilled worker (craftsmen, foremen, and kindred workers) occupational group. Building trades craftsmen, mechanics and repairmen, and skilled machining workers will account for most of the increase in the skilled worker group. More mechanics and repairmen will be needed to maintain, repair, and install the increasing amount of the more complex equipment used in industry. The widespread introduction and use of appliances in the home will require large numbers of appliance servicemen and other skilled maintenance and repair workers.

The operatives and kindred workers group is expected to grow at a much slower rate than total employment during the 1960-70 period. Nevertheless, these semiskilled workers will still remain the largest occupational group in our labor force. In contrast to the effect of mechanization in past decades, which led to the subdivision of skills and trades into a series of routine machine operations that could be performed by semiskilled workers, technological advances of the type known popularly as automation permit great gains in production without commensurate increases in the number of semiskilled machine operatives.

The continuing emphasis on mechanization in industrial operations points to a general relative decline in the proportion of industrial laborers in our work force, although the number in this occupational group will show little change in the 1960-70 period. The service worker occupational group, which includes workers such as those in private households, waiters, cooks, janitors, barbers, and policemen and firemen, is expected to grow more rapidly than the labor force, as a whole, in the 1960's.

Our look into the future makes it obvious that the young workers leaving rural areas and moving into our cities must bring more than willingness to work and a strong back when they seek work. In the job market of tomorrow, emphasis will be placed on education, training, skill, and competence. We must not let our young people seek employment without adequate preparation and training. This is our special challenge in the 1960's. Educational requirements for employment are rising, and we will have to concentrate on turning out better educated young people.

We must make an effort to reduce the number of young people who leave school before graduation. It is an arresting fact that one-third of all students who enter secondary school in the United States drop out before graduating.[4] As a nation, we are the loser because many of these school leavers are potential leaders who cannot make their full contribution to our society. It is inaccurate to think of school leavers as a homogeneous group. They are different in many ways. For one thing, according to a recent Bureau of Labor Statistics study, some dropouts had IQ's, based on standard intelligence tests, as high as those who graduated.[5]

We must explain to our young people that the amount and kind of education they get will determine their future occupations, the amount of unemployment they may face, and, in general, the kind of life they will lead. It is our job to let our young people know that a relatively short-term investment in training and education will pay dividends through the 30 or 40 years of a person's working life.

The guidance problem will be especially difficult in rural areas because many of our rural youth will have little opportunity to become acquainted with the employment requirements of industrial and other urban employers. This means that guidance counselors who work with these boys and girls must be especially well qualified and have a broad background of occupational information. With such knowledge, counselors will be better able to advise these students how to make a successful transition from their rural background to urban work.

---

[4] "Retention in high schools in large cities, 1957," Bul. 15, 1957, Office of Education, U.S. Dept. of Health, Education, and Welfare.

[5] "School and early employment experience of youth: a report on seven communities, 1952-57," BLS Bul. 1277, Aug., 1960, Bureau of Labor Statistics, U.S. Dept. of Labor.

Chapter 9

PHILIP M. RAUP
University of Minnesota

Economic Aspects of Population Decline in Rural Communities

MIGRATION out of agriculture is almost as old as human history. We have, in fact, defined economic development in terms that make the concept virtually synonymous with a reduction of the proportionate importance of agricultural populations. In the European setting, characterized by village-type agriculture, this has also been synonymous with the decline of the rural village. In the United States till the Second World War there was little evidence that the substantial decline of farm populations then under way was associated in a direct fashion with decline in rural villages.

In more recent years we have witnessed the emergence of a form of village-type agriculture in the United States, largely made possible by the automobile and by enormous investment in roads and transport facilities. As a consequence, the absolute and relative decline of population dependent on agriculture in many of the important sectors of the United States is today largely associated with a decline in the populations and status of rural villages. We are witnessing, in effect, a readjustment in the capital structure represented by rural service towns. This paper has three major purposes. The first is to delineate the changes in rural communities brought about by the truck transport revolution that has dominated rural American economic life in the twentieth century and to predict some future trends in this regard. The second is to examine the nature of the changing configuration of rural villages in American agriculture, the reasons that have brought it about, and some of the private and public costs associated with the change.

The relatively unfavorable level of agricultural incomes in the 1950's accentuated trends that were well established two decades earlier. The phenomenal increases in agricultural productivity per man, coupled with increasing requirements for a non-agricultural labor force in marketing, distribution, industry and commerce have precipitated off-farm migration and the decline of many small rural communities. In a fundamental sense they cannot be said to have caused them. The primary cause has been a change in availability of transportation at the farm level, symbolized by the motor truck, the automobile, and the hard-surfaced road. Campaigns of several decades ago to "get the farmer out of the mud" have had the added and hardly anticipated consequence of getting him, or his children, out of agriculture.

American agriculture is consequently over-equipped with small rural service centers. The network of these service centers was laid down under the predominant influence of railroad transport, in the important agricultural areas west of the Appalachians, in the South, and in the far West. Tradition has it that the primary determinants in the location of towns on rail lines were twofold: The distance between fuel and water stops for the ancient wood burning locomotives used on the first rail lines, and the feasible distance for a round trip to market by ox or horse team in one day. Each of these determinants resulted in a spacing of towns on a grid pattern roughly 6 to 10 miles distant from each other. An examination of railroad maps of about 1890 will indicate the "beads on a string" configuration of small villages throughout the key agricultural areas of the Middle West, largely determined by rail-line location.

These patterns of land use and townsite location were maintained and expanded in the early years of motor truck transport and rural farm-to-market road development from 1920 to the Second World War. In more recent years many "railroad towns" in rural America suffered severe shock as rail service facilities were curtailed. One aspect of this shock is seen in the conversion from coal to diesel fuel and elimination of the need for railroad division points at roughly 60 to 90 mile intervals. The more serious aspects result from the discontinuance of rail service, removal of trains, and elimination of daily runs that have dramatized the impact of truck transportation on rural towns whose initial location was dominated by the railroad.

This change has come about so swiftly that we have not yet witnessed its full impact. Fragmentary evidence can be read out of statistics on the bulk movement of farm products and supplies. In 1946, for example, 90 percent of all gasoline moving into North Dakota was carried by rail; in 1958, 86 percent of a larger volume was carried by motor truck. Rail carriers moved more than half of total gasoline into that state as late as 1952. The devastating impact of truck transport on rail freight traffic has thus largely been confined to the post-Korean War era.

The small "land locked" town off the rail line was given a new lease on economic life by the possibility of truck service for the inmovement of merchandise and the outmovement of products. This did not appreciably change the original pattern of secondary towns and small villages. The process of differential development for centers whose initial location was determined by rail services traces back to the days of first settlement. Where exceptions can be found, they relate principally to nonagricultural functions, particularly those associated with recreation and the exploitation of mineral resources.

As the network of interstate highways becomes open for traffic in the 1960's, we can expect to witness a new configuration of rural service towns, primarily influenced by these truck line arteries. The transportation revolution is still under way. Rural America has now clearly entered an era of "truck agriculture," but the consequences for the small town are still developing.

The major trends now apparent seem clearly to indicate a pattern of rural service towns in the last half of the 20th century that will be dominated by truck and feeder line transport arteries focused on the interstate highway system. Not only can we expect to see a continuation in the decline of small rural towns; we can also expect to see new configurations in the larger service centers that will replace them. They will not likely be widely spread over the rural landscape in a fashion that can be predicted from the current map of small-town locations. We can expect, in short, a sharply differential impact in the wasting away of small rural towns. Those remote from major road networks are not likely to see their functions taken over by one neighboring local but larger center; the region as a whole is more likely to surrender its supply and market functions to larger and remote market towns more advantageously situated with respect to heavy truck transportation.

The pattern of rural service centers that emerges may draw even sharper lines between rural and urban areas. Those rural communities and counties that are remote from major highway routes seem likely to become even more rural, by relative standards. We may be able to put this hypothesis to test when 1960 census of population data become fully available. Preliminary indications are that rural Midwest counties that have in the past had the highest ratios of "rural farm" population to total population have maintained these high ratios or even increased them. The decline of the small town may be less pronounced in these areas, but in contrast to more urbanized regions, the rural nature of these remote areas may stand out more clearly.

ECONOMIES OF SCALE FOR RURAL VILLAGES

This decline can be understood in terms of the changing requirements for a viable rural community. It will be instructive to begin by asking: What are the determinants of minimum tolerable economic size of a small rural town? In the past these determinants have been functions of the trade territories required to support local markets and minimum-scale service facilities required by rural farm and household consumers. In short, could the trade territory support a hardware store, a lumber yard, a bank, a blacksmith and machinery repair shop, a cream buying center, perhaps a cheese or milk processing plant, a grain elevator, plus schools, churches, and the like? Given the technologies of market assembly and merchandising of past generations, a relatively small rural place could support these minimum level functions. The prevalence of small rural communities of 100 to 500 population is ample testimony to this observation.

Technological changes in milk processing, grain handling, and livestock transport have all combined to raise significantly the minimum volume of business required to support efficient marketing agencies for agricultural products. On the supply side of the farm market, both for productive factors and family living requirements, parallel increases in minimum scale of business volume have taken place. The food supermarket, central bulk distributing stations for liquid fuels and gases, increasing scale of operation for feed mills, machinery repair centers, and banking and credit facilities have all played a role in this process.

As a consequence, many small rural towns are technologically obsolete. They command a trade territory that is inadequate for efficient marketing of farm products or for efficient provision of farm and family production and living requirements. In the terminology of economists, the "economies of scale" curve for the small rural town has shifted sharply to the right. In analyzing the reasons for this shift in the minimum economic size of rural communities, it is necessary to establish criteria by which minimum economic size may be measured. It is here proposed that the viability of a rural community is determined by the extent to which it is characterized by four key features:

1. A supply area adequate to provide a sufficient volume of products for the efficient operation of key assembly or processing functions. Examples are bulk milk handling equipment, grain elevators with cleaning and conveyor equipment needed to keep stored grain in condition, and

livestock auction markets with a sale volume large enough to attract competitive buyers.

2. A trade territory adequate to support the low-cost provision of producers' services and supplies. Examples are bulk feeds, formula fertilizers, liquid fuels, bottle gas, veterinary services, and machinery parts stocks and overhaul facilities.

3. An internal labor market sufficient to provide a range of job opportunities that will enable the effective utilization of the local labor force. Small communities, for example, are often unable to offer remunerative employment for women and girls.

4. A tax base and an economic structure large enough to permit efficient investment of social overhead capital in public utilities, educational facilities, churches, and recreational and amusement facilities. Water supply and sewage disposal are examples of public services that are frequently inadequate in the small town.

In each of these aspects, supply area, trade territory, labor market and tax base, the effect of recent trends has been to enlarge greatly the volume of business or size of market required for efficient operation.

It is important to recognize that the primary forces bringing these shifts about are not those directly associated with low farm incomes and low per capita purchasing power. The income position of American agriculture since 1945 has failed to progress in step with the nonfarm economy. This has had an important linkage relationship with the economic viability of small towns dependent on farm customers for their business volume. But low farm incomes alone have not sounded the death knell of many small towns. They were technologically obsolete at least by the outbreak of the Second World War; low incomes of recent years have simply accelerated our recognition of this obsolescence.

There is reason to believe, on the contrary, that higher levels of rural prosperity would hasten the process of small-town deterioration. With more money to spend on consumer goods, services, recreation, and education, many rural families would range farther from their farm homes in search of these service facilities than they now do. In the geographic distribution of American rural communities, for example, there is a rough correlation between high per capita farm income and widely spaced rural service centers. In general terms, the higher the level of farm income, the farther the farm family is prepared to go for its markets, supplies, educational services and recreational outlet.

If we can distinguish for the moment between the product-handling functions of small towns and their function as purveyors of private and public services, it is in service functions that their inadequacies are most apparent. In the private service sector this can be seen clearly in three fields: banking and credit, machinery maintenance and repair, and medical care. Small county banks are often shockingly inadequate to finance the credit needs of modern agriculture. In some states statutory limitations prohibit any single customer loan in an amount greater than 10 percent of a bank's capital stock and surplus. Many banks are so small that this requirement serves currently to exclude them from some of the credit functions needed in the community. This is particularly true in livestock areas in which beef cattle, hog-feeding, or turkey and chicken broiler production are concentrated. Where small size and statutory limits are not barriers, the lack of risk-spreading capacity dictated by the confined "trade territory" of local banks is often a major limitation on credit and community growth. These shortages in credit capacity can be read off a map of local interest rates for short-term loans. In the typical agricultural state, the rate of interest charged under a conventional 90-day personal note ranges from 6 to 10 percent, with the 10 percent rates almost invariably found in the smallest and most remote rural communities.

The provision of minimum-level machinery repair services follows the same pattern. Tractors with fluid drive, fuel injection systems, and complex components whose assembly and disassembly can only be accomplished with special jigs, fixtures, and hydraulic presses are commonplace on American farms. Their repair and maintenance is beyond the capacity of the traditional small town machineshop. For many farmers today, repair facilities and spare-part stocks are less available to them than was the case one or two decades ago. Complexity and variety in farm machinery design have lifted the minimum size of service territory needed to permit a reasonable spread for the heavy overhead costs that must now be met by machinery and parts dealers, and repair centers.

The difficulties faced by small towns in attracting or holding doctors, dentists, and hospital staffs are so well documented they require no further elaboration. As with farm machinery repair, the skills and equipment needed in the practice of modern medicine require a large volume of business if low unit costs are to be achieved. That the trade territories of small towns are often unable to supply this volume is illustrated by the fact that, in 1955, approximately one half of the incorporated communities in Minnesota were without the services of a locally resident doctor.

In the public sector, two aspects of inadequate service can also be identified: education and public utilities. James Bryant Conant, in his path-breaking study of American high schools, has observed that the minimum effective scale of operation usually involves an enrollment sufficient to produce a graduating senior class of approximately 100 students. This minimum scale of high school operation is in general beyond the level, and often far beyond it, that can be supported by small rural service towns. The volume of "business" needed to support the minimum tolerable level of public education through the high school has grown so rapidly that the small-town high school district finds itself at a serious disadvantage. This is dramatized by the fact that 20 percent of the public high schools in Minnesota find themselves unable to offer the minimum levels of mathematics required for entrance into college freshman algebra courses! The schools in question are almost all in small and usually remote rural communities.

In the public utilities sector, inadequate water supply, sewage disposal, and street and road maintenance have seriously handicapped the small town. The community offering substandard educational facilities and poor public utilities finds it virtually impossible to attract new industry, even where local labor supply might play an important role.

One important way in which rural population decline has handicapped the under-sized rural service center is through impairment of the tax base. A byproduct of population movement off of farms and out of rural communities is the collapse of rural nonfarm land values. In many small rural towns a platted lot and house are virtually unsaleable under present market conditions. We have witnessed in the 1950's the phenomenon of continually increasing farm land prices in the face of stable or declining farm incomes. No parallel increase in the value of small-town urban-type residential lands has taken place. On the contrary, there has been both a relative and an absolute decline in urban property values in many of the small towns of rural America. As a consequence, the capacity of these communities to support public services has been greatly reduced. Higher levels of dependence on state aid to roads and schools are evidence of this growing fiscal pressure. The problems of the small town are thus compounded. At a time when these communities should be upgrading their public services, their financial capacity to do so has slipped badly. A substantial destruction of property values in rural areas is under way. This has not been apparent in the statistics on farm land prices in recent years. We have no adequate statistics on land values in rural service towns and villages; if they were available, they would show declining values for many communities and consequent eroded tax bases.

There are important psychological and institutional barriers to adjustments for meeting this reduced capacity to finance the traditional functions of rural local government. For roads, streets, and highways this problem has been reduced through well-established programs of state and federal aid. No similar programs at the federal level have yet been developed for education. Rural communities, in fact, are often in the forefront of those opposing systems of federal aid to education. There is a disturbing lack of local realization that the cost of educating children who will not remain in the community to add to its labor force and income flow is a form of capital export. The typical rural community is peculiarly unsuited to engage in this form of subsidy to the urban and nonfarm sectors to which surplus rural youth will migrate. Until rural communities develop a more realistic appreciation of this fact, they create for themselves one of the most significant barriers to the adaptations required by the prospect of continuing rural population losses.

THE FULL INTEGRATION OF RURAL COMMUNITIES INTO THE MONEY ECONOMY

American agriculture is widely heralded as commercial and profit-oriented, conducted by businessmen-farmers who represent a high level of development in the application of business management techniques to agricultural production. In a comparative sense, and with the agricultural economies of most other countries in mind, this is an accurate portrayal. In an absolute sense, and in terms of motive forces associated with the price system and money economy in nonfarm sectors of the United States, the picture is inaccurate.

We can distinguish three phases in the development of a commercial agriculture, operating under the price directions made possible by a money economy. The first phase is characterized by the appearance of clearly-defined markets for farm products and a significant decline in home manufacture and processing for home consumption. The symbol of this phase of commercialization of agriculture might be the small rural town market place, or "fair." With the development of transportation, refrigeration, and efficient materials handling, a second phase emerges in which a substantial part of the contact between agriculture and the money economy takes place in distant processing or market centers. The symbol for the second phase of commercialization might be the large public stock yards, the central grain exchange, or an integrated dairy products plant.

As a consequence of the out-migration of rural populations, we can note the appearance of a third phase in the process of monetizing agriculture. Small assembly points and market service towns that played a key role in the development of present central market structures are now giving way to larger and highly nucleated market and service towns. The disappearance of smaller towns and the regroupment of their service functions into fewer and larger centers marks an almost total break from subsistence agriculture, home production for home use, and the processing of agricultural products on the farm. This is apparent. Less apparent but more important is the depersonalization of marketing and purchasing relations between farmers, the buyers of their products, and the suppliers of their needs.

Even in the highly commercial sectors of United States agriculture — the Wheat Belt, cotton in the high plains, or corn-hog-beef feeding in the Middle West there has long been a high degree of personal relationship between farmers and the nonfarm individuals to whom they look for markets and supplies. The typical marketing transaction in these highly commercial sectors did not take place in an atmosphere that permitted a complete operation of price motives and money considerations. There was always the personal relationship to be considered. The farmer was typically acquainted with the persons who bought his products, and from whom he bought his production and household needs. These were often neighbors; they went to the same churches; their children were thrown together in the same school systems; and there were many nonmoney considerations to influence the local market structure.

With a sharp upward movement in the size of efficient rural service towns, there has come a distinct break in this complex system of local rural interpersonal relations. The farmer seldom is personally acquainted with the buyer of his product in major sectors of United States agriculture today. Many of his contacts with suppliers of technical services, production requirements, or equipment and machinery are with people who are outside of his community and the social circles in which he moves.

The emphasis falls more heavily than before on price and money considerations; the personal equation in the marketing transaction has been reduced and in some cases virtually eliminated.

One important consequence is the fuller integration of agriculture into a money economy. Price considerations have been given freer rein, and the restrictions on bargaining imposed by a high level of interpersonal relationship are reduced. Even in the 1950's the spectacle of farmers who purchased their bread, butter, milk, and eggs from retail merchants was sufficient to cause a raised rural eyebrow. In the 1960's this is commonplace. One result is that the proportion of production needs and consumer goods now purchased from other firms has increased sharply in American agriculture. This increasing level of purchases from other firms and decline in the personal relationship represented by market contacts are support for the conclusion that major sectors of American agriculture are in the 1960's entering fully into the money economy for the first time.

A further consequence of this depersonalizing influence of a market economy can be anticipated. Larger rural market centers and depersonalized marketing can be expected to promote the growth of labor unions at primary levels of farm product merchandising and processing. With prominent exceptions, principally on the eastern and western seaboards, rural America has had little opportunity for direct contact with organized labor. This is rapidly changing. The small firms and personal relations that characterized rural communities of up to about 5,000 population have presented union organizers with unrewarding prospects. This changes abruptly as the scale of firm and size of town increase. As a rough approximation, we can observe that the "response curve" to union organizing activity turns sharply upward as town size increases through the 5,000 to 15,000 range. Larger firms appear; skills become more specialized, and group-centered motives gain in ascendency over the two-person relationships that have in the past been typical of the farmer's contact with the market.

An additional consequence of fewer and larger rural communities is thus likely to be seen in the growth of more direct contact between farmers and labor unions. In fields as dissimilar as foreign affairs and child training, it is axiomatic that it is the unknown that is feared. While direct farm exposure to union activity can be expected to result in a painful adjustment process, this is likely to be a short-run effect. From a long-run point of view, the expansion of labor unions out of metropolitan centers and into rural communities may lead to an increased awareness of common problems and healthier political relations between labor and agriculture.

CONCLUSION

It is reasonable to expect that there will continue to be an economic function for many small towns. Their role will be reduced in relative importance, but it is unlikely that the majority of them will disappear. Processes similar to those that characterize the disinvestment of farm capital are at work in the market centers that serve agriculture. Under-maintenance of physical facilities and stagnation at a low level of economic activity can proceed for several generations before they force the abandonment of farm land, or of rural towns. For many towns this process is well advanced. In the years immediately ahead we may have an opportunity to weigh more carefully the economic and social contribution that the small town can make.

Some insight into this future may be provided by a review of the early impact of the tractor and large-scale farm machinery upon agriculture. The early forms of mechanized agriculture were built around large units; too large for the typical farmer to operate economically. Later refinements increased the efficiency of smaller tractors and machines, and it became apparent that the technological limits set for minimum farm size were much lower than originally projected. The mechanization of production and the introduction of intensive levels of use of fertilizers, agricultural chemicals, and better seeds and feeds do not in themselves condemn the small farm as an efficient productive enterprise. Evidence is accumulating to support the view that credit limitations, inadequate market power and imperfect access to the fruits of education and agricultural research are much more significant limitations on the viability of the small farm.

It is here proposed that a comparable sequence of reactions to technological change is evident in small towns. There appear to be no compelling technological reasons why marketing and supply functions cannot be performed efficiently at relatively small scale. If the small town is technologically obsolete, it seems much more likely that this obsolescence is a consequence of our failure to develop external services and institutional structures adapted to small-town needs. Prominent among these deficiencies are credit, planning, and research.

It should be recognized that a pervasive reason hastening the economic decline of the small town is that it is largely outside the structure within which supervised mortgage credit is available for residential construction. In large urban centers the FHA loan, backed by direct or indirect government guarantees, has provided a decisive vehicle for the credit financing of residential housing. Small town dwellers are not excluded from these benefits, but they find themselves at a disadvantage in using them. Large-scale urban builders, flanked by credit agencies with national influence, have tailored our structure of residential credit to large-scale urban needs. The small-town resident and the small-town businessman find themselves between an agricultural credit structure tailored for farm production needs and an urban credit structure tailored for big-city requirements. If we search for institutional defects that contribute to the decline of the small rural town we could well begin with credit.

A similar deficiency can be found in the lack of access to research and technical services of a city-planning nature. Farm planning services are widely available, although not so widely used as we might wish. Larger cities in the past quarter century have recognized the contributions that can be made by urban planning, zoning, and research on urban problems. These forms of "external economies of scale" are generally unavailable to the small town.

The explanation for small-town decline is not necessarily to be found in immutable trends toward fewer and bigger farms and toward bigness in marketing and retailing functions. A part of the explanation lies in the absence, at the small-town level, of services that we recognize at the farm level under the names of supervised credit and agricultural research and extension. These services have become an established part of the institutional structure serving small business enterprises on the farm. They are often unavailable to small business in rural towns.

Off-farm migration and the changing structure of American agriculture are having profound effects on rural communities. Some of these communities are surplus to our needs for the services that they have traditionally performed. The extent to which they are "surplus" will not be accurately appraised until we have explored more thoroughly the steps that could be taken to render them economically viable. Surprisingly little research and public attention have been directed to these ends.

Chapter 10

MARVIN J. TAVES
University of Minnesota

Consequences of Population Loss in Rural Communities

THE CONSEQUENCES of population loss in rural communities are interpreted in varying ways. Some see such population decline as a disease, others as a sign of health. Some think of decline as a cause of malfunctioning in society, while to others it is a symptom of it, but not a cause. In this chapter population decline is recognized as being all of these at the same time. It is at once a disease to the loyal member of the declining community, a sign of healthy population redistribution to the proponent of efficient social and economic organization for an agricultural region with too many service centers; it is a cause of disaster to the small-town merchant, pastor, or club leader whose efforts are frustrated by declining numbers; it is a symptom of maladjustment to the demographer who studies the larger society.

HISTORICAL PERSPECTIVE

A brief historical review of Midwest agricultural service centers lends some helpful perspectives. Before 1900 the challenge facing rural communities was in large part one of sufficient growth to meet expanding demands of a growing population. Waves of in-migration required the creation of economic and social institutions in the frontier. They called for new stores, schools, churches, and streets. These were largely a "frontier solution" to provide for basic needs. Characteristic was the general store with a limited selection of a broad variety of goods and a multiplicity of functions. Functions often extended to that of news and financial center, social center and courtroom.

About the time these frontier communities approached apparent stability after the turn of the century, a new set of challenges was thrust on them: the demand for proliferation of service, expansion of social opportunities, secularization of outlook, and extension of cultural horizons. Industrialization opened new economic frontiers to replace those closed by westward expansion as urban technology invaded the thought and work patterns of rural life, and as isolation became unrealistic — both physically and socially — the agrarian ethic upon which these communities were based was shaken to its foundations. An urban society promoted rationalization in all phases of life; re-evaluation of life styles, daily culture, and Old World ideas, coupled with reform movements, resulted in new demands on rural life. In response, the rural community initiated consolidation and limitation of services, exhausted available means to meet the rapidity of socio-cultural change, and eventually approached a new form of stability through adjustments to a growing and encroaching urban society.

But a third challenge soon undermined the placidity and new traditionalism which rural communities developed during the first decades of the twentieth century. Wars, a heightened system of industrial complexes, an increasingly involved system of production and consumption, mass communications and transportation, and exchange of a traditionalistic for social ethic, all placed new strains on the rural community. The first had been a period of immigration and the second, one of internal growth, while out-migration characterized the last. For the first time, mass migration from farms, hamlets, and towns to growing industrial and metropolitan areas was observed. The responses on the part of community were to accede to the ways of an urban culture while at the same time restricting proliferation of new services and accepting the inevitability of second place as it continued to pour its redundant populations into the mainstream of an increasingly urban society. In effect, the sequence of events shows a series of responses to changing challenges — adjustments to external events and redefinitions of internal needs. The limitations of frontier solutions gave way to a maturation of local social institutions. Then expanding employment and social opportunities away from these communities created attractions with which the local community could not always compete. Urban-derived aspirations followed the advent of mass communications which made the rural community part of the great American audience.

Today folk values are being questioned; the inviolable sacredness of rural institutions is giving way to a secularism characteristic of urban life. A production orientation is yielding to emphasis on consumption activities. With these forces acting upon the rural community — and over time constituting external pressures and arousing internal motivations for change — the rural community has been pressed to meet the challenge of new ethics, values, and ideologies.

To this observer, today's population decline in rural

communities is above all a response to a challenge — an adjustment mechanism. Because of a relatively high population replacement ratio in such rural communities, it involves out-migration. Within this context out-migration, can be described as an adjustment device which individuals and families employ, and through which the community seeks new equilibrium.

This adjustment takes on different meanings for different persons. The resident of such a community adjusts to restricted employment, and to lack of social and educational opportunities by migrating to areas of greater opportunity. In turn the community is adjusting to lack in resources to carry its maturing population by restricting job opportunities and improvements which would keep its youth (the most mobile segment of its population) "at home." The larger society assists in the process with idealizations of opportunities in areas which can better utilize the labor force represented by the redundant populations of these communities — to the society this is an adjustment as well.

From this orientation the impact of population decline varies with the perspective. Thus one could ask, "What is its impact on the larger society; how does it affect its labor market, its standard of living, its cultural level, its total social and economic well-being?" The answers would often be in direct contrast if the same questions were asked with reference to the local community which sustains the population loss. Without implying any depreciation of this variation in significance of out-migration, the remainder of this discussion will deal almost exclusively with its significance for the residual, or sending, community.

It is to be emphasized that no attempt is made to either defend or deplore population decline in all rural communities. The effort is to assess its consequences. At the same time it is to be noted that the trend in the United States is toward specialization, centralization, and consolidation. In this process many small agricultural service centers become redundant. A selective survival is apparently most desirable.

This possible need for selective demise of rural communities is recognized by even as devoted a proponent of the small community as H. Clay Tate. In his book, Building A Better Home Town, he eulogizes thus:

> The small community is the balance wheel of our economic, social, and cultural order. It is the insurance policy against the loss of the individual's ability to determine his own destiny. In the small community the individual counts. Here he can own his home, keep close to the out-of-doors, and work, worship, and play with his neighbors. Here he can live a well rounded life with people who know him and who care about him. Here he

can establish roots and rear a family in a stabilizing environment. Here he can do more to provide his own security than any man in the large city.

Yet it would be a mistake to defend every community and every unit of government in the United States. Technology and the modern needs of man dictate that only those communities serving the needs of the people in them shall survive. That which no longer serves a useful purpose fades away.

Thousands of them belong now only to the archives, and thousands more are destined to follow them into oblivion. No formula can save them. None should be attempted. Too many weak communities threaten all small communities.

A rural community in a dynamic society has only very limited control over its destiny.[1] It must constantly adjust to changing demands imposed or generated by the rest of society.

STRUCTURAL LEAD VALUE CHANGES

It appears to be characteristic of our rural society that changes in its values trail after, and are a consequence of, changes in its structure in response to external pressures. A more rational process of change would be expected to reverse the pattern. Yet school consolidation occurred mainly in response to the smaller schools' inability to obtain teachers during and immediately after World War II — long after educators had pointed to the values of consolidation. Only after the structure of rural education was changing in response to externally generated demands did the value system in the rural community begin to favor consolidation. Consolidation was more a forced adjustment to forces beyond the control of the rural society (i.e. teacher and cost squeeze) than an appreciation of the functional (educational) values of consolidation.

So with consolidation of agricultural service centers, the value system of both the rural and larger society deplores their individual decline and fails to generate a rational program of reorganization. As a result, three villages too often struggle for social and economic survival where one consolidated community center could flourish at lesser per capita cost.

Rarely do inter-community businesses and social organizations appear to be consciously oriented toward encouraging selective survival of rural communities. Often small town churches, schools, and services are subsidized or staffed at submarginal return with no consideration of possible retardation of the

---

[1] For a discussion of the place of a small community in a dynamic society see Irwin T. Sanders, The Community, The Ronald Press Company, New York, 1958, pp. 146-54.

redistribution of service centers in a pattern commensurate with changing service demands of rural populations. Some exceptions are the attention given to the potential service area in distribution of Hill-Burton act funds for rural hospital development, the selective centralization of processing by the Land O'Lakes company, and the recent studies of potential parish consolidation by several major religious bodies. In these cases community population decline, or failure to grow, contributes to a decision not to enter, expand, or remain in a given community. In this case the impact of population decline is to add impetus to it.

In fact, probably one of the most significant impacts of population decline on the community is its snowballing effect; decline generates further decline. The process is quite apparent: as population declines the community finds it an increasing burden to add new services and provide new amenities offered by a dynamic technology and creative culture. As it lags in the march toward bigger and better stores, schools, churches, and banks, a retrenchment of goals takes place. No longer are community leaders encouraged to make it the greatest little town in the countryside. The emphasis turns to holding the line, making do with facilities and personnel as they are; the community stresses preservation of values, and glories in its past, while others dream of a greater tomorrow. In time its lag becomes apparent as retiring doctors are not replaced, store fronts become outdated, and the community's general appearance engenders memories of an earlier decade.

The most debilitating of all in this process appears to be pessimism generated concerning the declining community's future. It is this pessimism which constricts investment of finances, manpower, and enthusiastic leadership. Those with savings invest it elsewhere lest it depreciate with the decline of their town; those with children sacrifice to educate them for jobs elsewhere in the larger society, and those with free time fail to be inspired to apply it to community improvement. This self-regenerating decline is often halted only after the community has fallen well behind. Even then the thought is for maintaining the community for the present, not for building for the future. At this stage it begins to die with the passing of each of its business and social leaders; it becomes a village of old merchants, old houses, old people; a fading village which will weather and slowly crumble unless it finds a leadership which rekindles optimism. The importance of this optimism is reflected by Doerflinger and Marshall's study of Price County, a declining population area of Wisconsin. They conclude, "There is a need to encourage younger people to return and provide the skills, foresight, and leadership needed to move forward into the tomorrow."[2]

IMPACT BY TYPE OF OUT-MIGRATION

Within this frame of reference, the scope of this discussion is now focused on the more specific consequences of population decline upon the individual rural community. As is often true, the whole is more readily comprehended by viewing its parts. Out-migration is not the only, but is the major, source of population decline in today's rural communities. This out-migration consists in the main of individual youths (to about age 24); of some single individuals and families in their more productive years (approximately 25 to 60 years in age); and of a lesser number of older persons either singly or as members of a residual family (see Table 10.1). In turn the out-migration may result in either temporary, intermittent, or permanent absence from the sending community. The out-migration of each age group has a different impact from the rest. Obviously, the impact of temporary absence differs from that of permanent departure.

The specific impact of each of these types of out-migration must be largely a matter of intelligent conjecture since scientifically controlled observations of variations in sending communities associated with each type of migration are almost nonexistent. The consequences proposed for each type are, therefore, more in the nature of hypotheses growing out of limited knowledge than verified principles of social or economic behavior.

This fourfold typology of sources of population decline in United States agricultural areas is based on a number of assumptions:

1. This population decline is not a consequence of low birth rates and/or high death rates.
2. It is not a result of the dispersal of the center's population into its adjacent hinterland.
3. The chief source of decline is the net out-migration of persons seeking employment and/or residence elsewhere in excess of the number who replace them.
4. This out-migration is selective in terms of age, sex, and occupation.

[2] Jon A. Doerflinger and D. G. Marshall, "The story of Price County, Wisconsin," Research Bul. 220, University of Wisconsin, June, 1960, p. 3.

5. Replacements tend also to be selective but for the most part in a distribution at variance with that of the out-migrants.

6. The different types of out-migration each tend to have a somewhat unique impact upon the community.

The typology here presented is not exhaustive; in fact it obviously does not exhaust the various types of migration even on the continua of age, family, and degree of separation underlying this typological scheme. The intent here is to select a limited number of types which tend to be on the one hand relatively frequent, and on the other sufficiently different, to elicit a good portion of the variety of impacts that different types of out-migration can be expected to have on the declining rural community.

Out-Migration of Youth

By far the greatest population loss in declining rural communities results from the out-migration of persons between the ages of 16 and 25. One of the most thoroughly established demographic principles is that rural-urban migration selects persons on the threshold of adulthood and females in somewhat greater number than males. On the other hand, it may be questioned whether apparent occupational selectivity is a true selectivity or merely differential occupational development after migration. The argument that either the less, or the more, intelligent are drained off by this migration is largely lost in contradictory findings.

These gross data, however, tend to depreciate the impact which this migration can have on individual communities. It is not unusual for well over half of the high school graduating class in a smaller agricultural service center to leave the community within three years of graduation.[3] For most, if not for all of these communities, this out-migration of the best educated of the youth is not replaced by either a return of the out-migrants after further education or by others of equal training.

As noted in Table 10.1, where such out-migration is temporary (as in the cases of young men or women taking seasonal jobs, fulfilling selective service requirements in the armed services, or taking vocational training), the loss to the community may be offset, maybe even more than offset, by their higher quality upon return because of the experience. Their loyalty tends to continue strong,

[3] Marvin J. Taves, "Mobility among high school graduates, sociology of rural life," Sci. Jour. Series No. 4281, Nov., 1959, University of Minnesota.

Table 10.1. Some Consequences to Rural Communities From Loss in Selected Population Categories

I. Degree of Separation: Temporary or Occasional					
		Psychosocial involvement in community		Consequences to community	
Population category	Examples	Participation	Loyalty	Social	Economic
Youth: individual	Seasonal job Army service Higher education Vocational training	Low, but occasionally heightened	Strong - latent	Loss of leadership and interruption in participation • Return with potential for greater contribution and/or altered values	Reduced or some loss in consumption which may be more than replaced after return Burden when returning destitute; asset if better trained
Middle years: fragmented family	Seasonal work Contracting jobbing Armed service	Decreased for all members especially loss of some involvement	Oftentimes re-evaluation of community	Interest in possible subsequent migration Innovation of new ideas Abeyance of leadership: breaks in program continuity	Increased consumption and economic activity Vacationer takes money out of the community Reduces housing demands
Whole family	Extended vacation "Soil bank migrant" temporary job	Interrupted and reduced	Re-evaluation	Same as above but more pronounced	Reduced local consumption production and property values and credit losses
Older aged: whole or residual family	Family tourism Hospitalization or institutionalization	Reduced	Re-evaluation or idealization	Loss of older leadership Decreased dependency Variations in demand for social services	Reduced local consumption and re-allocation of savings

II. Degree of Separation: Permanent

		Psychosocial involvement in community		Consequences to community	
Population category	Examples	Participation	Loyalty	Social	Economic
Youth: individual	Job College and employment Marriage	At a minimum Curtailed Infrequent return to community	Gradual loss of identification Some idealization and/or disillusionment	Reduction of dependent age group Loss of youthful membership and potential leadership Reduced incentives, demands, and restriction of service opportunities Closure on social classes Status quoism - conservatism	Loss of consumption Loss of labor force Reduction in competition for employment opportunities Reduced tax base Lower production
Middle years: fragmented family	Employment Desertion Separation Institutional commitment	Curtailed Selective increase	Selective identification No strong view of total community Some disaffection	Selective exclusion Increase in dependency Greater welfare, legal, and religious demands for residual community	Reduced economic and productive contribution to the community Lower demands for some services
Whole family	Education Jobs Transfers	Effective participation is eliminated	Re-directed to receiving community	Exchange of self-direction for external guidance Reduction of membership Reduction of incentives Loss of vigor Reductions in goals and services Increased occupancy of multiple roles Drift toward anomie Increased fatalism or indifference	Failure to develop resources to highest potential Removal of manpower and economic assets Selective reduction in demand for services Concentration of economic control Selectively reduced overhead
Older years: whole or residual family	Retirement Transfer for health, etc.	Minimum persisent	Strong, although reduced somewhat	Allows new occupancy in old positions, disperses conservatism, reduces dependent age group, loss experienced leadership	Takes financial reserve out and reduces tax base Reduces local consumption and need for special services Reduces economic conservation

though latent. In the case of the chronic temporary migrant who sporadically leaves the community for brief periods of employment, the economic and social loss during his absence may never be made up.

The youth in the permanent migration category appears to represent a much greater loss to the sending community. He presumably leaves to attend college, to obtain vocational training or to take a temporary job; it is hoped he will return. Only at a later date does it become apparent that his farewells had far greater significance. This permanency of the original departure is more apparent in the case of the young woman who leaves the community to marry. In either case, from a socio-psychological point of view, participation in the community's on-going activities is reduced to a minimum, if not curtailed abruptly and completely. Sentiments of loyalty and identification with the community tend to linger. In time these sentiments, however, erode until they become insignificant as reminiscence and idolizing, rather than sharp appraisal of the community.

The ultimate social and economic consequences of the permanent out-migration of these youth are difficult to assess. On the one hand their departure for college and vocational training relieves the sending community of some of the burden of these costs as the young men and women take employment for at least partial support in the communities of their destination. Another portion of the cost is born by the public through taxes and other contributions to higher education. The remainder may come from the sending community via "checks from home." Pressure on job opportunities is likewise relieved for the sending community. On the other hand, their leaving also removes potential leadership, reduces the incentives and demands which youth tends to generate for innovation and improvement. One result is constriction of potentials for economic expansion and social improvement. This encourages closure of social classes and conservatism. In a very real sense, where the vigor and demands of youth outdistance the natural, economic, and social resources of the community, out-migration of the young may serve the functions of a safety valve without which uncontrollable pressures might result in even more painful adjustments not unlike the agrarian revolutions familiar in world history.

Economically the permanent departure of these young men and women represents sizeable losses in immediate consumption; but even more important is the potential loss of their consumption and that of their families. The loss of each young couple at age 19 represents a loss of four a decade later. It likewise represents a loss in manpower resources of that community. For the employer this represents a reduction in his labor supply but for the employee who remains it may represent at least reduction of competition for available jobs. In any case it has been shown that their leaving tends to be associated with reduction in the tax base, and it may also be presumed to be associated with lowered total gross product for the community.

As one basis for estimating the erosion of potential human resources from the point of view of the sending community, the following is suggested for discussion. In an agricultural service center of 3,000 population, with a contributory agricultural population of another 1,000, the local high school graduates a senior class of approximately 100 pupils annually. Recent estimates are that the cost of rearing a youngster to age 18, or high school graduation, amounts to approximately $20,000. Little, if any, of this $20,000 is returned to the community by productive employment before this age. If it may then be assumed that the investment in each of these young out-migrants represents a fair economic estimate of their worth from a strictly monetary point of view, and if it is further assumed that at least 50 percent (or 50 of them) will spend their productive years outside the community, then the loss in human assets from their out-migration amounts to approximately $1 million per annum for this community of 3,000 population. If this same logic is applied to the net annual rural-urban migration of some 275,000 youth for the United States the figure exceeds $5 billion per annum.[4] On the other hand, the dependency and social costs of such additional population, if borne by these communities because of the youth's failure to migrate, would be even higher. It is therefore suggested that this out-migration, costly as it might appear on the surface to the sending community, is a lower financial and social burden for it than would result from the damming up of this outflow of redundant population.

From the point of view of the larger society this redistribution of the labor force also represents an economically defensible adjustment whose consequences are more efficient production and higher productivity for the total society. In turn the migration of this population to centers of greater social and cultural opportunity should result in the fuller cultural development of the migrants. This again represents positive potential for the development of the society as a whole.

---

[4]Another way of estimating this transfer of economic potential is based on the earning potential of the out-migrants. At an estimated $2500 per migrant per year over a 40-year earning period, the potential personal income loss to a community of 3,000 population would be $5,000,000 each year ($100,000 x 50). Extended to the rural-urban youth migrants for the United States, the figure is over $27 billion per year.

All this assumes that there is no concomitant loss of values which living in smaller agricultural service centers generates. Fear for the reduction of such values has been expressed by A. E. Morgan and others who view the rural environment as the seed bed of morality, industriousness, and stability in the United States. More recent research shows the rural community to hold no monopoly in contributing to personality development. In fact, it often comes out second best behind the more urban centers.

The Productive Out-Migrant

That period of life from approximately 25 to 60 years of age, for want of a better term, is referred to here as the middle years. Temporary or intermittent out-migration of individuals, either singly or as members of a nuclear family, tends to be for purposes of temporary employment, for contract work in areas beyond commuting distance of the community, and for armed service or maritime service. In most cases, this results in decreased participation in the community's on-going social activities for the out-migrant and in selective changes in the social contacts of members of the family remaining in the community. There is a reduction in involvement for these remaining members, particularly in activities in which the absent member normally represents the family. In the husband's absence the wife's opportunity for participation in the auxiliaries of men's organizations would be reduced; in other ways the family's involvement in the web of social contacts is reduced when not all members are present.

For the unmarried adult who is temporarily or intermittently absent from the community, the impact is likely to vary with both the duration of absence and the pattern of absence. The impact should be associated positively with length of absence, but its association with seasonality or time of week is less predictable.

For any temporary migrant, the experience most likely initiates some reevaluation of his permanent community. When that community is already on the decline, this reassessment will most likely encourage additional out-migration. The experience away must also be expected to instill new ideas and encourage new tastes which the declining community does not wish to encourage. In addition there is some disturbance of on-going social and economic programs whenever a person or family either departs or returns. This is particularly significant in the case of persons occupying positions of leadership.

Economically, the impact on the community is negative when it results in loss of production and consumption, deterioration of property values, or loan delinquencies. Also detrimental is the return of the indigent, unless his consumption is paid for by welfare funds from outside the community. Even then the extent to which he is a true asset might be questioned. The impact can be positive when the unemployed breadwinner leaves for employment and sends back funds to support the remaining family or to pay debts in the community. More often than not a community will consider such a fractionation of the family disadvantageous to its social and moral well-being.

More of an impact is made by permanent out-migration of those in the more productive years. The consequences to potential economic activity and on-going social programs is similar to that already discussed with reference to younger migrants. When this involves dissolution of families, as in separation or divorce, social costs are added to economic losses. Such residual family members generally place heavier than usual demands on welfare, police, religious, and educational institutions. The loss of professional persons (teachers, ministers) who use the declining community as a stepping stone to better positions is a loss in the short view but a gain if the alternative be to do entirely without such services.

In contrast, where out-migration involves a transfer of persons potentially a social and economic liability, it means a reduced dependency load for the community.

The Older Out-Migrant

The impact of the out-migration of the older person is likely to have quite different consequences. Such persons presumably have been economic and social assets to their communities. They have developed financial reserves and experience. These they most likely largely take with them. Total economic activity is also reduced by their removal as consumption units.

But they also remove with them a measure of conservatism and demand for the specialized services associated with the aged (homes for the aged, for example). Their departure opens opportunities for leadership and employment to others.

Thus the impact varies with the character of the out-migrant.

CONCLUSION

An attempt has been made to assess some consequences of population decline within rural communities. Such consequences as increased ratios of dependent to productive age groups and of men to women because of age and sex selectivity of out-migration are well substantiated. Many of the other claims for consequences are based on widely scattered case studies, field surveys, personal observations, and inferences drawn from theory and common knowledge. These statements of consequences must, therefore, be treated more as hypotheses to be tested than axioms to guide action programs. There is a great paucity of research on the topic.

Population decline has been viewed as an adjustment mechanism whereby the rural community meets various challenges. At the time, these challenges include pressures from residents for a proliferation of the variety and quality of goods and services; and there are pressures from the outside toward increased efficiency derived from enlargement of firms through consolidation of service centers.

Whether the migration types proposed are in fact linked to the social consequences described may be questioned; but the phenomena are observable in the declining community. It is proposed that migration, as an adjustment device, has both detrimental and beneficial consequences for the community. If already in decline, migration may become the relief valve that reduces certain existing strains and stresses for the community's institutions. If not in decline, the sheer fact of out-migration may hasten gaps in the community's social and economic organization and lead to retrenchment simply by failing to recruit new members. Out-migration provides new opportunities for the migrant, but reduces the optional strategy of developing local potential and resources.

This investigation indicates a need for:

1. An extension of reliable knowledge concerning the positive and negative consequences of population decline in rural communities for the community, the migrant, and the larger society.

2. Indices to a community's potentials for growth which could form a more reliable basis to guide the selective encouragement or discouragement of investment. Of great assistance would be periodic measurement of community growth and decline in services, resources, or other strengths.[5]

3. Experiments in planned growth and restriction of small service centers to discover techniques for manipulation of the distribution centers in a free society, the responsiveness

[5]W. B. Baker, "Service centers," Royal Commission on Agriculture and Rural Life, Bul. 12, 1956, Lawrence Amon, Queens Printer, Regina, Sask., Canada.

of communities and possible unplanned consequences of such planned change.

4. Explorations of techniques or programs to reduce the economic and social costs in the consolidation of rural communities and the rationalization of the distribution of selected services among centers of various sizes.

The pursuit of the above would likely suggest a gradual redistribution of services and service centers. The process is already evident in the consolidation and specialization of educational, retailing, banking, library, health, and recreational facilities.

Chapter 11

LYLE W. SHANNON
University of Wisconsin

Occupational and Residential Adjustment of Rural Migrants[1]

ADJUSTMENT OF RURAL MIGRANTS IN URBAN AREAS

Rural-Reared Compared With Urban-Reared

THIS CHAPTER attempts to shed new light on the adjustment of rural migrants in urban areas.[2] Whether these findings can be generalized to other populations is problematical. But we do know that most of the other studies that have been carried out have only limited applicability to the case of migrants from the midwestern farm areas. Unfortunately, some of the most interesting studies of the consequences of migration have dealt with what might be termed the more "exotic" migrants.[3] As a consequence the findings have been somewhat foreboding and have given the impression that the adjustment problems of rural-reared persons are somewhat greater than they are in fact.

What we seem to know. When attempting to assess the adjustment of rural-reared migrants in urban areas, the usual approach

[1] The data on immigrant labor contained in this paper were obtained with the support of the Research Committee of the University of Wisconsin Graduate School, a three-year grant from the National Institute of Mental Health (Project RG-5342), the Urban Research Committee of the University of Wisconsin, and the Ford Foundation Urban Grant. These data are a very small part of the data that have been collected by interview and other techniques in connection with a study of value assimilation among in-migrant workers in Racine, Wisconsin. The author of this paper and Professor Robert McGinnis are co-directors of the project.

[2] Those who wish to pursue the extensive literature on adjustment should see Verne Wright, "Summary of literature on social adjustment," Amer. Soc. Rev., Vol. 7, June, 1942, pp. 407-22. Suffice it to say that the definitions of adjustment are countless. Adjustment will be operationally defined in several ways in the course of this chapter.

[3] See, for example, Grace Leybourne, "Urban adjustment of migrants from the southern Appalachian plateaus," Social Forces, Vol. 16, Dec., 1937, pp. 238-46; Morris G. Caldwell, "The adjustment of mountain families in an urban environment," Social Forces, Vol. 16, Mar., 1938, pp. 389-95; Lewis M. Killian, "The adjustment of southern white migrants to northern urban areas," Social Forces, Vol. 32, Oct., 1953, pp. 66-69.

has been to show how the migrant is faring in comparison with his urban-reared counterpart. While this approach is certainly acceptable and yields some provocative results, it is in a sense misleading because the cards are stacked. It is highly unlikely that the rural-reared will appear in a favorable light by comparison with their somewhat advantaged urban-reared counterparts. Studies with such a design tend to foster the impression that the rural dweller is indeed a rustic who cannot make out in the city. This we know to be incorrect.

Fortunately, such studies have often mitigated the impression that is presented by examining the varied adjustment of rural-reared urban migrants in relation to the time that they have been in the city. The differences in adjustment that at first seem to be so great between the rural-reared and the urban-reared tend to wash out over a period of time.[4]

A sampling of the research on urban migrants yields almost uniform conclusions. Ronald and Deborah Freedman found that the farm-reared are over-represented in low status positions, whether the measure of status is education, occupation, family income, or self-perception of status.[5] The farm-reared held low-status jobs and earned low incomes. These findings remained even when age, sex, color, and region of present residence were held constant. Not only did the Freedman study show that the rural-reared were lower on the average in terms of external criteria of adjustment, but that their self-concept was lower than that of their urban-reared counterparts. When asked which of four "class" names best represented their class membership, they said "lower" in disproportionate numbers. The Freedman study also indicated a lower level of political participation and a lower sense of political efficacy among the farm-reared than the nonfarm-reared.

Were the difference only one of participation in organized groups, there would not be quite so much to be concerned about inasmuch as numerous studies have shown that urban, working-class families do not participate in formally organized voluntary associations very much anyway.[6] The very low rate of participation

[4] See Thompson P. Omari, "Factors associated with urban adjustment of rural southern migrants," Social Forces, Vol. 35, No. 1, Oct., 1956, pp. 47-53. Omari's study of 200 Negro migrants in Beloit, Wisconsin, demonstrated that length of residence in Beloit was more highly correlated with socio-economic status and community satisfaction than any of a dozen or more other variables that were hypothesized to have some relationship to adjustment.

[5] Ronald Freedman and Deborah Freedman, "Farm-reared elements in the nonfarm population," Rural Soc., Vol. 21, Mar., 1956, pp. 50-61.

[6] Floyd Dotson, "Patterns of voluntary association among urban working-class families," Amer. Soc. Rev., Vol. 16, No. 5, Oct., 1951, pp. 687-93.

among the farm-reared does decline with time lived in the city, although those who remain manual workers never do come up to the level of their urban counterparts who become white-collar workers.[7] What often appears to be a low rate of participation among in-migrant workers is simply the normal rate of participation of people in that socio-economic stratum.

The apparent difficulty or relative slowness with which some rural-reared migrants become integrated into the formal and informal social organization of urban areas should not, however, lead us to the conclusion that the migrant finds himself in a sea of secondary contacts characterized by extreme casualness or formality, in contrast to the intimate, face-to-face primary group contacts he experienced at home. While it is all too true that the constellation of factors usually associated with the rural-urban dichotomy has made such a distinction, very little research has been conducted to actually test the hypothesis that these differences do exist. Research does show that primary group contact is in some respects more a characteristic of urban life than of rural-farm or rural-nonfarm life. Reiss' sample of Nashville, Tennessee, and adjacent rural-farm and rural-nonfarm respondents brought him to the conclusion that the average urban, employed male spent significantly greater time in primary contact than did his rural-nonfarm or rural-farm counterpart.[8] Harry Sharp and Morris Axelrod observed that mutual aid among friends and relatives is widespread in Detroit.[9] They found some difference between natives and migrants, with 80 percent of the natives reporting that help is given and received and migrants reported 66 percent over-all with variation up to 73 percent depending on the section of the United States from which the migrants came. But Omari's research in Beloit led him to conclude that having relatives in the city was not significantly related to either socio-economic status or community satisfaction.[10]

Note should also be made of Seymour M. Lipset's analysis of

---

[7] Basil G. Zimmer, "Participation of migrants in urban structure," Amer. Soc. Rev., Vol. 20, Apr., 1955, pp. 218-24. In a midwestern community of 20,000, rural-reared manual workers did not reach the level of officership positions in organizations that natives did but the difference was not great. Those with farm backgrounds reached normal officership status in organizations more slowly than did those with rural-nonfarm or urban backgrounds.

[8] Albert J. Reiss, Jr., "Rural-urban and status differences in interpersonal contacts," Amer. Jour. Soc., Vol. 65, No. 2, Sept., 1959, pp. 182-95.

[9] Harry Sharp and Morris Axelrod, "Mutual Aid Among Relatives in an Urban Population," Freedman et al., in Principles of Sociology, Henry Holt Co., New York, 1956, pp. 433-39.

[10] Omari, op. cit., p. 52.

social mobility in Oakland, California:[11] the smaller the community of orientation, the more likely the individual was to have spent a considerable proportion of his work career in manual occupations; the larger the community of orientation, the higher the status of the job held and the greater the likelihood that a man will be successfully upward-mobile. The relevance of this research is somewhat reduced by the fact that 250,000 was the most effective cutting point for size of community of orientation. In other words, the most effective predictor of occupational mobility was not rural vs. urban background, but rural and urban up to 250,000 vs. urban communities of 250,000 or more.

A further study is one made by Howard W. Beers and Catherine Heflin.[12] This research, conducted in Lexington, Kentucky, concluded that rural-rearing was disadvantageous on the average but that the range of distribution of rural migrants was such that many rural-reared persons were above the median of urban-reared persons. Rural-reared migrants were scattered widely throughout the city; ultimate social and economic status were not determined by rural-rearing.

Explaining the findings. Had the research thus far referred to come out differently, it would indeed have been surprising. Of more concern is what explains or accounts for these findings. Much has been said about personality adjustment; it is implied by some and stated as fact by others that rural life just does not develop the kind of people who take to city life. Personality is one of the slipperiest concepts with which we deal. There have been at least 100 different definitions of personality, and no matter which one is employed as operational, personality is still quite difficult to measure. If rural life does develop such a personality in people as to make them unfit for urban life, it is too late for us to be finding out about it. What is more likely is that the rural-reared migrant must go through a period of transition during which he learns about new statuses and the roles that go with them. During this period of transition the migrant may well have some conflict as he learns a new set of norms for the new social situations in which he finds himself. The facts of the case are that people are unbelievably plastic and that only a relatively small proportion of the rural-reared migrants find themselves in

---

[11] See Seymour M. Lipset, "Social mobility and urbanization," Rural Soc., Vol. 20, Sept.-Dec., 1955, pp. 220-28. The sample consisted of 935 principal wage earners chosen as a random sample of Oakland households after the highest and lowest socioeconomic areas of the city had been eliminated. Community of orientation was obtained by asking the respondents: "Where did you live most of the time between the ages of 13 and 19? Did you live inside the city limits? Did you live on a farm?"

[12] Howard W. Beers and Catherine Heflin, "Rural people in the city," Ky. Agr. Exp. Sta. Bul. 478, July, 1945, 19pp.

serious trouble simply due to the different pace of life and whatever else distinguishes the city from the country.[13]

But when the farm-reared youth or adult enters the urban labor market with less education and less experience than his urban-reared counterpart it would be most unrealistic to expect him to compete as effectively, at least initially. Every study has shown that rural-reared migrants are at a disadvantage educationally. This in itself is a difference that is measurable and meaningful in terms of the experience of rural-reared migrants.

Rural-Reared in the City Compared With the Country

The basis for comparison. Although the studies that have been cited comparing rural-reared with urban-reared make an important contribution to knowledge about the problem, they are not completely satisfying. The crucial question, it would seem, is whether or not rural-reared persons have bettered themselves by moving to the city.

There are two kinds of data to which we may turn in an effort to answer this question. The socio-economic status of the rural-reared migrant can be measured before and after and at intervals thereafter. This is an external criterion of change, and we shall presume that movement upward on a scale of socio-economic status is the intended direction of the migrant. It is likewise possible to employ something of an internal criterion, i.e., how does the migrant feel about the way that things are working out? Although this approach has been taken, it has not been as frequently used as has the former.[14]

Change in the status of rural-reared migrants. A study by Alvin L. Bertrand and Harold W. Osborne measured the increased level of living in the homes of persons who went to work in a local factory during the period from 1950 to 1957. The increase in level of living was greater for those who turned from farm to factory work during this period. Not only did their level of living go up but 96 percent of the factory employees attributed the higher level of living in the community to factory employment. Factory employees also increased their social participation during this period.[15]

[13] Lewis M. Killian concluded that the so-called hillbillies in Chicago were changing slightly in spite of themselves. Killian, op. cit., p. 69.

[14] See, for example, Eldon D. Smith, "Nonfarm employment information for rural people," Jour. Farm Econ., Vol. 38, No. 3, 1956, pp. 813-27. Smith's research on Indianapolis, Indiana, migrants indicated 44 percent feeling dissatisfaction and hoping or actively planning to return to farming.

[15] Alvin L. Bertrand and Harold W. Osborne, "Rural industrialization in a Louisiana community," Louisiana State Univ. Agr. Bul. No. 524, June, 1959, pp. 30-32.

Awareness that nonfarm work leads to a higher level of living and the goals for which they are struggling is demonstrated by expressions of choice of work desired. Ward F. Porter and William H. Metzler found that 90 percent of the persons seeking work from a formerly agricultural valley preferred nonfarm work.[16] Other studies have pictured farm youth as eagerly looking for work in the city.

It seems clear that, for the foreseeable future, a surplus of young and older workers from the farm will seek a solution to their problems in cityward migration.

THE ADJUSTMENT OF MIGRANT WORKERS WITH TIME AND ANTECEDENTS AS VARIABLES

Value Assimilation Among In-migrant Laborers

The Problem. The data to which we shall refer were collected as part of a 3-year study of value assimilation among in-migrant workers. The study is an attempt to determine which factors impede and which factors facilitate the assimilation of values in an in-migrant group. Interviewing in the community selected for study was preceded by a year of rapport-building, construction of schedules, pretesting in another community of a similar in-migrant population, and training of bilingual interviewers. The relative ease with which the interviewers obtained entry into homes that had in the past presented something of a problem to other groups can be explained in terms of the careful groundwork that was laid and the selection of interviewers who were not so likely to be immediately defined as outsiders. A 2-hour interview was conducted to collect the data required for a test of 12 general hypotheses derived from a theory of value assimilation.[17]

Selection of the sample. The in-migrant workers selected for study were Mexican-Americans, a group of in-migrant workers arriving on the scene in Racine, Wisconsin. They were concentrated in three areas in Racine at the time the first interviewing was conducted in summer 1959. A systematic sample was selected

---

[16] Ward F. Porter and William H. Metzler, "Availability for employment of rural people in the Upper Monongahela Valley, West Virginia," West Virginia Agr. Exp. Sta. Bul. 391, Morgantown, 1956, 43pp.

[17] The data collected were: place of origin, occupational status of respondent, parents, and grandparents, familial background and history, level of aspiration, job-seeking experiences, reasons for migration, conception of past and present place of residence, work experiences, patterns of influence and association, world views, ethnic attitudes, level of living, educational status of respondent and family, life style, and use of leisure time.

from a listing of the population built up from a number of sources during the year of preparatory work. A systematic sample of non-Mexican white residents was selected from areas adjacent to the areas of Mexican-American concentration. By this means it was hoped to obtain persons with somewhat similar social and economic antecedents. While this was difficult to do, the design of the study was such that it would have been highly undesirable to compare the Mexican-American group with persons whose antecedents would have at the outset marked them as entirely different persons. Hereafter, the control group of non-Mexican white residents will be referred to as Anglos and the Mexican-American as Mexicans.[18]

The bilingual interviewers were Mexican-Americans, trained for this particular study and imported from the pretest community. The Anglo sample was interviewed by white school teachers and social workers, recruited and trained for the task at hand.

Complete interviews were secured from 209 Mexicans and 189 Anglos. These interviews were coded and punched on IBM cards for analysis. The data presented in this chapter are only a small portion of those collected, and this relatively simple analysis has been made independently of a more systematic analysis of all the data carried out in the Numerical Analysis Laboratory of the University of Wisconsin.

Some characteristics of the samples. The samples in this study have the educational characteristics that might be expected. They play a part in the relatively lower mobility of the Mexicans when contrasted with the Anglos and point up that the migrant enters the industrial world with inadequate preparation compared with his urban counterpart. Table 11.1 indicates that the modal Mexican has from 3 to 7 years of normal schooling and that the modal Anglo has from 8 to 12 years of formal schooling. In this case it is probably not only a function of ethnicity and rurality but also a function of regional differences in the background of the respondents.

The modal Mexican was 35 to 45 years of age but the Anglos were quite dispersed, ranging from about 20 to 70 years of age.[19]

Ideally, it would have been easier to deal with the problem at hand had a good proportion of each sample been rural for

[18] Lest the reader be tempted to reject this study as another one dealing with an "exotic" population, it should be noted that ethnicity or race alone do not make an in-migrant group unusual or a very special problem. Eldon D. Smith found that the adjustment experiences of Negroes in Indianapolis were better than those of the whites. Smith, op. cit., p. 824.

[19] Omari found that age was significantly related to socio-economic status and community satisfaction. Omari, op. cit., p. 50. This may be a factor tending to maximize the differences between Mexicans and Anglos in Racine.

Table 11.1. Education of Mexican and Anglo Respondents by Sex*

Years	Mexican		Anglo	
	Male	Female	Male	Female
	(percent)	(percent)	(percent)	(percent)
No school	17	20	4	4
1-2	11	8	3	1
3-4	25	18	5	5
5-7	20	22	14	12
8	11	8	15	29
9-12	13	10	51	35
13+	2	1	7	8
Not ascertained	1	13	1	6
	100	100	100	100

*How many years of education have you (your husband) had?
Unless indicated otherwise, the following number of persons are in each subcategory of the sample: Mexican Male = 104; Mexican Female = 105; Anglo Male = 78; Anglo Female = 111.
Tests of the significance of differences will be used only when crucial to the acceptance or rejection of a proposition.

community of orientation. Since about 90 percent of the Mexican respondents were from Texas or Mexico there is some question as to just how urban their community of orientation might have been. Unfortunately it is not clear how many of the respondents grew up in the cities they have referred to as the place they grew up in, and how many have simply named this because it facilitated response to the interviewer's question or was more prestigeful than to say that early life had been spent in a small house on the edge of the community or some distance out. What we do know is that many of the communities referred to in response to the question on community of orientation did not have a way of life that is comparable to urban life in other parts of the United States. Furthermore, other questions elicited responses leading to the conclusion that the Mexican sample was far more rural than Table 11.2 would seem to indicate.

The annual income range within occupational classifications for the Mexican sample and the Anglo sample, and the distribution of annual income for each sample are presented in Table 11.3. The fact that annual income is not too closely correlated with occupational classification will account, at least in part, for some of the relationships to be found in the data at hand.

Table 11.2. Size of Community of Orientation of Male Respondents*

	Mexican (percent)	Anglo (percent)
Rural; open-country, farm	1	4
Up to 1,000	5	11
1,000 to 2,500	3	3
2,500 to 5,000	20	2
5,000 to 7,500	8	1
7,500 to 10,000	1	2
10,000 to 50,000	3	10
50,000 to 100,000	8	35
100,000 and over	27	5
Not ascertained	24	27
	100	100

*Where did you (your husband) live while growing up?

The Adjustment of In-migrant Workers

Changes in the way of life. The data in Table 11.4 were derived from two questions not strictly comparable. The Anglo respondent was asked how he thought the lives of people changed after moving to Racine. The Mexican was asked how he thought the lives of Mexicans changed after moving to Racine.

Mexicans believed that changes in their way of life were for the better. In most cases Anglos did not evaluate the over-all changes in way of life for people moving to Racine. Since 36 percent of the Anglos always lived in Racine they found this question difficult to answer. Only 3 percent of the Mexicans always lived in Racine. Here we see the Mexicans' evaluation of their particular situation contrasted with an evaluation of change for people in general. Without question, all groups interested in Racine's less fortunate were concerned about the status of the Mexican population. Comparison was made with long-term residents of Racine and with other groups that had acquired the wherewithal to live according to standards acceptable to the middle class.

Perhaps most interesting of all is the fact that so much of the concern over the "plight" of the Mexican-Americans revolved around the apparent lack of concern over their own sorry state of affairs evidenced by the Mexicans. This in itself was cause for great alarm on the part of middle-class persons. Knowledge of the environment from which the Mexicans came might have tempered local concern over the attitude of the Mexicans toward their present living conditions.

Table 11.3. Type of Job and Annual Income of Respondent or Respondent's Husband (1958)*

	Professional, technical, managerial, proprietor, clerical, sales		Craftsmen and foremen		Operatives (semi-skilled), maintenance and service, industrial laborers		Agricultural laborers, tenant farmers, peasants		Not ascertained		Total percent	
	Mex.	Anglo	Mex.	Anglo	Mex.	Anglo	Mex.	Anglo	Mex.	Anglo	Mex.	Anglo
$7,000 +	0	9	2	10	9	5	0	0	0	2	5	14
$6,000 to $6,900	0	8	5	10	17	5	0	0	0	1	11	13
$5,000 to $5,900	1	5	7	10	28	11	0	1	0	4	19	16
$4,000 to $4,900	0	2	3	9	60	16	0	0	4	3	32	16
Up to $3,900	1	9	1	10	28	26	1	0	4	8	20	28
Not ascertained	0	7	1	4	13	10	7	0	9	4	13	13
	2	40	19	53	155	73	8	1	17	22	100	100

*Approximately what was your total family income last year (1958)? Respondent's figure was not accepted if it was inconsistent with answers to the following questions: What is your (your husband's) hourly wage? How many hours do you (does your husband) usually work in a week? How many weeks do you (does your husband) usually work in a year? Does the family have any income besides these wages?

Table 11.4. Change Perceived Among In-migrant Workers*

	Mexican		Anglo	
	Male	Female	Male	Female
	(percent)	(percent)	(percent)	(percent)
Changes good	66	69	12	13
Changes half-and-half or not good	13	15	4	3
Change either not perceived or not evaluated or not ascertained	18	13	48	49
Always lived in Racine	3	3	36	35

*Sometimes you hear people talking about the way life is changed by coming to Racine. From what you've seen, what kinds of big changes take place in the life of [Mexican] people when they come to Racine?

If the respondent did not mention economic improvement, the neutral probe, "Any other changes?" was employed. The Mexican group was not quite so sure that economic changes could be positively evaluated. The Anglos were also slightly less sure of economic changes being for the good than they were in reference to over-all changes. The total mention of economic change is presented in Table 11.5.

Table 11.5. Economic Change Perceived Among In-migrant Workers*

	Mexican		Anglo	
	Male	Female	Male	Female
	(percent)	(percent)	(percent)	(percent)
Economic improvement	53	65	8	10
Economic disadvantages as well as improvement, or economic disadvantages	13	11	4	1
Economic change either not mentioned or not evaluated or not ascertained	31	21	52	54
Always lived in Racine	3	3	36	35

*If respondent did not mention economic improvement, the following probe was employed: Any other changes? Any mention of economic change in response to the original question or the probe is included in this table.

The next question was more direct: "How did your life change when you and your family came to Racine?" This question enabled the respondent to bring his or her own experiences into focus. In many ways it was a better question for the group with which we were dealing. Many of our respondents appeared to have had little time for consideration of the problems of the larger society. They were quite busy with their own struggle for survival from day to day, i.e., their focus of attention was on their own problems rather than on group problems.

The responses to this question are presented in Table 11.6.

Table 11.6. Change Perceived in One's Own Life After Migration*

	Mexican		Anglo	
	Male[a]	Female[b]	Male	Female
	(percent)	(percent)	(percent)	(percent)
Changes good	59	61	76	64
Changes half-and-half or not good	18	15	10	17
Change either not perceived or not evaluated	23	24	14	19
	100	100	100	100

*How did your life change when you and your family came to Racine?

[a] Mexican Male-Anglo Male test of significance: X^2 = 1.6750 1 d.f. Not Significant. With residual category included: X^2 = 3.4354 1 d.f. Not Significant.

[b] Mexican Female-Anglo Female test of significance: X^2 = .0043 1 d.f. Not Significant. The residual category was eliminated in testing for significance to avoid increasing the difference as an artifact of the data rather than the characteristics of the respondents. No difference will be considered significant unless it can be accepted at the .01 percent level of confidence; other levels of significance may be mentioned as a matter of information. With residual category included: X^2 = .0660 1 d.f. Not Significant.

The Mexicans answers indicated that Racine had not brought them significantly different improvement than it had the Anglo sample that was interviewed. A test of the significance of Mexican-Anglo variation, holding sex constant, indicates that Mexican males regarded changes in their own lives not significantly different than did Anglo males. At the same time that the Mexican males mentioned changes affirmatively, they made more frequent half and half, or unfavorable references than did the Anglos. Mexican and Anglo females differed even less than did Mexican and Anglo males.

When respondents were probed about economic advantages for themselves, they were even more hesitant. The Mexican male respondents saw fewer economic benefits for themselves than did the Anglo respondents. A test of the significance of Mexican-Anglo variation, holding sex constant, indicates that Mexican and Anglo males differ as do Mexican and Anglo females, although in a somewhat varied pattern. In neither case is the difference significant at the level established for this chapter, although the difference is closer to an acceptable level of significance for males than for females.

Table 11.7. Economic Change Perceived for Oneself After Migration*

	Mexican		Anglo	
	Male [a]	Female [b]	Male	Female
	(percent)	(percent)	(percent)	(percent)
Economic improvement	45	50	62	49
Economic disadvantages as well as improvement, or economic disadvantages	30	24	14	8
Economic change not mentioned or not evaluated	25	26	24	43
	100	100	100	100

*If respondent did not mention economic improvement, the following probe was employed: Any economic change? Any change in your level of living? Any mention of economic change in response to the original question or the probe is included in this table.

[a] MM-AM: $\chi^2 = 4.3980$ 1 d.f. $P < .05$ with residual category included: $= 4.0412$ 1 d.f. $P < .05$.

[b] χ^2 MF-AF: $\chi^2 = 3.8266$ 1 d.f. Not Significant. Residual category eliminated in testing for significance.

The Mexicans were aware of economic disadvantages in the Racine community to a far greater extent than were the Anglos. We shall see that their antecedents probably influenced their judgment of the situation. From the viewpoint of the Mexicans, economic improvement took place, even though one aspect of change may be favorable and another unfavorable. Among the Anglos there was perhaps recognition of the advantages that accrued to them in the city but not so much concern about the higher cost of living. The Anglos had become used to paying high rent in contrast to their Mexican counterparts who saw some economic advantage but had not yet adjusted to higher out-of-pocket expenses.

Reasons for coming to Racine and perception of change. The data suggest that it might well be fruitful to hold reason for migration constant and then examine perception of over-all change and economic change. Table 11.8 is made up of a number of collapsed categories of responses, consisting of basic economic reasons for migration and of a variety of reasons related to the family, as well as a few personal or idiosyncratic motivations for movement from previous place of residence.[20] Some of the economic motivations for migration could be classified as push and others as pull. It is clear that the Mexicans came to Racine for work, and we would expect that their satisfaction with the community would be greatly influenced by their experiences on the job and any changes that might come about in their way of life or level of living that are related to the economic institution.

Table 11.8. Reason for Moving to Racine*

	Mexican		Anglo	
	Male	Female	Male	Female
	(percent)	(percent)	(percent)	(percent)
Work-oriented reasons	63	61	18	17
Family-oriented, other	11	20	17	23
Always lived in Racine, Racine move not a major one	26	19	65	60
	100	100	100	100

*What would you say was the main reason that you came to Racine?

The average in-migrant Anglo moved to Racine during the 1920's and 1930's while the in-migrant Mexican moved in the late 1940's and early 1950's. How much their experiences were influenced by different economic conditions is not a part of our data, but suffice it to say that the Anglo interviewee has had a longer period of time to make whatever adjustments must be made in the city. We have already referred to other studies showing the relationship between integration into the social organization and time spent in urban areas, and it has likewise been noted that this proceeds more rapidly among those in the middle and upper classes than those who remain in the lower class in terms of occupational classification.

[20] A major move by a Mexican respondent refers to a move from Mexico or Texas to any non-Mexico-Texas location. A major move by an Anglo refers to a move from a place where a person lived the majority of his years before he was 12 years old. Tables dealing with reason for moving to Racine are based on responses to a question that tended to elicit from the female respondent, not her own reason, but the family reason for moving to Racine. For example: "I came here to be with my husband who was working in the foundry." Thus, the personal content of the female respondent's answer was subordinate to an economic motivation that took the family to Racine.

Table 11.9 develops from the questions that have been raised in earlier paragraphs.

When reason for moving to Racine is held constant, the difference between Mexicans and Anglos in their evaluation of perceived change becomes less.

Table 11.9. Over-all Changes Compared With Economic Changes Among Persons With Work-Oriented Reasons for Migration*

	Mexican[a]		Anglo[b]	
	Satisfaction		Satisfaction	
	Over-all[c]	Economic[d]	Over-all	Economic
	(percent)	(percent)	(percent)	(percent)
Changes good	63	50	79	55
Changes half-and-half or not good	15	28	3	12
Changes either not perceived or not evaluated	22	22	18	33
	100	100	100	100

*The questions referred to in Tables 11.4, 11.5, and 11.8 are the basis for data presented in this table. Mexicans = 129; Anglos = 33.

[a] Mexican, over-all change-economic change: $\chi^2 = 5.5589$ 1 d.f. $P < .02$.

[b] Anglo, over-all change-economic change: $\chi^2 = .9750$ 1 d.f. Not Significant. The t test indicated significance at the .05 level of confidence with the residual category included.

[c] Over-all change, Mexican-Anglo: $\chi^2 = 2.9375$ 1 d.f. Not Significant. The test indicated significance at the .05 level of confidence with the residual category included.

[d] Economic change, Mexican-Anglo: $\chi^2 = 1.7774$ 1 d.f. Not Significant. The residual category was eliminated in testing for significance in order to avoid increasing the difference as an artifact of the data rather than the characteristics of the respondents.

Over-all change was still more frequently evaluated as favorable by the Mexican sample than was economic change; the difference is significant for Mexicans but not for Anglos. The difference between over-all and economic satisfaction is significant for Anglos when the "t" test is used and a .05 percent level of confidence accepted. Economic motivations dominate the decision to move from prior place of residence and economic advantages accrued from the move, but even more extensive were the over-all favorable changes that took place in their way of life. Anglos expressed greater over-all satisfaction than did the Mexicans and somewhat greater economic satisfaction than did the Mexicans, but the differences are not quite statistically significant at the .05 percent level of confidence.

Size of community of orientation and perception of change. Since 9 out of 10 Mexican respondents had a Texas or Mexican community of orientation and more than 9 out of 10 of the Mexican male respondents had such a community of orientation, Table 11.10 is restricted to a presentation of perception of change in one's life by male Mexican respondents.[21]

If it is assumed that mention of change should be proportional to the number of respondents in each community of orientation category, the significance of any variation from a chance distribution of mentions may be tested by means of Chi Square.[22] Perception of change is not significantly related to size of community of orientation.

It is probably unnecessary to remind the reader that this finding is inconsistent with other research were we to assume that there is a positive correlation between external criteria of adjustment and respondent's own conception of how he is doing.

Another question on adjustment went as follows: "Some people feel that their lives have worked out just about the way that they wanted. Others feel that they've had bad breaks. How do you feel about the way that your life is working out?" Both Mexicans and Anglos were more responsive to this question than to the question on change. This is in part a consequence of the fact that it was answerable by those who had always resided in Racine and that this question came later in the interview after rapport had been well established by the interviewers. There was no statistically significant variation in satisfaction as related to size of community of orientation, with Mexicans and Anglos responding rather uniformly.

This study may in several respects have a population that reduces its likelihood of being generalizable to other urban areas. For one thing the ethnic variable makes some aspects of adjustment more difficult. In this case we can assume that ordinary, white, native-born rural-reared migrants will not have quite so many difficulties as their nonwhite counterparts. The data on community of orientation give us a relatively limited range with

[21] Although data on community of orientation are available for the males in the entire sample, the perception of change data are available for respondents only, i.e., a female respondent was asked to answer a question about husband's community of orientation but was not asked how he felt about change. The female respondent was asked about her own perception of change.

[22] Inspection of the differences between expected mentions and observed mentions shows that there is no consistent pattern of deviation of perceived changes from expected by size of community of orientation of respondents for either over-all change or economic change. Application of the test of significance to the difference between the theoretical distribution and the observed distribution indicates that there is no significant difference.

Table 11.10. Over-all Changes and Economic Changes As Perceived by Mexican Male Respondents Compared With Size of Community of Orientation*

	Over-all change[a]				Economic change[b]			
	Changes good		Changes half and half or not good		Changes good		Changes half and half or not good	
	Observed	Expected	Observed	Expected	Observed	Expected	Observed	Expected
Rural; open-country, farm	0	0	0	0	0	0	0	0
Up to 1,000	4	5	2	2	4	4	3	2
1,000 to 2,500	3	2	0	0	2	1	0	1
2,500 to 5,000	11	11	4	4	7	9	4	6
5,000 to 7,500	3	5	4	2	2	4	5	3
7,500 to 10,000	1	0	0	0	1	0	0	0
10,000 to 50,000	5	3	0	1	3	2	2	2
50,000 to 100,000	3	6	1	2	5	5	0	3
100,000 and over	19	17	5	5	14	13	12	9
Not ascertained	11		2		7		4	
	60		18		45		30	

*Only male respondents are included in this table since there is some variation in the distribution of town of orientation of males and females.

[a] Over-all change-community size: χ^2 Not Significant. } Different values obtained depending on how categories
[b] Economic change-community size: χ^2 Not Significant. } were collapsed but no significant χ^2 obtained.

Residual category eliminated from over-all change and economic change and from size of community of orientation when testing for significance. Expected frequencies are rounded and uncollapsed for presentation in this table. In computing Chi Square they were not. Expected frequencies were obtained by multiplying total "changes good" responses and total "changes half and half or not good" responses by the proportion of respondents from each size community of orientation.

each extreme end of the continuum missing. It is for this reason that we cannot expect to find the extreme differences in variables believed to be related to community of orientation.

The positive finding from the table is that people with quite diverse backgrounds migrate to urban areas, and even though their way of life is looked at with concern by their middle-class urban peers, they define it as having changed for the good.

It might be objected that migrants who were relatively successful were the ones who remained in Racine to be interviewed while vast numbers who tried to make the adjustment with less success were not around for us to interview. Indeed, that was a matter for consideration; 89.7 percent of the Mexicans interviewed in 1959 and in the sample for reinterview for a second time in 1960 were in the community and interviewed. Only 8.6 percent had left the county. This attests to a lower rate of mobility than had been anticipated.

There was a rather large amount of movement within the city and the county and considerable ingenuity was required in tracing down such mobile respondents. Their frequent in-area moves may be a factor in creating the impression that the Mexican population is more mobile than it is. Mexican-Americans are difficult to find and particularly so when a specific member of the family has been designated for interview.

Occupational antecedents and perception of change. The contrasting antecedents of the Mexican and Anglo samples have been touched on previously as factors in their differential response to change in way of life upon settlement in Racine. Enlarging upon earlier statements, it might be expected that variation between Mexican and Anglo evaluation of change would largely disappear if their antecedents were held constant. Although this might appear to be moving from the topic of central concern, it is not, for a large proportion of each group has agricultural antecedents, in spite of their responses when asked about their community of orientation.

In Table 11.11 expected mentions have been computed based on the total number of mentions and the proportion of each group with selected antecedents so that it is possible to see in which direction observed satisfaction differs from expected. The Mexican male respondents are compared with Anglo male respondents. Those with agricultural antecedents, whether they are Mexican or Anglo, have a disproportionate number of favorable over-all responses, while those in other occupational categories have disproportionately fewer favorable responses than expected.

That the Anglos whose fathers were in agricultural labor had more favorable view of change than did Mexicans is not surprising

Table 11.11. Over-all Change Perceived in Own Life of Male Respondent Compared With Occupation of Respondent's Father*

	Mexican[a]				Anglo[b]			
	Changes good		Changes half and half or not good		Changes good		Changes half and half or not good	
	Observed	Expected	Observed	Expected	Observed	Expected	Observed	Expected
Professional, technical, managerial, proprietor, clerical, sales	3	10	1	3	3	14	1	
Craftsmen and foremen	6		3		5		3	2
Operatives (semi-skilled), maintenance and service, industrial laborers	13	16	4	4	7	7	0	
Agricultural laborers, tenant farmers, peasants	29	25	4	6	17	11	1	3
Not ascertained	9		6		6		0	
	60		18		38		5	

*What was your father's occupation? How did life change for you and your family when you came to Racine?

[a]Mexican, change-respondent's father: $X^2 = 1.9219$ 2 d.f. Not Significant.

[b]Anglo, change-respondent's father: $X^2 = 6.3726$ 2 d.f. $P > .05$. Residual categories eliminated when testing for significance. Expected frequencies computed following procedure described in Table 11.10. Occupational categories collapsed as necessary for application of tests of significance.

considering the greater mobility of Anglos in comparison to Mexicans, their antecedents held constant. The Anglo variation in response, based on their antecedents, comes very close to an acceptable level of significance although the Mexican variation does not. What is important, however, is the uniformity in direction of the variation when antecedents are held constant.

The Mexican male respondents compare with Anglo male respondents in essentially the same way when economic change is considered. Just as in the case of over-all change, Anglos with agricultural antecedents observed more favorable changes in their own lives than did Mexicans with agricultural antecedents. That they did is not unexpected considering the difference in average income of Anglos and Mexicans with the same antecedents.

It could be argued that the Anglos with agricultural antecedents had somewhat better agricultural beginnings than did the Mexicans with backgrounds in agriculture, and that cannot be denied. This does assist in explaining a part of the differential mobility of Anglos and Mexicans with agricultural antecedents but this is not significant in respect to the central concern of this chapter.

Again it would appear that life in the city is not regarded as so grim if one has first experienced the country. Although it may be contended that this is a consequence of recent farm experience, that is to be doubted. The Anglo group had an earlier farm experience and their experience covered a sufficient span of years so as not to be based on a period of declining or rock-bottom farm prices.

None of the foregoing is meant to imply that rural life is unbearable. The smell of new-mown hay and the beauty of the pasture at sundown will linger with us forever, but that is far from saying that everyone can make the best possible living or other form of adjustment in a rural setting. The evidence indicates that people who have made the transition from rural to urban are not entirely sorry about it. That there is no comparison between life on one of Wisconsin's finest and most efficient dairy farms and Milwaukee's slums is not to be debated. The question, it seems, is entirely one of what kind of impact rural-reared persons make on the city and what kind of impact the city makes on them.

First job has also been compared with perception of over-all change, perception of economic change, and with responses to the question: "How do you feel about the way that your life is working out?" In each case there is no significant variation in response based on first job of respondent.

Size of community of orientation and occupational classification. In Table 11.13 the dependent variable becomes present job

Table 11.12. Economic Change Perceived in Own Life of Male Respondent Compared With Occupation of Respondent's Father*

	Mexican[a]				Anglo[b]			
	Changes good		Changes half and half or not good		Changes good		Changes half and half or not good	
	Observed	Expected	Observed	Expected	Observed	Expected	Observed	Expected
Professional, technical, managerial, proprietor, clerical, sales	3	8	1	4	2	4	1	3
Craftsmen and foremen	4		6		5	8	2	
Operatives (semi-skilled), maintenance and service, industrial laborers	11	13	6	6	5	5	2	4
Agricultural laborers, tenant farmers, peasants	23	20	7	10	14	9	2	
Not ascertained	4		10		5		0	
	45		30		31		7	

*What was your father's occupation? How did life change for you and your family when you came to Racine? Probe: Economic, level of living?

[a] Mexican, change-respondent's father: $X^2 = 4.4037$ 2 d.f. Not Significant.

[b] Anglo, change-respondent's father: $X^2 = 4.5892$ 2 d.f. Not Significant. Residual categories eliminated when testing for significance. Expected frequencies computed following procedure described in Table 11.10. Occupational categories collapsed as necessary for application of tests of significance.

of respondent or respondent's husband, and the independent variable is community of orientation of respondent or respondent's husband.

Responses of Mexicans and Anglos are presented separately. The expected number of respondents in each occupational category from each size community of orientation is computed on a basis of the observed number of respondents from each size community of orientation and the observed number of respondents in each occupational category. This procedure, i.e., the presentation of Mexican and Anglo data in comparison with two separate expected frequencies, may be criticized because it does not point up the quite different occupational distributions of Mexicans and Anglos and the fact that Mexicans are more or less limited to the lower three broad occupational categories of the four that are left when the data have been collapsed for presentation. That this is correct cannot be denied; this paper is not concerned with differential experience based on ethnicity alone. Attention is not focused on what everyone knows or expects to find, i.e., the contrasting occupational distribution of Mexicans and Anglos, but on the influence of size of community of orientation on present job.

There is no statistically significant variation in occupational status based on size of community of orientation for either the Mexican or the Anglo sample. This is in contrast to the findings as interpreted in most other studies. It is possible that certain characteristics of Racine industry have presented better opportunities for rural-reared in-migrant labor than have some of the other settings in which research has been conducted. If this is a consequence of some peculiarity of the Racine industrial setting, then it is a finding quite pertinent to the problem at hand. What are the characteristics of industrial communities where opportunities for integration are at their maximum?

Since occupational classification and income were not closely related in the sample, the relationship of size of community of orientation to annual income was investigated. There is no significant variation in income among either Mexicans or Anglos based on size of community of orientation.

Occupational mobility among in-migrant laborers. Neither of the samples consisted exclusively of in-migrant laborers, and the Mexican sample differed from the Anglo sample not only in its ethnicity but also in the time that it had been present in the city and in the process of integration. Nevertheless, one might hypothesize that one of the sharpest differences will occur when Mexicans and Anglos are compared on the relative amount of mobility that they have evidenced between first and present jobs. Here we will have the influence of ethnicity, the influence of being

Table 11.13. Size of Community of Orientation and Present Job*

	Professional, technical, managerial, proprietor, clerical, sales		Craftsmen and foremen		Operatives (semi-skilled), maintenance and service, industrial laborers		Agricultural laborers, tenant farmers, peasants	
	Mexican[a]	Anglo[b]	Mexican[a]	Anglo[b]	Mexican[a]	Anglo[b]	Mexican[a]	Anglo[b]
Rural; open-country, farm, up to 1,000	0	3	2	9	11	12	0	1
1,000 to 7,500	1	1	3	3	53	6	1	0
7,500 to 50,000	0	6	2	9	5	5	0	0
50,000 to 100,000	0	20	3	19	11	22	1	0
100,000 and over	0	1	6	3	37	5	2	0
Not ascertained	1	9	3	10	38	23	4	0
	2	40	19	53	155	73	8	1

*Data from question referred to in Table 11.2 and: What is your (your husband's) present job?

[a] Mexican, community of orientation-occupation: $\chi^2 = 1.7207$ 6 d.f. Not Significant.

[b] Anglo, community of orientation-occupation: $\chi^2 = 10.0773$ 6 d.f. Not Significant. Residual categories eliminated when testing for significance. Expected frequencies computed procedure described in Table 11.10. Occupational categories combined as necessary for tests of significance.

longer in the city, of educational differences, and of a broader range of first jobs. It is this variety of factors playing a part in determining relative social mobility that makes it so difficult to categorically state, as is sometimes done, that a particular group are disadvantaged because of their "rural" or "farm" background.

In Table 11.14 the number or proportion of respondents in each category of first job and the number or proportion of persons in each category of present job are used as a basis for determining the expected number of persons in each subcategory of present job. These expected frequencies are computed on the assumption of equal likelihood of rising or falling on the continuum within each category of first job in proportion to the over-all change that has taken place in the occupational status of the total Anglo group or in the total Mexican group. Statistically significant variation from this indicates that it is more propitious to have commenced work at one level rather than at another.

In the case of the Anglos there is a statistically significant difference between the distribution of present jobs and the model based on the assumption of equal probability of rising or falling, without regard to first job. Most of the difference takes place at the upper levels, indicating that the pattern of Anglo mobility is affected by first jobs at the higher levels but not so much at the lower levels. The disproportional mobility among Anglos takes place as they move up and out of every category and fail to move downward out of the higher job statuses in which they have started. Anglos and Mexicans have the same experience in one important respect. Respondents whose first job was in agriculture moved out of agriculture and into positions as craftsmen and foremen at the same rate as did persons whose first jobs were in the operative category.[23] In other words, Mexicans and Anglos have similar experiences as far as mobility at the lowest level is concerned but they are differentiated by the greater mobility of Anglos at other levels. All of the factors that we have been considering play a part in this very sharp difference in Mexican-Anglo mobility, and it should neither be assessed to ethnicity nor to rurality alone.

---

[23] See Clopper Almon, Jr., "Origins and relation to agriculture of industrial workers in Kingsport, Tennessee," Jour. Farm Econ., Vol. 38, No. 3, 1956, pp. 828-36. Almon's research indicated little difference in the work records of those with farm and nonfarm backgrounds in two major manufacturing plants in a predominantly agricultural area. It did not make any difference whether workers were reared in farm or town, had industrial or only farm experience, they had essentially the same employment records. More than half of the workers were from farm backgrounds. Promotion to the semiskilled level went to those with previous experience in skilled trades or truck driving rather than to men direct from the farm. General manufacturing experience, however, did not appear to give any advantage over one fresh from the farm.

Table 11.14. First Job and Present Job of Respondents or Husbands of Respondents*

	Professional, technical, managerial, proprietor, clerical, sales		Craftsmen and foremen		Operatives (semi-skilled), maintenance and service, industrial laborers		Agricultural laborers, tenant farmers, peasants		Not ascertained
	Observed	Expected	Observed	Expected	Observed	Expected	Observed	Expected	
Present Job - Mexican					First Job - Mexican[a]				
Professional, technical, managerial, proprietor, clerical, sales	0	0	0	0	1	0	0	1	1
Craftsmen and foremen	0	0	1	0	6	7	8	8	4
Operatives (semi-skilled), maintenance and service, industrial laborers	3	3	3	4	43	41	47	48	59
Agricultural laborers, tenant farmers, peasants	0	0	0	0	0	1	3	2	5
Not ascertained	2		0		2		14		7
	5		4		52		72		

Present Job - Anglo	First Job - Anglo[b]								
Professional, technical, managerial, proprietor, clerical, sales	14	5	3	4	9	13	3	7	11
Craftsmen and foremen	1	6	9	5	15	15	9	8	19
Operatives (semi-skilled), maintenance and service, industrial laborers	4	8	6	7	24	21	13	11	26
Agricultural laborers, tenant farmers, peasants	0	0	0	0	0	0	0	0	1
Not ascertained	0		2		4		2		14
	19		20		52		27		71

*Data from questions on occupational history.

[a] Mexicans: First job-present job: $X^2 = .4405$ 4 d.f. Not significant.

[b] Anglo: First job-present job: $X^2 = 27.97$ 6 d.f. $P > .01$. Expected frequencies computed based on proportion of persons in each category of first job and number of persons in each category of present job. Residual category excluded. Categories combined as necessary for tests of significance.

SUMMARY

Studies of the adjustment of rural-reared migrants in urban areas

When the rural-reared urban migrant is compared with urban-reared city dwellers the rural-reared migrant is found in lower status positions no matter which measures of status are selected. But research also shows that status differences based on size of community of origin disappear over a period of time. The rural-reared migrant becomes more and more like his urban-reared counterpart.

Comparisons of this type are in a sense misleading. The question would be better put if we asked, "How much did the urban migrant have of whatever he valued before he came to the city and how much does he now have of whatever he still values or has come to value as a consequence of urban life?" This formulation is applicable to either measures of level of living or to expressions of satisfaction. Research is scarce, but what we have indicates that status is improved through migration to urban areas and integration into the urban-industrial society.

The adjustment of migrant workers

A sample of in-migrant Mexican-American workers had a favorable perception of the changes that occurred for Mexicans in general and for themselves. Anglos perceived the changes that occur as predominantly favorable and in the case of economic change had more favorable perceptions of their own changes than did Mexicans.

Anglos who moved to Racine for work-oriented reasons perceived over-all changes for themselves more favorably than did Mexicans. Both groups perceived over-all change more favorably than economic change.

Size of community of orientation and perception of favorable change did not have a significant deviation from a distribution based on the assumption of no relationship. The same was true for size of community of orientation and present job.

Occupation of respondents' fathers, as a measure of their antecedents, was compared with perception of change. Anglos with agricultural antecedents had more favorable perceptions of change than did others.

When first job and present job were compared for Anglos and Mexicans, there was a significant difference between the model of equal movement out of one occupational category and into another and the observed situation for Anglos, but not for Mexicans. This was based in part on the position of the Mexicans in the occupational structure.

REFERENCES

Bulletins

BAIRD, A. W., and BAILEY, W. C. Farmers Moving Out of Agriculture. Miss. Agr. Exp. Sta. Bul. 568, Oct., 1958.

BEERS, H. W., and HEFLIN, C. Rural People in the City. Ky. Agr. Exp. Sta. Bul. 478, July, 1945.

BERTRAND, A. L., and OSBORNE, H. W. Rural Industrialization in a Louisiana Community. La. Agr. Exp. Sta. Bul. 524, June, 1959.

PORTER, W. F., and METZLER, W. H. Availability for Employment of Rural People in the Upper Monongahela Valley, West Virginia. W. Va. Agr. Exp. Sta. Bul. 391, 1956.

Books

FREEDMAN, R., HAWLEY, A. H., LANDECKER, W. S., LENSKI, G. E., and MINER, H. M. Principles of Sociology, Henry Holt and Co., New York, 1956.

ROGOFF, N., Recent Trends in Occupational Mobility, The Free Press, Glencoe, Ill., 1953.

Journals

ALMON, C., JR. Origins and relation to agriculture of industrial workers in Kingsport, Tennessee. Jour. Farm Econ. 38:828-86, 1956.

CALDWELL, M. G. The adjustment of mountain families in an urban environment. Social Forces. 16:389-95, 1938.

DOTSON, F. Patterns of voluntary association among urban working-class families. Amer. Soc. Rev. 16:687-93, 1951.

FREEDMAN, R., and FREEDMAN, D. Farm-reared elements in the nonfarm population. Rural Soc. 21:50-61, 1956.

HEBERLE, R. Social consequences of the industrialization of southern cities. Social Forces. 27:29-37, 1948.

KILLIAN, L. M. The adjustment of southern white migrants to northern urban areas. Social Forces. 32:66-69, 1953.

LEYBOURNE, G. Urban adjustment of migrants from the southern Appalachian plateaus. Social Forces. 16:238-46, 1937.

LIPSET, S. M. Social mobility and urbanization. Rural Soc. 20:220-28, 1955.

OMARI, T. P. Factors associated with urban adjustment of rural southern migrants. Social Forces. 35:47-53, 1956.

REISS, A. J., JR. Rural-urban and status differences in interpersonal contacts. Amer. Jour. Soc. 65:182-95, 1959.

SHARP, H., and AXELROD, M. Mutual aid among relatives in an urban population. In Principles of Sociology, Freedman et al. pp. 433-39.

SMITH, E. D. Nonfarm employment information for rural people. Jour. Farm Econ. 38:813-27, 1956.

WRIGHT, V. Summary of literature on social adjustment. Amer. Soc. Rev. 7:407-22, 1942.

ZIMMER, B. G. Participation of migrants in urban structure. Amer. Soc. Rev. 20:218-24, 1955.

Chapter 12

R. L. MCNAMARA
University of Missouri

Impact of Rural Migration on the City

THE PATHS OF MIGRATION are many; within localities, from farm to city, regional, city to country – all have had great significance in the development of this nation. The concern here is primarily with the meaning of migration from rural areas to cities. At the outset, I believe we should recognize the traditional relationship of country and city with respect to population replacement or maintenance of numbers. Cities were not able to maintain their numbers through their own replacement power, and so, many of the earlier students of the field were correct in their observation that the country was the seedbed of replacement. The upsurge of the birth rate generally has somewhat changed this relationship, but the great growth or urban industry with its demands for manpower has sustained the need for recruits to supply labor in urban industry.

Likewise, large numbers of persons employed in agriculture found themselves in a disadvantaged position as the agricultural economy was making needed adjustment to modern conditions. This together with the continued high fertility of rural areas, particularly those areas remote and less productive of opportunity, has resulted in high out-migration rates from rural areas to cities and industrialized areas generally.

Migration has had momentous effects on society both at the point of origin and the point of destination. The result is one of general observation: many of the established social structures of the home society have been disrupted. In this connection rural sociologists have very properly pointed out the distressing effects on homes, neighborhoods, and on many of the processes for maintenance of satisfying social living. In the city, migration, though not forgetting its benefits, has resulted in conflict with competing ethnic groupings; has brought about maladjustment of the economic situation including sometimes the cheapening of labor; and serious congestion in certain urban areas.

Rural migrants have contributed to the relative surplus of

persons in the economically productive ages of the urban population. In 1950, persons aged 20 to 49 in the urban population of the United States constituted 46 percent of the total, but the proportion in those ages in the rural-farm category was only 31 percent. Also, the ratio of dependents to gainful workers is relatively low in urban areas.

But apparently we must deal with the fact that we are an urbanized nation. As Gulick puts it, "It may well be a generation before we have a satisfactory description and analysis of what is happening to us in and around the great cities as America becomes urbanized and a new metropolitan culture comes to dominate our life. From now on most Americans will be born, grow up, live, work and die in great metropolitan complexes; some in cities, some in expanding suburbs, but mostly in urban surroundings. From now on we are an urbanized civilization."[1]

Now whether the city we think of is St. Louis, Detroit, Leopoldville, Bombay, or Bangkok the headlines concerning growth and problems of adjustment are essentially the same. Migrants entering a world of strangeness from one of easy familiarity produce what one writer has called the "waking sickness," not just a physical, emotional, or social illness, though it has aspects of all three, but a disorder of rapid social change.[2] The following comment, though its setting is a continent away, could very well be one we might hear in urban field studies here. "The house was different; the food was different; the people were different; suddenly the world was full of strangers, behaving strangely. The family was different too. There was no supporting network of relatives, no grandmother to give advice, no grandfather to make decisions. The problems were different; there was talk of police and passes, jobs and jails. The roles were different; mothers worked away from home, and children — if lucky — went to school."[3]

From a world of readily recognized norms for social and personal conduct, the migrant is literally in a world he never made — for him an atmosphere of normlessness, where his reference points are vague or unknown, and where his usual behavior which has long given him identity and satisfaction is termed deviancy.

The pessimistic tone of this chapter thus far could be taken to mean that there is an unfailing regularity of maladjustment of recent rural migrants in the city. This is far from true, for many

[1]Quoted from Population Bulletin, Sept., 1960, p. 128.

[2]H. Jack Geiger, "When Africans Go To Town," Saturday Review, Sept. 3, 1960, pp. 43-46.

[3]Op. cit., p. 44.

migrants, probably most of them, are adjusting to their new environment, supporting themselves, and staying out of trouble. Nevertheless, the difficulties of a considerable minority confront city people, their public and private agencies, with trying social and economic problems. Focusing in the central city and particularly in specific areas, distressing reports and judgments are brought to public attention. For example, in a major midwestern city receiving large numbers of migrants from the rural South, law enforcement officials and social agency workers estimate that: (1) 50 percent of the major criminal activity involves southern migrants; (2) 50 percent of the juvenile delinquency involves children of southern migrants; (3) 30 percent of the help given by relief agencies is received by southern migrants; and (4) 20 percent of the southern migrants are unemployed. All this in an urban center in which a small segment of probably not more than 10 percent are southern migrants of recent origin.

One should hasten to observe, however, that what is perceived to be proper conduct in the city may not "square" with habits of the newcomer and that the migrant in the city is a vulnerable, highly visible person because of, among other reasons, his manner of speech, of dress, his understanding of courtesy and cleanliness. None of these marked him unusual or deviant in his place of origin but may result in his being a central participant in conflict situations in the city. Hesitancy to accept the newcomer and conflict with the strangers are not new in this country. At an earlier time, complaints were made against German immigrants in the city because "they drank beer and sang songs on Sunday" and against the Italians because they "frolicked in the streets" on festival days. The descendants of these ethnic groups, now quite urbanized, may in their turn now be calling attention to the "improper" behavior of rural migrants and their repeated violation of rules of the game.

It would appear that the recency of migration is an important consideration. Learning the ways of the city is not accomplished quickly. It must be remembered that newly arrived migrants are not culturally deprived persons but rather that they bring with them, from a different setting, a full load of custom and tradition with knowledge of "what works" in interpersonal and inter-group relations. To state their relationship as a hypothesis: (1) as diversity between the migrants' culture of orientation and urban culture increases, maladjustment also increases; (2) as isolation prior to migration increases, maladjustment also increases; (3) as education increases, maladjustment decreases. Adjustment as used here is a very general term. An individual is personally adjusted if he is relatively satisfied with life as he experiences it. An individual is socially adjusted if he manages to avoid violating the mores and laws of the society in which he lives and if he manages to avoid serious conflict in his relationships with others. Of course, conflict with others includes interpersonal conflict, strife between the person and members of groups to which he belongs, and inter-group conflict or strife between the individual and members of groups to which he does not belong.[4] Carefully planned research is badly needed on adjustment of rural migrants in the city, and these need to be focused so that action programs of private and public agencies are clearly indicated and can be most promising of success.

However engrossing the situation of the individual migrant and his family may be, it should be seen as a part of the general phenomenon of population redistribution. The statements made earlier in this chapter on this point may be made more specific by referring to a preliminary statement by Clarence Senior writing for the American Society of Planning Officials.

BACKGROUND

Internal migration involves about one person in every five of the total population: approximately 30 to 33 million persons have moved their homes annually each year since World War II. Almost all move into new neighborhoods; over 5,000,000 have moved from one state to another each year.

Much of this movement represents a continuation of the long-time trend of our population from country to city. Metropolitan areas contained about 30 percent of all our people in 1900 and about 60 percent by 1956. Most estimates for 1975 reach at least 66 percent.

Many of the new urban dwellers come relatively short distances geographically, but if they have come from farms, they are likely not to know as much about the complexities of city living as would be desirable. Studies have found that it takes 5 to 10 years for newcomers from the farm to equal the voting participation rates of the older urban residents, for example.

Large numbers of the migrants must bridge both long geographical distances <u>and</u> great cultural differences, since much of the movement is between regions of the country. Many come from those sections of the country where large numbers of persons are disadvantaged when judged by any of the usual indices

---

[4]Adapted from "Migration and adjustment," a design for research on urban adjustment of the rural migrant in St. Louis, Robert L. Hamblin, pp. 2-3 (unpublished).

such as high death rates, high birth rates, widespread illiteracy, low per capita income, high proportions in agricultural, forestry, and extractive occupations, etc.

PREMISES

A. Internal migration will continue and probably increase if the speed of economic development is maintained or improved.

B. It is essential to the health of the entire national economy that migration continue and even increase, in the interests of efficient allocation of human and other natural resources. (There are at least 1,200,000 "surplus" farm families, according to the recent Rockefeller Brothers report on the United States economy, for example. A forthcoming report from Resources for the Future advocates speeding up internal migration.)

C. The migration is often wasteful in time, money, and energy. It penalizes many of those who pull up their stakes to travel in search of a job, or a better job, or better life chances for their children. Often tiny life savings are gambled on the move to the city. The move may well turn out to be relatively successful economically; often it is harmful to family life and to the personal development of individuals involved.

D. The migration also often helps contribute to the further complication of life in large urban areas. Probably most city dwellers do not understand the dynamics of urban change; that the "emptying out of the central city" and the "flight to the suburbs" have a natural history of many decades is not widely realized. The entry of conspicuously different ethnic groups into areas which have been declining steadily for years dramatizes the deterioration, may well cause further "flight," and may lead to deterioration in human relations. The stranger becomes both the symbol of the end of an era and the "cause" of urban blight.

E. Successful urban living involves a variety of patterns of learned behavior:

1. The newcomer must learn, and learn rapidly, how to cope with new and strange problems. Habits learned in different, and usually simpler, surroundings do not make for satisfactory results in the new environment. Customary ways of making a living, keeping house, raising children, visiting friends and neighbors, playing, and worshipping, may all, and all at one time, be called into question. Matters treated casually in the old environment may, in the new, suddenly become invested with high emotional content (e.g., disposal of refuse). Added to all

these puzzling changes often goes the reduction in self-esteem which comes from being labelled as a "problem," from being treated as a member of a conspicuous "minority," instead of as a person.

2. The "host" people also must learn to cope with new situations, to understand what is happening and how to help speed up the adjustment process. Neighborhood and city transitions can be brought about peaceably and without major personal, social, economic, and political disruption. However, citizens must be aware of the factors involved and organize to guide the process.

The task would be far too extensive to document the impact of these changes on the city, but some general statements may be made. The development of suburban areas along with loss or little change of population in the central city has meant often the moving out of middle-class families and their replacement (or partial replacement) by lower-income families. The net result may mean a considerable reduction of tax revenue simultaneously with a greatly increased need for schools and other public services.

It may be well to consider the school as an example of the impact of migration on urban centers. The school is always a key factor in the adjustment of the migrant whether one considers rural schools where our potential migrants receive their formal training or city schools where children of migrants are in attendance. Limited training of many rural migrants from south Missouri who are in St. Louis may mean simply that these people had not advanced far enough in school to receive the kind of training (vocational and otherwise) for which they were best suited. Or it may mean the school was not offering the choices of training most useful in an area where at least half the young people will not remain but will live their adult lives in the city. In any event, the reality of the situation is that few job opportunities exist for those of limited skills. In response to this type of problem among rural migrants, the Ford Foundation in St. Louis and several other cities, as a part of its "Great Cities" project, is financing "on the job" training administered and conducted by the city school system. This program is being well received by both employers and employees. Following a well-established American pattern, private support will continue until it is demonstrated that such training programs should become the responsibility of the public school system. Then we must face such logical questions as — who should pay the bill, and should training in urban trades and industries be a primary concern of the rural areas that are characterized by high out-migration?

Another project in St. Louis financed by the Ford Foundation is that of arranging for special classes in English composition and remedial reading for children of migrants. In part, this has been developed because of the high "drop-out" rate of migrant children. It is intended to develop comprehension of written material and to stimulate interest in communication by writing. Professor Corey in a half jesting, half serious piece has called attention to making the school a meaningful life experience as well as a highly disciplined formal learning situation.[5] Actually, school people do recognize this need, but acting on the need involves greater school expenditures and undoubtedly a re-orientation of the role of the school in our society.

To conclude, it would appear that redistribution of our population will continue, a major part of which will be movement of rural people to urban residence; that the "stranger" will continue to confront urban people with difficult problems of personal and community adjustment; that adjustment is a two-way street; that new services in the schools and in social agencies, for example, are needed to smooth the way for newcomers; and that carefully designed studies can provide the knowledge to speed assimilation and thus reduce personal tension and social and economic loss.

[5]Stephen M. Corey, "The poor scholar's soliloquy," Illinois Education, Dec., 1958.

Chapter 13

T. W. SCHULTZ
University of Chicago

A Policy To Redistribute Losses From Economic Progress

THE ROUTE assigned to me is not on the high road of traditional analysis paved with roles and factors having impacts and effects which produce trends and which lend themselves to cold, positive analysis with explanations and projections. I am to take the low road of policy full of opinions, beliefs, and values and hot with controversy. Here one proceeds at his own peril. The conventional way to reduce the risk is to camouflage one's values and to wrap the mantle of academic innocence about himself. I have decided to walk it unprotected although I do so with trepidation.

The concept of labor mobility is too rich for my appetite. I want a simpler concept, one that abstracts from sociological and cultural factors, relevant as they are, to some of the issues before us. I want to restrict my treatment to the actions of people who change jobs to improve their economic positions based on economic motivations. Why, then, do people change jobs in this restricted context? They do so because earnings to be had from the old jobs have fallen, or those from new jobs have risen, or the people involved have improved or have lost ground in skills and knowledge to do useful work.[1] It will be convenient to think of these changes as transfers of human resources which entail costs and returns. By jobs I do not mean only work that is done for someone else for a wage or for a salary. People can be self-employed, or they can be entrepreneurs. Thus, I wish to include all forms of human effort that enter into economic endeavor. Although the concept of changing jobs does not necessarily require a change in occupation or in location, the core of this problem confronting farm people does entail a change in occupation and as a rule also in location.

[1]Various combinations are, of course, possible. Nor do I exclude young people entering the labor force. They should be treated as changing from the "job" of studying (students) to a traditional job. Old people "retiring" also are to be included. I do, however, wish to abstract from changes in job preferences.

The economic test is based on resource allocation theory; the particular allocation before us is that of labor and its employment. The circumstances are those of an expanding economy in which both jobs and human resources are being altered fairly rapidly over time. Under these circumstances it is difficult to conceive of changes in jobs, representing the demand for workers with particular skills and knowledge, and the changes in human resources, making up the supply of workers with their skills and knowledge, paralleling each other so closely that no person would have to move or enter upon a new occupation in matching jobs and workers. The circumstances that characterize our kind of economic growth give us a conception of an economy in which there is a vast amount of internal migration and many transfers among occupations over time. Thus, in examining jobs and human resources by occupations, industries, and areas we are guided by the hypothesis that adjustments between jobs and human resources are the order of the day.

I shall first review our traditional policy and then propose an alternative policy which is, so it seems to me, more appropriate for a rich country such as ours and for our kind of economic progress.

OUR TRADITIONAL POLICY

Let me begin with a sketch of the principal attributes of our traditional policy. Its heart is the distribution of windfall gains and "unforeseen"[2] losses from economic progress. The rules of the economic game are that these particular gains and losses are to be absorbed by labor (including management) and by those who own the nonhuman resources as changes in demands and supplies reveal themselves in their respective markets. The rationale of this policy is that economic progress entails all manner of demand and supply changes. The discovery and accumulation of additional resources alter in many ways the quantity and quality of resources whether we treat them as inputs or as stocks of capital, rendering productive services. Thus, there is the belief that the relevant changes are not only numerous but that they also take many turns and twists that cannot be anticipated and, thus, planning and policy to cope with them are not possible. There is the further belief that these changes as a rule occur slowly and gradually, that they are widely diffused and that the resulting

[2]Not all of these losses are necessarily wholly unforeseen as I shall argue later in this chapter.

windfall gains and losses are not accumulative in the way they come to rest on the particular workers and resource owners. Lastly, and of great importance, there is the strongly held belief that these particular gains and losses are the essential inducements to get labor and owners of resources to make the necessary adjustments called for by economic progress. Thus, it should surprise no one that it has long been held that it is the better part of wisdom to let the chips fall where they may. In line with that wisdom, we have evolved our traditional policy which lets and which requires labor and those who own the nonhuman resources to absorb the windfall gains and the "unforeseen" losses that occur as a consequence of economic progress.

This policy has not escaped criticism, and there have been many protest movements. The classical treatment of rent and its implications that landlords acquire an unearned income is a major part of this criticism. Free trade (in corn), the nationalization of land, and the single tax have been put forward to reduce or to give to the state this unearned income from increases in rent. The sorry history of the poor laws following the social and economic disorganization attendant upon the industrial revolution and the movements in protest belong here. So does the public outcry against the enclosures. Again and again workers have tried to protect their jobs from the adverse consequences of the introduction of new machines. There then came the mounting protest to the fluctuations in employment caused by the uneven process of economic growth with its booms and recessions; as a result, governments now employ fiscal and monetary measures to reduce these fluctuations and provide unemployment payments. Farmers and peasants in western countries have also protested, predominately against two features; namely, against the wide fluctuations in farm prices and against secular declines in prices of the products they produce and sell. Farmers, however, have not distinguished between losses in earnings from their own effort (their labor and management) and changes in the return to land and to other forms of capital they employ in farming caused by economic progress.

Yet, the traditional policy has prevailed. It has done so in spite of much criticism and many protests and even when one takes into account the public measures that have been taken to modify and to supplement this policy. The core of this policy remains intact in the sense that we let, or require, labor and the owners of resources to absorb the windfalls and losses from economic progress. The values and beliefs underlying this policy are best revealed in the ever-present and formidable question: How else can one maintain the essence of an open, market economy?

AN ALTERNATIVE POLICY

Let me now present an alternative policy and the reasons in support of it. Ideally, the objective of this policy is to ensure individuals they will not suffer losses caused by economic progress. How to identify these losses and how to protect individuals against them are no doubt important, practical matters. Before turning to them, however, I want to consider what such a policy would do to incentives in general. It would redistribute the losses, but it would not alter directly the windfall gains from economic progress that labor and owners of nonhuman resources now absorb. These gains, accordingly, are not to be captured (indirectly they will be modified). This policy, therefore, lacks symmetry. But it is of critical importance not to take away these gains because they become the (remaining) incentives to induce labor and resource owners to make the required adjustments. It is assumed, here, that these losses are much smaller than the gains and, therefore, that the net aggregate gains from economic progress are not only large but large enough to provide an effective system of incentives. The asymmetry, therefore, is an essential part of this policy because it makes possible maintaining the substance of an open economy.

Before considering the ways and means of making this policy effective, there is the question: How well grounded are the beliefs about economic progress on which our traditional policy rests? Are the gains and losses from economic progress widely distributed? Among consumers, yes. But not so among producers. What this means is that consumers gain qua consumers although some of them lose in their capacity as producers. For example, a decline in real costs in producing farm products as a consequence of economic progress soon benefits all consumers, including farm people, purely in their capacity as consumers, but some farm people can lose more as producers than they gain as consumers from this process.

Producer gains and losses from economic progress are by no means evenly distributed. Consider only the losses as these are revealed to us in what we call the "depressed areas." Areas dependent on coal mining were long depressed. New England textiles was another. Other industrial activities also leave entire communities seriously depressed as a consequence of supply and demand changes arising from economic progress. Much of our agriculture, because of the rapid rate of improvements in the production possibilities in farming, because of the slow rate at which the demand schedule for farm products shifts to the right, and because of difficulties in adjusting to these changes, becomes depressed. Surely no one can any longer maintain that these producer losses from economic progress are distributed at all evenly among occupations, industries, and areas.

Moreover, many of these producer losses from economic progress are accumulative. That is, they continue to mount and to burden particular occupations, industries, and areas over long periods of time. Northern textiles, coal mining, and agriculture have been up against such losses from economic progress for many decades. Surely the end is not in sight for agriculture.

There is, also, the belief that these producer losses cannot be dealt with by policy and by appropriate public measures because none of them can be foreseen. They are thought to be in the realm of the unknown, i.e., losses that occur as a result of pure uncertainty. Here, again, the evidence does not support such an extreme position. Particular classes of people as workers and even some owners of nonhuman resources are absorbing such losses not because no one knew that these losses would occur but because some people are caught in a process from which they find it exceedingly hard to extricate themselves. Older farm people are thus caught. The salvage value of their skills if they were to leave agriculture is even less than the reduced earnings they can win for themselves in farming. The quasi rent on what they have invested in skills and knowledge to farm falls because, even though younger people leave agriculture, there is a long lag.

We know full well that much of agriculture is in for losses that are a consequence of economic progress for years to come. The rub here is not that there is no relevant knowledge but that some farm people cannot act on it in ways to escape serious losses for themselves.

What about the belief that any attempt to redistribute these producer losses from economic progress will inevitably undermine and ultimately destroy our open, market economy? I have shown that the essence of our incentive system can be preserved by giving free rein to the windfall gains from economic progress. True, this means that these gains will have to carry a larger load, in fact the entire burden of inducing people to make the necessary adjustments called for by economic progress. But this is not the whole of the story; the present distribution of these losses in many situations gives rise to a kind of reverse English because they undermine the capital and credit position of workers and of the owners of the nonhuman resources who absorb these losses and because no small amount of capital is required to extricate oneself once one is caught in such a situation.

In the case of agriculture, weight must also be given to the fact that some of these producer losses from economic progress falling on farm people are a consequence of our public policy to support agricultural research and disseminate the new knowledge from such research so it will be adopted rapidly and effectively. The new and better production possibilities that have characterized our agriculture and that are continuing to take place in farming are in no small part a consequence of such public programs.

LOGICAL BASES AND PRACTICAL DIFFICULTIES

Returning, then, to the proposed policy, as already set forth, its purpose is to ensure in principle that laborers and owners of resources would not be made worse off as a consequence of economic progress. Is such a policy feasible? What is the logical basis for determining the lines of action to be taken? Let me narrow the question for a moment by focusing on that part of economic progress which we achieve through agricultural research.

Assume the following: That the annual rate of return to resources at the margin employed in agricultural research is 50 percent (thus, a marginal rate that is far higher than the existing rates of return to alternative investments at their margins); and, that as a consequence of the new, useful knowledge from this agricultural research three things happen: (1) the real relative price of farm products falls to the advantage of consumers; (2) the real value of the wealth represented by land used in farming falls to the disadvantage of landowners; and (3) less farm labor is required in farming, making migration from farms necessary and, as a result of the lag that occurs in this adjustment, the earnings for human effort in farming fall relative to what they otherwise would have been to the disadvantage of the farm labor force, especially so for those who are self employed.

Should a community under these circumstances allocate more of its resources to agricultural research in order to take advantage of the relatively high marginal return available to it from this source? The answer is yes, but only if there is some way of reckoning and reconciling all gains and losses. The problem here is on the same footing as are gains and losses from removal of an import tariff, and the treatment rests on the principle of compensation. The gross gains, in our case, to consumers are larger than the losses of landowners and of farm people as workers so that there is a net gain to be had after compensation, and accordingly, the community could be better off.[3]

[3]Assume here that the costs of administering such compensation is zero.

There is, then, a logical basis for implementing the proposed policy. There are, nevertheless, some practical difficulties. What is the basis for distinguishing between losses from economic progress and all other losses that occur? What are the forms of compensation that are efficient in achieving the objective of this policy? Is it feasible for our government to administer such compensation? These are difficult questions, but they are no more formidable than those that arose in our efforts to cope with mass unemployment.

The losses from mass unemployment is the analogue of the losses from economic progress, and I find it an instructive analogue in taking a bearing on our problem. We do well to remember that there were many serious objections to any policy which deals with mass unemployment. Many people, lay and professional, firmly believed that any public measures to treat this unemployment would seriously impair the economy; now, too, there are many who look in the same way upon measures to deal with losses from economic progress, as is clear from some of the objections to the "depressed areas" bills that have been advanced by Congress. There are some who thought, in the case of mass unemployment, that public measures were unnecessary because if only wages were more flexible there would be no such unemployment. Similarly, there are those who believe that the resource mal-allocations caused by economic progress would rapidly correct themselves if only market prices were free and flexible.

Yet out of our trials and errors and from what we have learned about booms and recessions, there is now a strong consensus that economic stability is an important objective to be achieved through public measures. There are, as we all know, still substantial disagreements about the appropriate fiscal, monetary, and other measures for achieving this objective of economic stability. There also are unemployment payments, and these, too, are still far from satisfactory. The point is that the question asked in the study of mass unemployment is no longer, "Should there be a policy to cope with it?" That question has been settled in favor of having such a policy. The question now is, "How can it be done more efficiently than is now the case?" But we are not at this stage in dealing with the losses from economic progress. Neither our analytical work nor the public policy debate is addressed to the question of ways and means. The issue still before us is comparable to the first, namely, "Should there be a policy to cope with the losses from economic progress?" The burden of this chapter has been to show that such a policy is warranted because of our kind of economic growth, because of the uneven way the losses from economic progress are distributed and the welfare implications of unequal distribution of such losses, and because there is a logical basis for redistributing these losses through public measures.

A STARTING POINT FOR IMPLEMENTATION

In implementing this policy, there are good reasons for beginning with the losses borne by labor including the self-employed and management, and for leaving aside until later how best to treat the losses that owners of resources bear as a consequence of economic progress. In the first place, we have a strong precedent for doing so in the early approach to mass unemployment: when unemployment insurance was undertaken, no "insurance" was provided for unemployed plants and equipment, although at a later stage tax laws were altered so firms could spread their losses. Secondly, the adjustments confronting labor are as a rule subject to a longer lag than there are for nonhuman resources. Human beings have a much longer productive life than do most forms of reproducible physical capital. Thus by doing no more than not replacing the machines and tractors that wear out, the stock is rapidly reduced over time, whereas people retire from the work they are doing only after four decades or more of work. A third reason is in the fact that workers, because of compelling cultural reasons, are unique in producing not only their own replacement but for good measure add to their numbers. Imagine how different the farm problem would be presently if no farm children had been born these last several decades! Also, in the case of agriculture, the human investment in skills and knowledge required to farm is very substantial, and the demand for these particular skills and knowledge elsewhere in the economy is indeed small. Lastly, there is the obvious fact that most members of the labor force are tied to families, and those in agriculture in addition are rooted in communities which they are reluctant to leave. We do well, for these several reasons, to concentrate on labor in treating the losses from economic progress.

I can do no more than mention the types of public measures that are likely to prove useful in achieving the objectives of this policy. Two broad lines of action are open to us: (1) measures to accelerate the adjustment process; and (2) measures to compensate those who nevertheless bear losses. Note the parallelism, once again, to what has been done in dealing with mass unemployment: there have been various measures to reduce the fluctuations in business activities with a view of attaining economic stability and thus to achieve more nearly continuous full employment; there also have been payments to cushion the losses in earnings from unemployment.

To accelerate the adjustment process does not mean that the goal is to eliminate the lag in this adjustment altogether any more so than the goal of economic stability is to eliminate all fluctuations in business. Even though it were possible to devise programs that would eliminate this lag, it would undoubtedly be all too costly to do so. What is implied, however, is that the lag presently is all too large in the sense that much could be gained from a reckoning of costs and returns by reducing it substantially.

Rate of Unemployment

The rise and fall in unemployment of the range that we have been experiencing since World War II and the fluctuations in business activities with which this unemployment is associated, appears not to have had any large influence upon the domestic demand for United States farm products. Nevertheless, the longer run welfare position of people in farming has been seriously affected by periods of large unemployment which have reduced sharply the nonfarm jobs available to off-farm migrants. The positive correlation between unemployment and off-farm migration has been discussed in an earlier paper (see Chapter 4).

Agricultural leaders have been altogether shortsighted in concentrating so much of their attention on the current level of farm prices and income and overlooking the serious adverse implications to their welfare, of the high rate of unemployment and the mistakes in monetary and fiscal decisions that lie back of this excessive unemployment. We can and should do much better in reducing the rate of unemployment than we have in recent years. Moreover, to do so is of great importance in accelerating the adjustment process under consideration.

The Investment Component in Skills and Knowledge

Human investments in skills and knowledge play a large and complex role in our adjustment process. Some skills and knowledge are specific to farming, and some are not specialized. Young people have many years during which they can realize on new investments in themselves whereas old people do not have this opportunity. In general farm people who are both young and well educated, e.g., have completed high school without specializing in agriculture, have both a relatively large investment that they can transfer to advantage and have time enough to warrant making additional investments in themselves to acquire the required nonfarm skills and knowledge. But those farm people who are not young and who possess mainly the skills and knowledge that are specific to farming have little to transfer, and they have too few years remaining to warrant new investments of this type in themselves. These farm people are trapped in agriculture. Their one ray of hope is that enough of those farm people who are not caught, as they are, will migrate to accelerate the adjustment and thus minimize the losses they will have to bear as a consequence of economic progress.

Our objective here is to accelerate off-farm migration. Most off-farm migrants are restricted largely to the lower paid, unskilled occupations. To enter upon better jobs and to climb the occupational ladder more rapidly, these off-farm migrants must acquire particular skills. To do this requires substantial resources. A strong case can be made for the position that the costs of such new investments can and should be borne on public account because it would induce more farm people to leave agriculture and thus accelerate the adjustment process and because the social gains often exceed the private gains when all costs and returns are taken into account, including the important fact that the children of the farm families that transfer are going to be better located with reference to job opportunities when their children enter the labor force. It should not be very difficult to develop programs to do this.

Homesteads in Reverse

This proposal which I made some years ago continues, so it seems to me, to have merit in coping with an important aspect of the problem under consideration. The recent work of Glenn Johnson, concentrating on the divergency between the buying and the selling prices of some classes of inputs used in farming to explain both the "excess capacity" and the large number of obsolete (inefficient) farms in parts of agriculture, lends strong support for this line of action to accelerate the necessary adjustments. In a well conceived program of this kind, account should be taken of both human and nonhuman assets used in farming and to this extent the preceding section of this paper may be treated as an integral part of homesteads in reverse.

The advantages here are of two types: (1) One can treat the problem confronting older farm people arising out of the characteristics of their skills and knowledge, already discussed, and (2) one can also help alleviate the difficulties that farm people face in disposing of the physical farm assets they have acquired and thus induce them to leave farming. Various types of programs can no doubt be developed in this framework. The Conservation Reserve Program under the Soil Bank Act is one such. By renting whole farms for a period of years, especially in areas that are probably close to being marginal for growing crops including hay and pasture under existing circumstances, it is possible to assist some farm families to transfer out of farming. Grants to assist farm families to acquire nonfarm homes, to cover the costs of moving to the new place of residence, and to undertake the study and on-the-job training to acquire new skills and knowledge, represent still another relevant approach. Then, too, special programs to purchase particular farm assets at a price that would enhance substantially their salvage value for those farm families that want to leave farming, have a role to play in accelerating off-farm migration.

The specific lines of actions that I have considered above are each designed to reduce the supply of workers in agriculture and thus to keep the earnings for human effort in farming from falling as low as they otherwise would drop. These measures are comparable to the function of fiscal and monetary measures in dealing with the problem of mass unemployment inasmuch as they reduce the need for unemployment insurance to compensate workers at least in part for losses in earnings from unemployment. But it is altogether likely that even with good programs of the type outlined above, there will be losses from economic progress borne by human effort in farming for years to come.

Lastly, then, in order to compensate farm people in their capacity as workers and not in their capacity as owners of the productive physical assets used in farming, a program is warranted that will channel some income payments to farm people based wholly on the amount of farm work they do. It would be desirable to make these income payments dependent upon the rate of unemployment. A simple rule would be to make no payments whatsoever whenever unemployment is 4 percent or less and to undertake such payments whenever unemployment exceeds 4 percent. Even a flat rate per hour of farm work done, with all of its shortcomings, might be workable as a beginning.

Chapter 14

ROBERT K. BUCK
Waukee, Iowa

A Commercial Farmer Views Labor Mobility Needs

IN OUR DISCUSSIONS of labor mobility, one might get the impression that agricultural labor is immobile. Compared with most other nations, farm labor in this country is highly mobile.

From 1920 to 1960 the net reduction in farm population due to migration averaged over 23 percent per decade. Since 1940 more than 40 percent of the farm labor force has shifted to nonfarm work.[1]

Many farm people have actually moved to urban areas. Many others continue to live on the farm but commute to off-farm work. In 1950 there were approximately 2 1/3 million persons living on farms whose major occupation was in nonagricultural employment. In 1954 it was estimated that 28 percent of all farm operators worked off farms 100 days or more per year.

It is clear that labor on American farms has been moving and is continuing to move. The number of openings each year for new farmers on commercial farms is not large. It has been estimated that only 10 to 15 percent of farm boys reaching 20 years of age between the years 1954-63 are likely to find good farming opportunities on farms which can net more than $2500 per year.[2]

For many different types of farming situations, the production economists in the USDA and the land grant colleges have found that no less than $10,000 worth of total farm marketings is needed to enable the operator to realize at least $2500 per year for his labor and management. It is obvious that a great deal remains to be done in the reorganization and the enlargement of many commercial farms now selling less than $10,000 worth of products.

---

[1] "Migration to and from farms – 1920-54," USDA Report, AMS-10 Dec., 1954. Gladys K. Bowles, "Net migration from rural farm population 1940-50," USDA Stat. Bul. No. 176, June, 1956.

[2] Karl Shoemaker, "Opportunities and limitations for employment of farm people within and outside farming," USDA Fed. Ext. Serv. Mimeo., 1958.

This much-needed reorganization cannot possibly be accomplished without a continuation of at least the present rate of out-migration so many uneconomic units can be enlarged.

My view, as a commercial farmer, of the mobility needs in agriculture can be summarized as follows: (1) The most important need is to keep the "pull of jobs" working through adequate growth in the nonfarm sector of the economy. (2) We can and must do better in providing needed education and training, information, and employment service aids and even transfer aids to those who must find non-farm employment. (3) We should not count on continued or even accelerated movement of labor from rural areas to make a significant dent in the crucial problems facing commercial farmers in the decade ahead.

PULL OF JOBS – THE MOST IMPORTANT NEED

Farm people have a large interest in this country maintaining a rate of economic growth sufficient to provide jobs for our rapidly growing labor force. If the jobs are not available, discussion of mobility of farm labor becomes somewhat academic.

We must face up to the problem of chronic and persistent unemployment, which in recent years has approached 5 million persons even in the boom years of the cycle.

Hendrix states flatly, "Underemployment does not result from ignorance or other individual failing. Instead it is a general economic problem resulting from the structural and growth characteristics of the general economy."[3]

The crucial question is not "How can excess farm labor be pried loose from the farm?" Surely evidence is clear that when the opportunities are available, labor on American farms has moved out of agriculture in record numbers. If we have the growth and the jobs are available, then the question of labor mobility in agriculture or anywhere else becomes a fairly manageable problem.

OTHER MOBILITY NEEDS

The largest number of rural people seeking jobs off the farm during the 1960's will be youth. Next after job opportunities, their greatest needs will be education and training. A recent study by the National Planning Association indicates that many youths leaving the farm are not well enough trained to compete on

[3] William E. Hendrix, "The economics of underemployment and low incomes," paper presented to Southern Agricultural Workers, Birmingham, Ala., Feb. 1-3, 1960.

even terms with urban youth for town and city jobs.[4] Countless studies indicate that rural youths are not getting a fair deal in education – either in technical training or in higher education.

The expansion in jobs in the 1960's will be in occupations requiring skills and training. Most projections indicate no increase in number of jobs available for unskilled workers. Without adequate training, many of these youngsters leaving American farms will be headed straight into the unskilled jobs.

Another serious problem which many rural youth face in finding jobs is the distance they live from industrial centers. For many of them, getting a job means moving completely out of their home community. They often have to make this move with very little knowledge of what jobs are available and with inadequate training or skills.

For established farmers, the most serious obstacle is age. For obvious reasons farmers reaching 35 or 40 years of age find it difficult and costly to shift to nonfarm work. A change in occupation may involve a movement of the family to a completely strange community at considerable distance.

Some established operators lack the training and skills for many of the jobs available in urban areas. But I believe we tend to give undue emphasis to this point. I live near the Des Moines industrial area. For several years I have observed farmers whom I know getting a job in a manufacturing plant and soon operating a fairly complicated piece of machinery. A young man who worked for me for a year demonstrated only average skills as a farm worker. He shifted to employment in Des Moines and within a year was operating a tire-making machine. I don't believe there is general understanding of the level of skills and abilities required these days for farm work, especially that needed by the operator of a family farm.

In my opinion, a great many of these skills and abilities are not specific to farm work. Many of the established operators who want to shift to nonfarm work do have the basic qualifications. Of course they would benefit from special training. But because of the nature of the labor market, the distance they live from industrial areas, and other factors such as age, many established operators are at a distinct disadvantage in competing for nonfarm jobs.

With the continued improvement of highways, there is an increasing practice for farmers or members of their families to commute fairly long distances to work. It is common to drive 30,

[4] Vocational Training for Rural Youth, National Planning Assoc., Special Report No. 58. Washington, D.C., Sept., 1960.

40, or even 60 miles to and from work every day. This type of mobility, shifting to nonfarm work but continuing to live in the country, tends to be neglected in our studies. It is of growing importance. Many rural communities are working frantically to attract or develop industry and some progress is being made, but it is my impression that growth of new industry since World War II has become even more concentrated around existing industrial centers. It is hard to believe this is deliberate national policy in an age of possible nuclear warfare.

I should think development of long-range policy for dispersal of new industry (not into every local community but around moderate sized industrial clusters such as Waterloo, Mason City, Des Moines, Davenport, etc.) would contribute greatly to reduce underemployment on farms.

One of the current programs which shows promise is the Rural Development Program. Techniques have been developed for making greater use of local, state, and national resources in a coordinated approach to rural development. One of the promising aspects of the program is the evidence that local leadership and initiative can be developed for improving local facilities in education and training, for developing local industry, and for making use of already existing private and public institutions and agencies.

I believe that if we set our minds to it, we can develop a national policy and necessary programs to alleviate greatly the problem of widespread underemployment on farms in the United States. First and foremost we can maintain the rate of growth that will provide the job opportunities. We can improve the educational opportunities for rural youth – opportunities for technical and vocational education as well as for college training. We can improve on vocational guidance and testing and job placement services for rural youth and adults. We can even provide economic aids for established farm families who seek off-farm employment, but who find the costs of moving prohibitive. We can continue and accelerate programs for developing water and other resources across the country and for establishing new industry in areas of heavy underemployment of labor.

I have been talking about migration from rural areas – from commercial farms, noncommercial farms, part-time farms, rural residences, etc. Lumping all of agriculture together as if it were a homogeneous whole has serious limitations in analysis of such matters as resource mobility. I should like now to examine the question of labor mobility as a solution to the major economic problem of commercial agriculture.

THE POINT OF VIEW OF COMMERCIAL AGRICULTURE

How important is migration to the solution of the basic problems of commercial agriculture, that segment of our agriculture which supplies 80 to 90 percent of the products marketed? Speaking broadly, the basic problem of commercial agriculture is: (1) chronic overproduction with downward pressure on prices and incomes as well as heavy accumulation of surplus stocks by government and, (2) constantly rising costs of off-farm inputs.

What is needed for commercial farms is a balancing mechanism for gearing production to market outlets. If accumulation of surplus is to cease and if farm prices and incomes are to be maintained at satisfactory levels, some means must be found to enable commercial farmers to produce at less than full (around 90 to 93 percent) capacity for at least the next decade, but at the same time maintain the farm plant in good working order for the growing needs of the years ahead.

There are numerous reasons why this country must create conditions which permit a continuation of the large migration of labor from the rural areas of this country, as indicated in the earlier sections of this chapter and by other chapters. I would suggest, however, that we will be quite unrealistic if we regard out-migration as an important solution to the immediate problems of commercial agriculture.

We continue to underestimate the increasing productivity of new capital and new technology. Who among us would have guessed that movement of labor off American farms would be as great as it has been since 1940, and who would have foreseen that such a rapid rate of out-migration would not have gone a long way toward bringing production into balance with market needs?

Over 82 percent of commercial farms had less than $10,000 worth of farm marketings in 1954. These farms accounted for about 42 percent of all production. John Brewster, of the Agricultural Research Service of the USDA, suggests that these could easily be replaced by half the number. He suggests that if this were done it would make possible a substantial increase in farm output with just the present technology.

Actually, there is evidence that movement of labor off strictly commercial farms has slowed in recent years. McElveen estimates practically no change in the number of commercial farms (sales of $2500 or more at 1954 prices) from 1944 through 1959 and guesses very little further reduction by 1964.[5]

---

[5] Jack McElveen, "Family farms in a changing economy," Agr. Info. Bul. 171, Table 4.

1939	1.9 million commercial farms
1944	2.1 million commercial farms
1949	2.1 million commercial farms
1954	2.1 million commercial farms
1959	2.1 million commercial farms (unpublished estimate)

Labor mobility in commercial agriculture must be concerned largely with mobility of members of the operators' families and with operators themselves. Wilcox and Cochrane state, "Only 323, 444, or 9.7 percent, of all commercial farms reported regular hired workers during the week they were enumerated by the census in the fall of 1954."[6] I doubt they would average 2 workers per farm. Regular hired workers on commercial farms, therefore, must number between 300,000 and 600,000.

It is my observation that farms employing one or more regular hired workers are usually well organized so that a near minimum of labor is employed. Even with continued application of new technology, it is my guess that the reduction in labor force on these well-organized commercial farms will be negligible during the 1960's.

The point I wish to make is this — even if out-migration from rural areas continues at one million persons per year, relatively few will come from the strictly commercial farms (those, for example, marketing more than $10,000 of products annually and who account for at least two-thirds of all farm marketings). Out-migration from rural areas should not, therefore, be expected to contribute importantly toward bringing farm output into line with demand during the next few years.

I don't minimize the need for reorganization and consolidation on many smaller commercial farms. It is an important area of needed agricultural adjustment, but obviously not a "cure all."

In some of our discussions we appear to believe that needed farm consolidation and reorganization accompany off-farm migration automatically. I believe that more research is needed to observe and evaluate what actually happens to the resources left in agriculture as labor moves out.

When farms become available as a result of operators moving to nonfarm work, it is my observation that the land is often absorbed by owners or operators of farm units of already adequate size and in some cases of large-scale units. The operator of the marginal unit who desperately needs to enlarge his business is at a distinct disadvantage in competing for the land as it becomes

[6] Walter Wilcox and Willard W. Cochrane, Economics of American Agriculture, 2nd ed., Prentice-Hall, N. Y., p. 403.

available, either through rental or through purchase. Without any clear public policy on this question it is very possible that 10 or 20 years from now there will be a substantial increase in the number of large-scale farms and a continued and growing disparity between the large-scale farms and the marginal units. This can happen even if out-migration continues at the present rate or at an accelerated rate.

Commercial farmers are concerned with the long-run effects of adverse selectivity in who leaves and who stays on the farm. There is evidence that a relatively higher proportion of the more energetic and the better trained and educated rural youth are leaving the farm. This suggests the need for greater attention being given the problem of "How are new farmers to become established on modern, highly capitalized farms?"

In closing I should like to stress again the overriding importance of sufficient economic growth to provide job opportunities for underemployed rural people. A continuation of at least the present rate of out-migration is essential for the needs of many rural youths, and for operators of many small farms. For strictly commercial farms, however, the over-rapid introduction of new technology resulting in persistent excess capacity is likely to be the tough issue in the 1960's. If we come to grips with this problem, we'll have to go beyond the classical concepts of "shifting labor out."

Chapter 15

F. L. FERNBACH
AFL-CIO

Organized Labor Views Labor Mobility Needs

THE WAY the subject of this conference was phrased suggested a particular emphasis on the need to expedite the movement of manpower out of agriculture. Consequently, I will make a few observations about the problem of absorbing under-employed members of the rural population into more rewarding occupations in the cities. I will also mention the possibility of increasing off-the-farm job opportunities in rural areas.

I would like to make a few observations about what seems to me to be an even more basic question. I refer to the priority problem of keeping the right people mobilized in agriculture — those competent farm operators whose enterprises and managerial skills presumably should be preserved, and the hired farm wage earners who continue to have an important function in today's agriculture.

Although this is not the place to consider the extremely complex over-all problems of American farm economy, nor am I prepared to do so, I cannot forego the observation that public preoccupation with farm surpluses creates a widespread impression that a large part of America's agricultural enterprise must be liquidated speedily.

We are told, on the other hand, that actual annual farm output is no more than about 7 or 8 percent greater than what is being consumed. What is more, we know that there are vast good uses to which more of many of our agricultural commodities could be put.

Contrary to statements of the well fed, millions of American families still do suffer from inadequate diets. In addition, there are certainly useful purposes which export of more of our food and fiber overseas could be serving. Furthermore, instead of our stockpile of agricultural commodities being viewed as a scourge, it seems prudent to maintain a very substantial reserve against the possibility of national emergency. Thus, a minor redirection of the agricultural production effort, on the one hand, and a major effort to constructively utilize more of the abundance that our farmers are able to produce, on the other, are important aspects of a policy for a sound and healthier agricultural economy.

At the same time, it is evident that the problem of underutilized manpower continues to plague the rural economy and does, indeed, demand a solution. Long existing rural poverty – a situation that is hardly related to the operation of our commercial agricultural establishment – continues unabated. Furthermore, the spectacular growth of agricultural productivity – the product of the farmer's hard work and ingenuity and of government financed research and education – continue to reduce our farm manpower requirements.

Spurred thus by rural poverty and productivity growth, there has been a long history of out-migration from the countryside, and, inevitably, it will continue. Yet, it appears doubtful that migration by itself can resolve deep-seated economic dislocations within American agriculture.

At the heart of the problem, there remains the inability of most farmers – if left to the vagaries of the market place – to secure an income commensurate with their contribution to the welfare of society. Economic justice simply is not guaranteed by the unhampered and capricious operation of the law of supply and demand.

The American labor movement is well aware of the nature of the problem; it is somewhat comparable to some of our own. Just as we trade unionists have sought a measure of protection from the brutality of the unhampered determination of the "price" paid for labor in the market place, so do we understand and support the legitimate effort of farmers to establish a few protective "rigidities" of their own in an effort to achieve well-being and security.

The AFL-CIO, in testimony before the Committee on Agriculture of the House of Representatives on March 22, 1960, said:

> Over a quarter of a century ago, it seemed that most Americans had accepted the principle that federal cooperation is essential both to insure adequate production to meet the nation's food and fiber needs and to insure a decent livelihood for those who produce it. Long ago, the American labor movement supported federal programs not only to help raise farm family incomes through price supports, but to expand farm credit, conserve our soil, insure crops against damage and strengthen rural cooperatives. We have also supported measures to improve the housing, health, and education of those who live in rural America.
>
> .... just as fair wages and other legitimate production costs, plus a fair return on capital, are necessary elements in the price consumers expect to pay for industrial products, so, too, a fair return for those who work in agriculture is a necessary element in the price we pay for food and fiber.

These preliminary observations are an effort to put first and basic things first, as I see them. Of course, we are committed both by conscience and by the Employment Act of 1946 to a national effort to help under-utilized members of the rural labor force secure adequate nonfarm jobs. It seems to me to be even more important, however, to concurrently protect and improve — through a better system of income supports, through a measure of control and redirection of output, and through a greater effort to distribute more of our abundant food and fiber — the livelihood of many people whom a properly functioning agricultural economy should be able to utilize and adequately reward. Failure in this undertaking will end the wide diffusion of ownership and operation of American agricultural enterprise, and it will intensify the problem of mobility far beyond its present dimension.

Before turning to other matters, I feel compelled to add a few words about hired farm workers, and particularly the domestic migrants, a group of our fellow Americans that national policy now seems bent upon degrading. How else can one interpret the deliberate exclusion of these workers from the protection of the National Labor Relations Act (the right to organize), the Federal Fair Labor Standards Act (the right to decent hours and minimum pay), and denial of unemployment insurance benefits and workmen's compensation under the laws of almost all states?

Even worse, we apparently are determined to liquidate many of these American workers right out of our agricultural system while at the same time Public Law 78 allows more and more foreign contract workers to be brought in.

It is incredible that nearly a half million imported laborers are now being allowed to work in our fields under the sanction of a program that could be justified only by manpower shortages during a war emergency. Yet, Public Law 78 remains on the books because of public indifference and because about 50,000 large and politically powerful agricultural producers — less than 2 percent of the nation's farms — have become happily adjusted to enjoying the benefit of an assured adult male work force at cut-rate wages in preference to the employment of their fellow citizens at American wage rates. It is little wonder that these specially favored, highest income farm operators want to continue this program indefinitely.

The substandard status of so many of our agricultural wage earners can hardly be justified by the argument that their employers can do no better. In 1954 — the latest year for which official census figures are available — less than 5 percent of all our farms accounted for 70 percent of all expenditures for hired farm labor. These were our largest and most profitable farm enterprises. On the other hand, about 53 percent of all our farms used no hired workers at all, and on another 33 percent the farmer and his family performed nearly all the work themselves. Clearly, the low status of the farm laborer — and particularly the migrants — is neither attributable to this 86 percent of smaller American family farm enterprises, nor can an improvement in the farm laborer's lot be viewed as a menacing addition to their operating costs.

Even more significant, this 86 percent of all our farms is in direct competition with the 5 percent at the top that account for 70 percent of the total farm wage bill. To the extent that this small segment of our largest growers continues to maintain sweatshop conditions of wages and work, it continues to enjoy an unfair advantage over family-type farms by getting one of the significant elements of its production costs at bargain rates. Thus, the exploitation of the hired farm laborer has the inevitable effect of lowering the value of the labor of the family farmer and, hence, his family income.

The function of the hired farm worker in our agricultural system is an important and honorable one, and the opportunity for Americans to fulfill it under conditions of decency and dignity must be assured. Is it not appropriate that all those who plead for higher standards of rural life include this too-long neglected and exploited segment of the agricultural labor force in their appeal for justice?

While we must pursue public and private policies to safeguard work opportunities in agriculture, and to make them more rewarding — for operators and hired hands alike — it is evident that poverty and rising productivity continue to require the rapid absorption of substantial numbers of the rural labor force in nonfarm occupations. In fact, I have heard reference to a target of one and a half million new nonagricultural jobs — primarily for farmers among the nearly 50 percent who now produce less than 10 percent of our commercial output — as a reasonable objective for the 1960's.

Three major obstacles stand in the way of the fulfillment of this goal:

The first is the inadequate training of our rural labor force for today's increasingly competitive urban labor market.

The second is the lack of facilities to inform rural workers about the requirements for and availability of off-the-farm jobs.

The third, and most important, is the lagging rate of new job formation due to inadequate national economic growth.

It is hardly necessary for me to belabor the fact that effective competition in today's highly specialized labor market increasingly requires a higher order of general educational achievement and vocational skill.

What is more, technological progress in American industry — as in agriculture -- is rapidly raising production, but with a smaller labor force. During the first six months of 1960 there were actually one and a half million fewer production and maintenance jobs in our factories than there were in the same period of 1953. Most of the job growth in this 7-year period has occurred in clerical and professional occupations in the private sector of the economy, and in local, state and federal government. To compete for these jobs, a high school education as well as vocational skill is increasingly a minimum credential.

Unfortunately, those members of the rural labor force for whom jobs are needed now have ended their formal education some time ago, although many might be responsive to vocational retraining to prepare them for nonfarm employment. Nonetheless, because poverty too often breeds upon itself, it is urgently necessary to improve the educational opportunities of their children so that they may be prepared for the choice of job alternatives on or off the farm.

Unfortunately, the quantity and quality of public education in areas where the need for out-migration is most acute is even less adequate than in rural America generally. To upgrade both general and vocational educational standards, school district consolidation should be accelerated. This would maximize the effective use of limited local resources. In addition, a broad program of federal aid for education must be initiated. Organized labor has long supported federal legislation to help achieve a higher minimum educational standard for all American children. Those who now are schooled in rural areas will be major beneficiaries of enactment of such a program.

Under-employed and jobless rural workers need better information about locations of and qualifications for city jobs — even in other states. The responsibilities of the United States Employment Service should be expanded for these purposes. More rural employment service centers should be created to provide job counselling and to bring jobs and job seekers together even on an "interstate" basis. Moreover, relocation loans should be provided to assist needy out-migrants for whom jobs have been found.

Here it is well to observe that more than the agricultural labor force would be aided by this expanded effort. Between the first half of 1953 and the same period of 1960, the number of jobs in mining decreased by 200,000 and in railroading by 400,000.

Many of the jobless who were formerly employed at these occupations live in small and remote towns and are part of our rurally based and presently under-utilized labor force.

Most important, however, if all these under-utilized persons and, ultimately, their children, are going to enjoy satisfactory job opportunities, the rate of national economic growth must increase substantially.

From 1940 to 1953 – the years of defense preparation, World War II, the post-war boom, and the Korean War, during which the gross national product was rising rapidly – net migration off the farms approximated 13 million people. Since then, the rate has gone down sharply, and the reason is not hard to find.

In the 7-year period from the first half of 1953 to the first half of 1960:

The American labor force grew by 6,000,000 persons.

But employment grew by only 3.9 million jobs.

As a result, the jobless more than doubled from about 1.9 million in 1953 to about 3.9 million in 1960.

During these same years, as we have seen, production and maintenance jobs in manufacturing, and employment in mining and on the railroads, actually declined by more than 2,000,000.

At the same time, farm employment also declined by about 1,000,000.[1]

Meanwhile, as has been pointed out, most of the employment rise of the past 7 years has occurred in clerical, technical, and professional occupations for which displaced factory, railroad, mine and farm workers do not easily qualify.

Because of lagging economic growth and job creation, the seasonally adjusted unemployment rate for the first six months of 1960 stood at 5.1 percent of the civilian labor force, and in 1961 it stands at 5.7 percent. In contrast, the rate was 2.7 percent during the first half of 1953. Moreover, according to the latest report of the U.S. Department of Labor, 42 of the 150 major labor market areas of the United States are now suffering from a substantial labor surplus, which is defined as unemployment of 6 percent or more.

And what of the job needs of the future?

According to a recent Department of Labor study, 26,000,000 young workers will be entering the labor force in the 1960's. The net increase in job seekers – after allowing for withdrawals for all reasons – will be the highest in our history. By 1970, there

[1] From a statement by George Meany, President of the AFL-CIO, submitted to the Subcommittee on Automation and Energy Resources of the Joint Economic Committee of the Congress of the United States, July 29, 1960.

will be 87,000,000 Americans able and willing to work. The American economy must create an average of 1,350,000 additional civilian jobs each year during the 1960's. In contrast, our labor force was expanding at the rate of only about 800,000 per year during the 1950's.[2]

In the face of mounting unemployment and under-employment throughout the United States, even during so-called "prosperous" years, there is little hope that a million and a half rural workers (the estimated need by the Department of Labor) will be absorbed into nonfarm jobs unless the rate of economic growth is rapidly increased. If we fail, both rural and urban workers will be engaged in brutal competition for an inadequate supply of jobs in an ever more competitive labor market.

As we seek a faster rate of national economic growth, is it desirable and is it feasible to achieve more job creation in the smaller communities of rural America?

Today, nearly 2 out of every 3 Americans live in 209 metropolitan areas which occupy only 6 percent of the land surface of the United States. What is more, of a total population increase of 26 1/2 million during the 1950's, 85 percent of the growth occurred in the already tightly impacted metropolitan areas.[3] All of us have a stake in arresting this trend.

During the 1950's, America invested over $300 billion in new plants and equipment, and the amount should be substantially greater during the 1960's. Surely, enlightened public policy should prod more of this growth toward rural areas where abundant human and material resources and potentialities are available for utilization. I avoid use of the word "exploitation" advisedly. Too often rural communities have, indeed, encouraged their own exploitation by "run-away" employers who demand free plants, sweat-shop wages, and special tax exemptions as the price of relocation. Communities which seek to lure this kind of establishment should be forewarned that the effort seldom produces even a temporary asset; in due time most of these fly-by-night employers move on to even greener pastures, leaving unemployment and frustration behind.

As the American economy grows, expansion into areas outside metropolitan centers should occur for wholly legitimate economic, social, and security reasons. Many people in our rural labor force may conceivably prefer to live and work in communities where they have their roots. Land and other production costs may often be lower than in the impacted cities. From the

[2] "Manpower: Challenge of the 1960s," U.S. Department of Labor.

[3] "Population of standard metropolitan statistical areas, 1960 and 1950," PC(P3)-4, Bureau of the Census, Oct., 1960.

standpoint of national security, too great a concentration of people and industry is clearly hazardous and should be avoided.

Public awareness of the desirability of a strong rural economy, based upon a prosperous agriculture and expanding nonagricultural enterprises that neither degrade the worker nor the community in which they locate, is increasing.

Support for the objectives of the Rural Development Program of the Department of Agriculture, initiated in 1956, is widespread. Passage of the Area Redevelopment Act by the Congress on two occasions is of even more significance. If it had not been vetoed, it now would be providing technical assistance, industrial development loans, community facility aid, and vocational retraining to low-income rural communities as well as to chronically depressed industrial areas. Congressional support for this legislation is evidence of a growing public conviction that no part of America should be viewed as expendable. Indeed, with our population expected to reach 225 million by 1975, and to soar to 335 million by the year 2,000, development of the economic potential of all parts of the nation is essential if Americans are to have a decent place in which to work and to live.

It may seem surprising that a city-bred spokesman from organized labor should stress the importance of a more decentralized national economy in which the values of small town and rural life would be preserved.

Perhaps those of us who spend weary hours battling through the city traffic to our workplaces and home again, who suffer from inadequate recreational facilities, urban slums, and a score of other ugly aspects of city blight, are most aware of the value of a more remote and restful place in the sun.

If, at another conference, attention is focused on the problems of the impacted victims of urban America and their growing mobility needs, I am sure a large group of trade unionists will be eager to attend.

Chapter 16

BURTON SEEKER

Dow Chemical Co.

Business Views Labor Mobility Needs

THE AGRICULTURAL employment situation has led several observers to comment that the greatest farm surplus problem we face today is the surplus of farm people – especially farm youth.

I take issue with this analysis of the situation. It is not that there aren't substantial numbers of people in need of better employment than they now have in farming. Rather, my dispute is with the idea of considering people a surplus commodity. As a representative of business and industry, my contribution amounts to a report that on all levels of employment, qualified men are not in surplus, they are in demand.

Our expanding economy is creating new jobs every year. In the case of my own company, our payroll at present is some 15,000 persons larger than it was in 1950. Industry needs an ever increasing labor force.

There has been especially rapid growth in the field of commerce we have dubbed "agribusiness." This field has its roots in the fact that many of the functions once performed on the farm are now done for the farmer by industry. For example, the farmer once bred his own motive power or swapped with his neighbors for it. One of the big jobs in farming was to produce enough hay and grain to feed draft animals. Today the farmer buys trucks, tractors, and gasoline for cash. This has created the farm implement business, now doing some $3 billion in business annually. Similarly the mushrooming feed industry has taken over the farmer's job of providing rations for his livestock.

Marketing of agricultural products has also changed vastly. Where the consumer once bought wheat or even wheat ground into flour, he now buys enriched bread, sliced, double-wrapped, and baked fresh daily. Because of these farm functions taken over by industry, one set of statistics shows that we now have 10 million people on the farm, backed by 15 million employed in industries of farm supply or distribution and marketing of farm produce.

The sum of the situation is that good jobs are available in our expanding economy. Beyond that, the fact of farm experience in itself can be most valuable to the man on the job market today.

For one thing, fields of industry related to agriculture offer a great number of jobs in which farm experience is a valuable asset. Beyond this is an attitude that I have encountered repeatedly among employers causing them to favor farm-experienced employees for jobs that have nothing at all to do with agriculture. The attitude involves the idea that farm-experienced people have more of the ingredients of success: a willingness to work hard, inventiveness and ingenuity to work things out, a mechanical aptitude or "feel" for machinery and a simple, honest philosophy of life.

I have endeavored to develop specific information on the business and industrial situation by discussing the matter in some detail with the men in charge of employment at Dow's main production plant at Midland, Michigan. I have chosen this course because I feel data developed this way are really more meaningful than highly generalized statistics drawn from a superficial surveying of the whole industrial field. I feel that the general impressions I am able to convey can be taken as a reasonable pattern for the whole of industry.

First let's look at the types of jobs available: Of all Dow employees at the Midland location, two-thirds fall into the grouping of "hourly" employees — that is, those who are paid according to the time clock. Of the hourly help, 10 to 15 percent fall into the classification of unskilled workers; 15 to 20 percent can be called semiskilled men, and 65 to 70 percent are skilled craftsmen or tradesmen.

The other third of our payroll is the professional group. The primary distinction is that these people work for a fixed salary. Of this group, less than a third are included in the "technician" category usually held by men with limited scientific or professional training. The balance of the group are fully trained men with the potential for unlimited advancement.

The point that I want to bring out is that in both instances not only the better paying jobs, but the majority of all jobs, are to be found in the upper ends of the employment brackets. This is the result of a substantial trend over a period of years brought about by the advancing technology of industry. Automation, for example, may be replacing men on some jobs, but it is taking the tedious jobs of unskilled laborers. On the other hand, automation is creating a demand for highly skilled technical people who can design, build, and service such a labor-saving machine. Therefore, the majority of the new jobs being created are higher paying jobs, although they place greater demands on the skill and preparation of the workman.

Age is another significant factor on the job market. Generally speaking, the older the man is when he moves off the farm, the more difficult the task of finding really good employment. The problem in this case is the fact that when the adult farmer leaves his farm to look for a job, he usually does not bring with him any special skills or experience that make him valuable in business. His new employer will have to provide him with some sort of job training to qualify for a good job. If the employer is to expect a reasonable return on his training investment, he must know that the employee is young enough to put into enough years of productive work to justify the training. The cut-off point on age varies considerably with the type of job under consideration. The older man coming from the farm will probably have to accept a more menial, less rewarding job in industry. A man in his 20's or early 30's still has time to develop skills that will command good employment. In best position of all is the farm youth still in school who is wise enough to plan his education to provide for the changing times.

Let me digress momentarily to introduce another basic thought regarding the economics of employment in industry.

The thing that is forcing men off our farms today is the complex of factors which demands $25,000 in capitalization for every farm worker. However, the situation is no different in industry where it now takes $15,000 to $17,000 capitalization, on the average, for every worker. Our advancing technology is steadily raising this figure. The Dow Chemical Company represents our technical, highly mechanized, industry where it takes $40,000 to put one man to work. There is an ancient quotation to the effect that "a laborer must be worthy of his hire." The question that faces us today is just how can the farm-trained individual be worthy of his hire in business or industry.

To develop the picture, let us consider the various types of jobs found at Dow's Midland plant.

First there is the category of the unskilled workman. This includes section hands on the railroad, loaders, packers, and similar laborers. The job requires a normal mentality, usually a grade school education and primarily the ability to work hard. This echelon is the starting point for most hourly employees, although most of them rather quickly advance to better jobs. A certain proportion of these workers, however, lack the desire or the ability to advance.

Men of virtually all ages are hired for these jobs. In Dow's case, the cut-off point on age comes at 55. New men are usually not started beyond age 55 since they would not qualify for full benefits under our employee program.

As I mentioned earlier, this unskilled labor category includes 10 to 15 percent of the hourly employees or 7 to 10 percent of the total payroll. These jobs are fewer than they were in 1950 because mechanical power is replacing manpower on so many heavy jobs. This proportion can be expected to drop even further as the trend toward mechanization continues, although our employment people feel there will be an eventual levelling point after which there will always be a certain, limited demand for unskilled labor.

Next are the semiskilled workmen. This group would include truck drivers, intermediate operators, and various types of service personnel. The majority of these men are high school graduates, although this is not a requirement. This group constitutes 15 to 20 percent of the hourly staff or 10 to 13 percent of the total payroll. The types of services these men perform seem to match pace with other changes in industry, and the proportion of employees in semiskilled positions will continue to hold steady.

Two-thirds of the hourly men, or 45 percent of our whole staff, are skilled workmen. These are the electricians, machinists, the top operators, and the laboratory technicians. These men are in demand, and it is in this category where the expansion in payroll size is taking place.

Membership in the skilled workman category is the objective of virtually every hourly employee. Men reach skilled ranks through training and advancement. Two channels of advancement are open. First, a given number are set up as apprentices and pursue a combination of on-job training and home study. Upon completion of their work they automatically become journeymen. Apprentices are selected from the non-skilled workmen category with requirements including high school education with a good record in shop and mathematics courses.

The second avenue of advance is that of the tradesman's helper. Helpers are also selected from the unskilled category for advancement. In this case, requirements are based more on the man's native ability to do the work than on his background training. The helper works with various technicians for a period of a year and then goes into training. Upon completion of training the helper must await an opening for another journeyman appointment before he can gain this status. The primary difference is that the apprentice's previous training allows him to advance far faster on the job.

Age is a factor in this type of advancement as well. Men over 40 years of age are not considered for a start in these training programs since they simply would not have time enough to practice their trade to pay for the schooling. I might point out, however, that the age limit was earlier set at 30 but raised 10 years on evidence that the older men proved to be more steady and reliable employees.

Criteria for advancement among hourly employees are largely on the individual's personal aptitudes rather than fixed criteria. Our employment people report that the biggest failing they find with most job applicants is an inadequate background in high school mathematics and science courses. All new employees are given an examination in eighth grade arithmetic. Fully half of the candidates fail to make a passing score on the test. They do feel that considerable progress is being made in this regard although the matter still needs emphasis.

The unskilled worker is destined for difficult times as our technology advances and competition stiffens for the decreasing job possibilities in this area. This is not to say that everyone needs a college diploma to qualify for employment. Our employment people still insist that for the bulk of jobs available on an hourly employment basis they would rather put their faith in a good, sharp man with a high school diploma and good marks in math and science than in a bachelor's degree holder in some general college course.

The field of professional employment offers a slightly different picture. The usual rule in this case is that the individual pursues his training in college and then goes directly into his chosen line of work. This limits opportunities for men attempting to enter the professions after years of farm work. Even though the individual may have been brilliant in his college years, he will find himself sadly rusty if he attempts to return following several years of absence. The field does offer virtually unlimited opportunity to farm youths who decide to study and pursue a professional career.

Professional positions — that is, men paid on the basis of a fixed salary — constitute one-third of our total payroll. This proportion is rising and can be counted on to become an ever greater part of the total employment picture.

Our professional people can be divided into one-third which are the trained technicians and two-thirds which are the full professional people with virtually unlimited possibilities for advancement.

The technician group comes to its job with either a four year or two year terminal course in a given field. This group would include jobs such as accountants, draftsmen, and the lab technician who carries out a project after it has been set up by the research scientist. These are good jobs and are rated as important by the company. There is opportunity for advancement within technician ranks. A few well-qualified individuals gain full professional status and can continue up from there.

Jobs as technicians do carry requirements for training prior to hiring although requirements are relatively modest. This field is certainly one that should be given consideration by the farm youth still in school or even the younger man leaving farming. Qualifications for these jobs can be met, in many cases, with two year courses of study or through night school or extension courses offered by many universities.

The full professional positions are held by men well qualified in fields such as the sciences, law, or engineering. These jobs, of course, are very good jobs with more attractive pay and very good opportunity for advancement. Industrial concerns may not be quite so strict in requirements for attainment of advanced degrees as is true in college work, although it is none-the-less true that the better the man's preparation, the better his career opportunities.

The advancing technology of business today does demand the specialist who is highly knowledgeable in his chosen field. However, on top of this demand for specialty continues the demand for characteristics of the well-rounded individual. Perhaps the primary consideration here involves effective use of the English language. Assuming an equal break on technical competency, the breaks will always go in favor of the man who works well with people and has the ability to communicate his ideas to others. These are aspects that should never be overlooked as the student prepares himself for his chosen career.

SUMMARY

In summary, I would draw several points from our experiences at the Dow Chemical Company which doubtless can be applied to the whole of the business and industrial field:

1. Our expanding economy is creating new jobs which can absorb people leaving the field of farming. This does not necessarily mean that a good job awaits everyone making the change, since requirements for industrial employment are increasing and the job seeker must be able to offer some skills or abilities that are in demand.

2. The trend is definitely that of declining opportunities for unskilled workers, and the majority of new jobs are being created

for skilled laborers, technicians, and professional people. This shift in job distribution means better pay for the average wage earner on one hand, but on the other places greater demand on the skills and abilities of the job applicant.

3. Age is a considerable factor governing the mobility of farm people. In best position are the farm youths, still in school, who can study and learn any trade or profession within their abilities. Men in their 20's and 30's still have time to acquire special skills that command good jobs in business. In many cases this training can be had on the job. Men from 40 to 55 will probably have to settle for more menial, less rewarding jobs unless they bring special skills with them. In the most difficult position are those men of 55 and over who will find it hard to make any substantial change in their economic situation.

4. There will doubtless always be some opportunities available to the unskilled workman to find gainful employment, although these jobs are declining steadily.

Chapter 17

LAUREN SOTH
Des Moines Register

The General Public Views Labor Mobility Needs

IN COLONIAL TIMES, when 80 to 90 percent of the people in this country lived on farms, mobility of labor between farm and nonfarm occupations was a matter of vital concern. Probably no one thought of the problem in such terms, but early American leaders were eager to develop manufacturing and trade, and this certainly required mobility of farm labor to new jobs.

The same is true of the underdeveloped countries of today's world. The success of their economic programs to raise per capita income and consumption turns on transferring labor to more productive occupations.

It is true that, theoretically, economic growth and rising per capita income do not require a transfer of labor from farming to nonfarming occupations. Christian Engel's law – the larger the family income, the smaller the proportion spent for food – implies that a higher real income in the world can only be achieved by reducing the proportion of human effort on food production. But in any individual country this may not be true. A country could specialize in agricultural production and reach a very high level of income through trade without a rise in manufacturing or services.

In practice, however, most countries get richer by expanding industrial production. So mobility of resources, especially of labor, and especially from agriculture to manufacturing, has very high priority among the requirements of economic growth.

THE RELATIVE NEED FOR AGRICULTURAL MOBILITY

When a country has 80 percent, or even 50 percent, of its labor engaged in agriculture, the necessity for mobility to permit its transfer to nonfarm activities stands out clearly. But when a country already has less than 10 percent of its labor in farming and more than 90 percent in nonfarm activities, as the United

States has, the case for increasing the mobility of farm labor, from the viewpoint of the general public, is not a compelling one.

Only one of five additions to the United States urban population came from farms between 1940 and 1950. Certainly the proportion has declined from this level in the 1950-60 decade and will be even less in the future. Clearly, industry, trades, and services no longer depend mostly upon emigrants from agriculture for most of their work force.

The total labor force in the United States now is between 72 and 73 million, including the members of the armed forces. Of this total, according to the U.S. Department of Labor, less than 6 million are in agriculture. Thus about 8 percent of our total work force is engaged in primary agricultural production. Rather large changes in this agricultural work force would have comparatively little significance in the total picture.

For example, let us say the agricultural work force were to be reduced by 2 million in the next 5 years. This would be a reduction in the farm labor supply more than twice as fast as that which occurred in the 1950-60 decade. It would be a decrease of 33 percent in 5 years, as compared with 25 percent in the 10 years of 1950-60. Even this massive change in agriculture, which most of us would agree is unlikely to occur, would be only a ripple in the total nonfarm labor market. Maybe that's an exaggeration. It would be a ripple, a 3 percent addition to the nonfarm labor force, but it certainly would not be a wave that would be of immense influence on the total national product.

Economic policymakers, private and public, should always seek to improve efficiency in use of resources, labor especially. Converting resources to new uses is a problem that is ever present. New technology, changes in international trade, changes in demand, impose on the economy the need for changing its product mix and changing the distribution of its work force.

The contrast I am trying to draw here, in very broad strokes, however, is the contrast between the farm-nonfarm adjustment needs of a poor economy and the farm-nonfarm adjustment needs of an advanced industrial economy. The inefficiency of having two or three million under-employed people in agriculture in the United States is a matter of indifference, relatively speaking, compared with the urgent need for converting farm labor to other employment in, say, India.

The assumption up to this point is that the transfer of labor from farming to manufacturing, trade, and services is a wholly good thing and ought to be encouraged, because it will increase the total output of goods and services in line with consumer demand – Engel's law again. I have argued only that the urgency of this problem is not very great in the United States, because we are fairly well adjusted as it is, and don't have much farther to go.

These are concepts of economic development that are almost universally accepted, at least within broad limits. The Communists, the democratic socialists, the old-fashioned capitalists, and the new-fashioned capitalists all agree on the desirability of reducing the labor force in agriculture and putting more people to work producing goods and services beyond the material necessities of life.

Christian Engel, incidentally, thought that about 80 percent of family income for the material necessities was "normal." He was writing in the last half of the nineteenth century. That seems a very high percentage of family income for food, clothing, and shelter today. It gives us a picture of how the standard of living, and I mean standard in its literal sense, has climbed in the last 100 years.

AGRICULTURAL EMPLOYMENT AND THE TOTAL ECONOMY

But now let me examine farm labor mobility from another aspect. The practical world has a very annoying way of not fitting the theoretical models of the social scientists. The theory that it is always meritorious to transfer people from farming to other occupations runs into some stubborn facts in the American situation.

I have noted that the proportion of agricultural labor to the total is so small it is of little consequence – whether it stays put or moves out of agriculture. But let us look at the farm labor force in relation to the number of unemployed workers in the economy. Take my hypothetical 2 million displaced farm workers and compare them with the number of unemployed, which has been averaging around 4 million in 1960 and 1961. Obviously, adding 2 million to the number of people seeking work in nonfarm jobs within a 5 year period would be quite a jolt. The general public would not be indifferent to that.

In the practical situation, we must recognize that, so long as there are sizable numbers of unemployed in the cities, agriculture performs a public welfare function by keeping excess people on farms beyond the requirements of the industry. From the public viewpoint, agriculture helps to keep down the rolls of unemployed in the cities – and also the public expenditures for relief in the cities.

Thus one could make an argument that it is more economic to maintain surplus labor in agriculture, and under-employment in agriculture, than to increase labor mobility — in the absence of a faster rate of total economic growth and "full" employment or a strong demand for nonfarm labor. However, this would be shortsighted, even if expedient.

The public has a deep long-run concern in agricultural adjustment from the viewpoint of improving the quality of the human resources involved. The young people growing up on the poorest farms in this country will not be assets to the community in the future. They will lack education, job training, social adjustment, and even the health of their contemporaries in the cities. Thus it is in the public interest to provide better opportunity for these young people.

This does not necessarily mean "moving families out" of rural areas. It may mean bringing nonfarm jobs to rural communities. But it certainly does mean providing more productive employment for the heads of many rural families, rather than public welfare — public assistance — which becomes demoralizing.

It is always better to spend public money and public effort on adjustment of an industry which is declining in its need for labor, rather than to subsidize or protect the labor in place.

The public also has an interest in mobility of farm labor from the viewpoint of social justice and equality. The economic benefit to the whole community from better agricultural adjustment may be small — but the moral benefit of living up to community ideals is large.

Another public consideration which must be given some weight in this matter of farm labor mobility is the social value of maintaining a rural culture and an industry of individual family enterprise.

Is there really a rural culture in the United States these days, or is farm life so urbanized as to blur any distinction? Although we all talk a great deal about preserving the family farm and preserving the values of rural life, actually our agricultural education agencies, private business, and most other influences on agriculture have been in the direction of eliminating rural culture. In spite of this, it is conceivable that the people of the United States, once they gave the matter thought, might want to keep a family farm system of agriculture at some extra cost.

I have little doubt, myself, that preservation of a rural culture is the principal reason for the subsidies to agriculture in Great Britain. The traditional reason of maintaining a sure food supply in case of war really doesn't make much sense in these days of nuclear weapons. If all-out war comes, it won't last long, and food output won't be much of a factor. Anyway, Britain would have to depend on North America for food as it did in the last two wars. So I think Britain actually subsidizes agriculture in order to maintain a bit of rural life in that highly urbanized island, though that is seldom mentioned as a reason.

Maybe we are coming to the time when we will do the same in the United States. Maybe we will want to maintain a free enterprise agriculture, rather than allow it to go the way of other industries into highly organized large units with hired labor.

The public interest in rationalizing the agricultural industry in the United States thus is somewhat mixed.

On the one side, it is in the public interest to transfer labor out of agriculture to increase the value of the national output and to equalize economic opportunity. The public interest also would be served by providing better educational opportunities for young people in rural areas, as a source of manpower and womanpower for the nation in the years to come. There is a national interest, too, of course, in reducing farm subsidies by getting agriculture into better adjustment in the economy.

Against these arguments for public action to rationalize agriculture, we have the fact that agriculture is not very large in the total national economic picture, so the potential gain is small from rationalization. From the public viewpoint, therefore, special agricultural adjustment programs, retraining programs, subsidies for transferring to new locations, and the like might not be considered justifiable at a time when 5 percent of the nonfarm labor force is unemployed. If national economic policy calls for unemployment of about this level, as a means of restraining inflation or simply because a fuller degree of capacity employment is held to be impractical, then special agricultural mobility programs would be hard to justify.

Under a policy of full employment and more rapid economic development, however, it would be sensible to carry on a vigorous program of agricultural adjustment. Making excess agricultural labor available for nonfarm work in such circumstances would contribute to a larger total national output and a faster rate of economic development.

But the national policy of full employment must come first. You can't carry on an agricultural adjustment program effectively without an active labor market in the economy as a whole. Indeed, it might well be more economic to maintain surplus labor in agriculture under conditions of 5 to 7 percent unemployment in the rest of the economy.

Finally, the public interest in labor mobility in agriculture is more than an economic interest, or at least it may be more than an economic interest. The public may want to maintain a larger agricultural industry and more farm families than could be justified on straight economic grounds. Within the 1960's, I believe, the nation ought to make a decision on this point, because we are nearing the time when agriculture may change rather rapidly to large-scale units, with a great deal of hired labor, specialized and integrated into nonfarm business.

If there are no social values worth preserving in the agricultural industry, then there is no reason not to push the rationalization development rapidly. If there are social values we want to maintain, then action will have to be taken.

FACTORS AFFECTING MOBILITY

The most important factor that influences the migration of farm people to cities seems to be the demand for nonfarm labor. When unemployment is high in the cities, the movement of people off farms slows down.

Mobility of farm labor seems not to be closely related to changes in income advantage or disadvantage in agriculture within wide limits. According to economic theory, to move resources out of an industry, there must be some income disadvantage, and presumably the greater the disadvantage the greater the movement. However, I can see little correlation of this kind. During the period of federal farm price support and subsidy programs, the movement of people out of agriculture has been as rapid as at any other time or even more rapid.

Those who have argued that farm subsidy programs would reduce the mobility of farm labor cannot develop proof on the record of the years 1940-60. This is not to say that the logic is wrong but only that other influences appear to be far more important. One of these, perhaps the strongest, is the desire for urban living. Despite all the propaganda about the advantages of rural life, most people prefer to live in cities.

It may be that the disparity of farm income has been so great farm income subsidies have not altered the pull of higher-paying nonfarm jobs at the margin. That is, the subsidies haven't made enough difference to hold people in agriculture. And I suspect that the disparity of income people will accept rather than make the effort to move out of farming has narrowed in recent years. Farm people in this country in this age, for the first time in history, are beginning to believe they <u>should</u> have incomes equal to those of city people. If they don't have that kind of opportunity, they will move out.

Farm price supports, other subsidies, and educational aids to agriculture should be carefully designed so as not to interfere with the mobility of agricultural labor, of course. However, it seems evident to me that farm income supports could be considerably higher than they have been without blocking the migration to nonfarm activities. Farm programs of the kind we have had or are likely to have will not "freeze" labor in agriculture.

The mobility argument also is used to oppose minimum wages in agriculture. However, low wages in agriculture may in many cases operate to keep labor in that industry. With cheap labor, management has less incentive to use workers at high levels of productivity and to minimize the use of labor. Importation of workers from Mexico and Caribbean countries, along with the lack of minimum wages for American farm workers, may provide some incentives for farm workers to seek other employment outside of farming. On the other hand, this situation may influence farm owners and managers to maintain people in the farm labor force. Among the relatively uneducated workers who supply the hired labor in fruit and vegetable areas particularly, the market incentive probably is less powerful in its effect than it is with management. A higher minimum wage would cause management to reduce farm labor and, I suspect, would help mobility more than low farm wages.

But nonfarm jobs must be available. Information and job counseling for the workers and raising minimum wages are not enough if there is little demand for nonfarm labor.

Workshop Session: Chairman, **L. M. THOMPSON,** Iowa State University; Resource Person, **ROBERT ISENBERG,** National Education Association; Recorder, **EDWARD AITON,** Federal Extension Service

Chapter 18

Modifications in Rural Education in Relation to Mobility Needs

I. PRESENTATION: Robert Isenberg

ANY THOROUGH CONSIDERATION of educational opportunities available to rural youth should include 4-H club work, scouting, and the programs of other agencies as well as what is done through the public schools. From the standpoint of any individual young person now residing in a rural area, such a program may actually be the dominant determiner of vocational choice and pursuit and possibly, therefore, mobility from agriculture. Hence education as a social process should be considered in its broadest outlines. Acknowledging this, let me limit my remarks to educational programs as provided by the public schools.

The public schools in the rural areas of this country are vastly different from what they were 10 or 12 years ago. The one-teacher school is rapidly disappearing. Since the end of World War II, the number of school districts has been reduced by reorganization and consolidation from more than 100,000 to only slightly more than 30,000. This process is continuing, really only beginning in some states, and further reductions can be expected. Better educational programs possible through larger school districts, coupled with the relatively easy access made possible by school buses, have made this substantial "new look" possible.

But even as this kind of organizational modification has taken place, the circumstances within which educational programs operate have changed even more. Reorganization of school districts is not adequate to provide for expanding educational needs. The school districts which have been newly formed and are now being reorganized are not capable of finding solutions to the problems associated with the topic of this conference. A discussion of modifications in educational systems as they relate to public schools, to rural youth, and to mobility needs must therefore be concerned with modifications which might be made more than with those already accomplished.

While a long list of problems characteristic of public education in rural areas and smaller communities can quickly be developed, let me generalize these into three basic areas. Rural public schools at this time:

1. Offer a program severely limited in scope of opportunities.
2. Are lacking in expertness in nearly all specialized areas.
3. Are inadequately structured to provide either the scope or expertness that is needed.

With respect to limitations in scope it would not be unfair to say that most rural high schools continue a major emphasis on a college preparatory program — a college preparatory program that may be lacking in advanced mathematics, physics, or chemistry or all three, or may be lacking in modern foreign language training; a college preparatory program supported by limited laboratory facilities and equipment and usually a most limited library. In reorganized districts the chances of rural youth are somewhat greater. In addition to a more complete college preparatory program there will also often be programs in vocational agriculture and/or industrial arts, homemaking, and introductory business education. Other vocational opportunities are seldom available.

In terms of the absence of expertness, my reference is to the general lack of access on the part of rural schools to educational specialists — guidance counselors, school psychologists, instructional supervisors, curriculum consultants, and other such specialized personnel who can assist in developing and maintaining a quality educational program.

Both of these areas can be expanded in considerable detail, and both are very closely and directly related to our topic. But let me single out of the third general problem area — the lack of adequate organizational structure — two modifications which must be made if educational opportunities available to rural youth are to equip them for a satisfactory adjustment to the changing social and economic circumstances which they are certain to meet, ready or not. Other aspects of this structural area may be filled in to some extent in our later discussion.

The first modification which I want to single out is the reorganization and redirecting of what those of us who work with educational organization call the "intermediate administrative unit." An intermediate unit is an administrative organization which functions between the local school districts and the state education agency. It is an area or regional unit. Increasingly apparent is the need to reorganize this administrative structure so that its base of operation is adequate to operate efficiently a program of specialized educational services. Such research as is presently available indicates this would require an area with a minimum of 10,000 pupils. This type of modification would furnish a structure — within the same educational framework which provides all public elementary and secondary education — that can develop adequate area vocational educational programs so urgently needed for so many rural youths. But a revamped intermediate unit can do much more. It can establish on an area basis an instructional materials center (films, tapes, exhibits, etc.), a central library service, a broad program for various types of handicapped children, and also provide the specialized kinds of personnel which local school districts are unable to provide. The beauty of this kind of modification is that this can be done on an area basis, efficiently and economically, without destroying the autonomy of local school districts and the close identification which people have to their local school system. What I am describing here, much too briefly, is an organizational device for supplementing local school districts even after they have been reorganized in those areas where educational shortcomings continue. While some modifications in this area have been made, most are yet to come. It might be sufficient to say that up to the present time separate efforts are being made for the reorganization of intermediate units in 19 different states.

The second aspect of organizational structure which I want to mention is finance. Before substantial educational improvements will be possible, some changes in the manner in which schools are supported will need to be made. Rural areas are, generally speaking, the least able to tax themselves to support the diverse kind of educational program which present and future social and economic circumstances call for. There are a number of factors which contribute to this inability. Let me mention a few:

1. The disproportionate number of children to be educated in relation to the number of people in the maximum economically productive age groups — a need for education that is inverse to tax paying potential.
2. The general absence of industrial tax base — local taxable

valuation consisting largely of residential and agricultural real property.
3. An actual declining real property valuation in some areas.
4. The impracticality of local tax revenue from sources other than real property.

Such generally limiting characteristics of rural areas with respect to financing education operate in many areas today to an extent that the maintenance of even a most inadequate rural education program is a great burden. When we add to this the kind of expanded educational effort which is implied by the preparation of rural youth for virtually certain mobility to urban areas, the task of overhauling our concepts of how education should be financed should seem obvious.

Let me conclude with another and yet unmentioned problem with respect to educational modification. This one is perhaps the most difficult and most serious of all. Crudely put, it is that a seeming majority of people in agriculture, however imposing may be our identification of necessary modifications in relation to necessary mobility of rural youth, simply do not want and strongly resist these modifications. Rural people work hard to maintain the inadequacy of the educational status quo.

II. DISCUSSION

It has been recognized for many years that the dropouts from elementary and high school are greater percentagewise among rural youth than among urban youth. From the standpoint of the nation as a whole, this will be a serious problem in the decade of the 1960's. It is estimated that 7.5 million young workers entering the labor force in the '60's will not have completed high school. About 31 percent of these will not have advanced beyond the eighth grade. It is expected that 30 percent will drop out in the ninth grade and 39 percent will drop out in the tenth and eleventh grades. This is becoming a critical problem for two primary reasons: (1) the population and, therefore, demand for products of labor, will not grow as rapidly as the labor force in the 1960's, and (2) with the advancement in technology of production on farms and in factories, the demands for skilled and well-educated young people will be increasing, while the demands for unskilled and poorly educated people will be decreasing.

During the decade of the '50's, the population of the United States was growing faster than the labor force. There was virtually full employment during this period of rapidly expanding industrial economy. A young person entering the labor market was not penalized for lack of skill or education to any appreciable degree because industry was willing to train him for the job to be done. As we look to the future, industry will have greater choice from a greater supply of labor. The unskilled, poorly educated young worker will be at a serious disadvantage.

The curricula of our public schools have generally been oriented toward college preparation. Students who lack interest and aptitude for college find the college preparatory courses unsuited to their needs and drop out with inadequate preparation for job opportunities. There is a great need for increased vocational training in our public schools. At the present time, 35 percent of high school graduates enter college, and only about half of these earn a degree. So we might say rather conservatively that about 20 percent of the high school graduates are expected to complete a college degree program.

The academically talented students need an even more rigorous high school curriculum than is presently required in most high schools. They need strong preparation in English, mathematics, and basic science courses. Many of our high school curricula represent a compromise between a rigorous college preparatory program and a terminal general high school curriculum.

Vocational education is seriously lacking in most high schools, particularly in rural areas. Probably the high cost of vocational education has been the greatest factor in its lack of adoption. However, there is a general prejudice toward vocational education because of the image that the typical American family has developed as a goal for its youth. Perhaps too much emphasis is placed on "a college education for every youngster."

Vocational agriculture has been criticized because it competes with academic subjects in the curriculum of the college-bound youth. Critics of the program appear to be unaware of the importance of a vocational subject in developing interest in a career. In Iowa, for example, about 15,000 boys finish high school each year. About 2,000 of these have had vocational agriculture. Of the 500 freshmen entering the College of Agriculture of Iowa State University, about 275 come from the 2,000 who took vocational agriculture. This means that only about 225 of the agriculture freshmen come from the group of 13,000 who did not take vocational agriculture in high school.

It should be recognized that over 90 percent of our beginning farmers in this country will not have attended college. Their formal education for their life's work will have to come from high school. Yet only half of our rural high schools today offer vocational agriculture. There have been suggestions that vocational agriculture should be cut back so that other forms of vocational training might be financed. This would not be a desirable solution to the problem.

Greater attention needs to be given to counseling in high school. Better guidance will help students understand the kinds of occupations for which they might prepare and will enable them to be better prepared for the career of their choice. Furthermore, counseling will have the effect of keeping students in school for a longer period of time. Rural areas are in particular need of more guidance counselors.

The guidance role is becoming so important in our rapidly changing economy that we cannot leave the job to the high school guidance counselor. He can be of much help and can be the consultant for many allied groups who can help with the total program. A community should not assume that employment of a guidance counselor will solve the problem of guidance. Every organization working with youth, particularly rural youth, should give considerable attention to career exploration. This type of program can be tied in with programs of 4-H, YMCA, YWCA, Boy Scouts, Girl Scouts, and other youth groups. Communities can develop apprentice programs so that high school students may obtain work experience in libraries, hospitals, offices, factories, and other establishments.

SUMMARY

1. Our major thesis or concern is with the life-adjustment problems of youth in relation to the world of work.
2. Equalization of rural-urban youth opportunities should be a major national educational goal.
3. Communities need to examine their educational services with the view of a complete, well-rounded set of facilities and educational opportunities.
4. Guidance and counseling services need improvement and strengthening.
5. The tax structure must be revised to accomplish the job of providing a comprehensive school system, offering both vocational training and preparation for college.
6. School personnel need to recognize other agencies, services, and facilities and cooperate with them.
7. Some of the major problems relate to motivation, attitude, parent interest, and community indifference. These problems exist in urban as well as rural areas.

Workshop Session: Chairman, **ROY HUFFMAN,** Montana State College; Resource Person, **MERVIN SMITH,** Ohio State University; Recorder, **WALLACE OGG,** Iowa State University

Chapter 19

Modifications in Farm Policies As Related to Mobility Needs

I. PRESENTATION: Mervin Smith

PAST FARM POLICIES have given very little attention to the transfer of labor within farming or between farm and nonfarm employment. In fact, the so-called farm problem generally has not been defined as a labor resource problem. It usually has been defined as a farm price problem and sometimes as an income problem. The low income is believed to be the result of chronic overproduction and the slowness of some farmers to adjust to changes brought on by rapid adoption of new technology.

A fundamental modification needed in farm policies is an improved analysis of and recognition of the problem which mainly is the maladjustment of the resources in farming — both in the aggregate farm production and within the individual farm. The human resource adjustment is the most critical. Probably the main reason why farm policies have not been more successful is the failure to recognize the need for transfer of human resources out of farming. Economic theory would tell us that if we are to increase the return to a resource factor such as labor (farmer), an effective way is to reduce the supply of that factor. We need much more understanding of the farm problem if we are to develop improved farm policies.

Since the adjustment of human resources has not been considered to any extent, some of our farm policies slowed down the mobility of farm labor. This is debatable though, and more research is needed as a basis for developing improved policies.

In evaluating farm policies we are assuming some general over-all objectives. One of these is progress or economic growth. This means increased productivity and adoption of improved technology. We want agriculture to continue, as it has in the past, to contribute greatly to progress and therefore to increase its productivity and efficiency. Another general objective is that we want farmers to share in the benefits of this progress at least in proportion to their contribution to it.

In light of present maladjustments in farming we will further assume that there is need to (1) speed up transfer of labor to off-farm work, (2) improve the balance of land, labor, and capital on individual farms, and (3) upgrade quality of labor staying in farming and of that moving off farms.

In considering how farm policies might be modified to meet mobility needs, we will examine how all alternative programs might affect labor adjustment. Present programs and new proposed programs will be considered.

Direct Price and Income Programs

With no government price, income, or other programs, more farm labor might be squeezed out of farming. It is subject to debate, however, how much faster people would leave the farm without any price or income supports. Nonfarm incomes have nearly always been higher than farm incomes with or without price or income supports. Studies of the net migration from farms since 1920 tend to show that migration has been higher when farm prices and incomes were increasing and lower when prices and incomes were decreasing. This may not be due to the prices themselves, but it is likely that off-farm employment opportunities were greater when farm prices and incomes were increasing.

Price supports and storage programs, multiple pricing, and direct income payments tend to retard labor transfer from farming. However, evidence seems to indicate that other factors are much more important in determining the amount of migration from the farm. Farm labor would be influenced if incomes were subsidized directly or indirectly through prices. Most of these programs have been selective as to commodities and can influence the relative profitability of some commodities compared with others. As a result, farmers may be slow to shift labor resources from those supported commodities to production of other commodities.

It has been proposed that direct income payments be given to farmers seriously affected by rapid technological changes. While this may alleviate the low income situation with some farmers, it may retard the adjustments that eventually must take place in labor, land, and capital resources. Otherwise maladjustments may accumulate and either income payments will need to be increased or incomes will continue to be depressed.

Demand-Expanding Programs

Such programs as school lunch, domestic consumer subsidies, foreign trade programs, and development of new uses in agricultural products, are not for purposes of influencing mobility of human resources in agriculture. It might be said that to the extent they expand demand they would alleviate the need and pressure for transferring farm labor to nonfarm jobs. Even if demand and production were more nearly balanced, underemployment would still be large in farming. Changes in technology require recombination of the resources in farming. Most of it involves substitution of capital for labor and therefore requires a transfer of labor out of farming if we are to have most efficient combination and use of resources.

Demand-expanding programs alone will not solve the so-called farm problem. Other programs to facilitate labor adjustment will be needed to complement these demand-expanding programs. Changes and shifts in demand require changes in the combination of resources even within the farming sector of the economy.

Supply-Restricting Policies

There are a number of procedures which have been used or are proposed for restricting farm production or supplies. These include marketing quotas, compulsory crop land adjustment or allotments, voluntary land retirement, and some form of capital or new technology rationing or restrictions. This also might include direct programs for transferring labor out of farming. At most they require restriction in supply of production resources, some more than others.

Marketing Quotas. The use of marketing quotas is not a direct approach to facilitate labor mobility. However, it can have some influence on the labor resource. Some difference would occur if the quotas were transferable or negotiable. If they are effective in reducing production, greater underemployment in farming (maladjustment of labor) likely will result. If the same farm labor is left in farming, each unit of labor will be less productive or efficient. Negotiability of quotas may encourage more mobility and adjustment. Those farmers who are able to buy or obtain additional quotas will have the advantage. Those unable to obtain quotas may be encouraged to move out of farming faster, and the sale of their small quotas may help finance their transfer. Tenant farmers and croppers especially might be forced or squeezed out more quickly. On the other hand, the older, less able farmers who have limited resources may hang on longer if prices are held up for them, even though with low production their incomes are held up only slightly. Young farmers may have more difficulty in getting started because they will have to obtain sufficient quotas and this will represent additional investment.

With negotiable quotas it could be expected that areas with the most comparative advantage would have a reduction in labor mobility and those with less comparative advantage would have more labor transferring out. In other words, good areas would bid away quotas from poor areas. This would likely raise problems in certain communities as to support of social, educational, and other services as well as the prospects for local business. The volume of products moving through local marketing channels, as well as the volume of farm supplies to farmers, would be reduced in the disadvantaged areas. This might reduce opportunities for farm labor to obtain employment close by in related agricultural industries. Such adjustment in labor and production is probably important for general progress of society; but it might mean that complementary programs, some of which might deal directly with adjustment of the labor resource, would be necessary.

Compulsory crop land adjustments or allotments. To reduce the land resource devoted to crop production, compulsory allotments might be used. This is not a direct approach to labor adjustment. There would be a difference in the effect on labor resources depending on whether or not allotments were transferable. With transferable allotments the effect on labor would be similar to the effects with marketing quotas. The farmer unable to obtain more allotments would tend to be at a disadvantage.

Voluntary land retirement program. About the only difference between a voluntary land retirement program and a compulsory program is that payments to farmers would be high enough to cause enough of them to volunteer retirement of their land. This is not a direct approach to labor mobility, but it would have considerable influence in encouraging transfer or retirement of labor from farming.

Some research has been done bearing on the conservation reserve, a type of land retirement program. Wallace Barr and others at Ohio State University are completing a study in this area, and their preliminary findings indicate that labor mobility is facilitated by the conservation reserve. The primary objective of the conservation reserve has been to reduce the land used for crop production. However, reduction of farm labor can be considered an important byproduct. It encourages older farmers to retire sooner, and it encourages some part-time farmers to quit cropping the land. Many of these continue to live on the farm and do the maintenance work required under the conservation reserve. However, it was found that the farmers, other than the part-time or older farmers, who do not have an off-farm job opportunity, are very slow to enter the conservation reserve. Many of them indicate they will not use the conservation reserve until they find other employment. There is some evidence that availability of the conservation reserve may encourage a few farmers to search for other employment and to train for other employment sooner than they would otherwise.

It is questionable whether the conservation reserve can help middle aged farmers with very few resources of land and capital to move out of farming. According to the Ohio studies, these farmers are not generally attracted to the conservation reserve. Many of them who would transfer to nonfarm work have not been able to find such employment. Often the amount of land they have to put in the conservation reserve is so small that their returns would still be low and possibly be reduced.

There is some evidence that, with the 28 million acres now in the conservation reserve, those farmers have been pulled out of farming who are easiest to attract. It might be more difficult to obtain labor transfer with the conservation reserve as the amount of land in the program is stepped up to 60 or 80 million acres. This raises a question as to the effectiveness of different methods of land retirement, particularly as to whether parts of individual farms or whole farms are retired and how much it is concentrated in better land or marginal areas. The success of a land retirement program will depend considerably on its effect on and relationship to farm labor transfer. It is highly important to have complementary programs dealing with transfer of labor out of farming to go along with any expanded land retirement programs.

It is important that broad complementary planning and development programs on land, water, labor, and capital resources be initiated. This would be related to a greatly expanded rural development program. Land and labor resources cannot be dealt with entirely separately. We have failed to stress the importance of having a number of concurrent programs that are complementary within a broad frame of development.

Farm labor transfer program. Proposals have been made for a direct farm program to increase and speed up farm labor transfer to nonfarm jobs as a means of improving welfare and income of all farm people, both those remaining on the farm and those transferring to some other job. Such a program would have about four main parts: (1) Financial assistance – grants, loans, or both – to farmers desiring to change occupations; (2) expanded services of employment agencies for farm labor to test, counsel, and place those who want to transfer to nonfarm jobs; (3) special training programs for nonfarm jobs, including vocational and trade and industrial training as well as how to make social and living adjustments when transferring to new communities; (4) expansion of occupational guidance programs for farm youth, including occupational opportunities and personal qualifications for success.

An explanation of this type of program is made in the publication entitled "Fewer Farmers," by Riley Dougan, published by the Farm Foundation and the Center for Agricultural and Economic Adjustment.[1]

A study is being completed by Reginald Harlan and others at Ohio State University on willingness of farmers in a southern Ohio county to move from farming. Only about 22 percent of the farmers were really satisfied to remain as they were as farmers or part-time farmers. Another group of 33 percent said they were not satisfied but were too old to do much about it. About 43 percent said they were willing to take training for off-farm jobs if they have the opportunity, and most of them were willing to travel 20 to 25 miles to take this training.

In this study about 15 percent of the farmers would move if they could obtain a nonfarm job. About 33 percent said they would sell or rent their farm and move to take a nonfarm job if their moving expenses were paid.

This study and other studies indicate that there are many farmers who would transfer from agriculture if they had opportunity to do so. It also indicates that there are many rural people who are eager to develop skills so they can more readily compete for nonfarm jobs. Apparently we need more vocational, industrial, and trade schools in local areas, and these would have a strong impact on labor transfer and efficient use of human resources. These could be combined with junior colleges and high schools, or they might be separately operated. These should be for all people, including rural and urban, who need training.

A direct labor transfer program should be complemented by

[1] This is one of a series entitled, "The farm problem – what are the choices?"

an expanded educational program on farm management and adjustment for the remaining farmers. Greatly improved management training will be needed by future farmers if they are to operate larger and more efficient farm business.

With a direct mobility program farm labor transfer could be speeded up considerably, perhaps as much as doubled. These programs likely would do more to improve incomes of farmers remaining on farms as well as those who move to other occupations than any other policies. It would enable us to continue progress in technological advancements in agriculture. It would benefit the rest of society in that the progress and advancement of technology would be encouraged with improved quality and skills of labor, both in and outside of farming. It would increase productivity of our total labor force.

The importance to agriculture of national economic growth and full employment cannot be overstressed. It would be desirable for us to include as an objective of employment policy the mobility of underemployed labor off the farm. Employment opportunities off the farm must be available if our farm policies include the transfer of farm labor to nonfarm work.

I believe the greatest problem in agriculture is the adjustment of human resources. Unless we adopt policies to speed up mobility of farm labor, society will force upon us programs which may retard and stifle economic progress and growth. We have been too timid to discuss labor mobility and strongly advocate programs and means to achieve ends which we know are desirable. Much more research and educational work is urgently needed on mobility and adjustment of our human resources.

II. DISCUSSION

The first point considered is the political feasibility of direct action to increase mobility. There is considerable consensus that direct action to increase mobility would receive strong political resistance. Mr. Fernbach has indicated that in "sending" communities, businessmen were the focal point of this strong resistance, while in the receiving communities, organized labor tended to resist direct action. It is generally agreed that Congress is very sensitive to this resistance.

Mobility of labor would help in that sector of agriculture where the income problem is the problem of low output per farm. There are strong doubts as to whether an increase in mobility would help on the aggregate output, price, and income problem. It is generally agreed that transfer of labor would probably be effective only if the transfer continued to the point where labor became a limiting factor. Under these circumstances, transfer of labor would induce extensive farming and might have some effect on output.

The discussion then moved to consideration of whether positive supply control was needed in commercial agriculture. There is no consensus that such definite action as positive supply control is needed, nor is there agreement on the means for bringing it about.

The following points are generally agreed upon.

1. Government policy on supply control has conflicting aspects. There is a reasonably close balance in the amount of money spent on supply control for American agriculture and on the amount of money spent that would tend to increase output. Output-increasing expenditures include such things as the Agricultural Conservation Payments and Land Reclamation.

2. Some nonfarm uses of agricultural land, such as recreational use, might be politically acceptable. In some limited areas recreational use of agricultural land might absorb almost as much labor input as farming now does.

Some of the following points are raised in connection with positive supply control.

1. Area development might or might not contribute to positive supply control. In some places it might actually compete with supply control. Mr. Fernbach has indicated that if area development was to be acceptable to organized labor, it would need to be on the basis of expanding enterprise, not on the basis of encouraging industry to move in because of low cost labor.

2. There is some disagreement with the expression vigorously stated by Mr. Garver that the supply control problem should be handled primarily by relying on competitive prices and resource allocation.

3. The question is raised as to why we have moral judgments against curtailing education and technology and yet consider that land retirement is perfectly appropriate as a positive means of supply control. We need to consider carefully the social goals of supply control. Is the social goal of supply control based on the idea that we simply cannot adjust rapidly enough to technological progress and, therefore, we must intervene to reduce the income impact of technological progress on farmers? If this is the case, then policy should recognize that adjustment and positive supply control action should be related to each other.

As a summary the following two points can be made:

1. Programs have not been designed to promote mobility.
2. Perhaps we can have positive policies for education and training, for full employment, and for area development which would have indirect effects on the mobility of agricultural labor.

Workshop Session: Chairman, **A. L. BERTRAND,** Louisiana State University; Resource Person, **JAMES S. BROWN,** University of Kentucky; Recorder, **MURRAY A. STRAUS,** Cornell University

Chapter 20

Programs Related to Family and Community Adjustments As Affected by Mobility Needs

I. PRESENTATION: James S. Brown

DISCUSSIONS IN THE CONFERENCE implicitly focused on the "agricultural heartland." There are vast differences between regions, and it is important to differentiate both facts and policy according to region. At the same time, since contemporary American society constitutes a single national social and economic system, the most effective types of policy consider both the unique features of each region and the interrelation of regional and national economy. In short, we need to make policy on a national level, but policy which is regionally differentiated and flexible. More specifically, Dr. James S. Brown recommended that:

1. Each region must prepare its people for participation in a national society, but they must do so in ways appropriate to the region.
2. Policy must be oriented to full development of human potentialities. This requires looking at the needs of agriculture and industry as means rather than ends in themselves.
3. The metropolitan region should be a major unit for research and policy since it represents the kind of ecological structure which now dominates the American scene.
4. The southern Appalachians are a region of chronic, severe depression. Prosperity elsewhere in the nation merely affects the relative depth of depression in this region. Programs for this

area need to help the population prepare for migration and to migrate most efficiently.

5. The idea of the economy as a manageable unit subject to government intervention for purposes of stability or stimulating growth is now widely accepted. Hence, there is favorable climate for programs which are needed to enable the family and community to adjust to agricultural changes.

Using eastern Kentucky as an example, a number of these points were illustrated. The great problems in a region such as this are human problems, and not technological problems. In eastern Kentucky, 40 percent of the population has left in 10 years. Hence, motivation to economic betterment via migration can be assumed since these people are closely attached to their local communities. Although the area is agriculturally marginal and although there is heavy out-migration, the felt need on the part of the local populace is for agricultural specialists to re-establish the region agriculturally — a clearly impossible task.

Despite this continued local demand for agricultural aid, and despite the reflection of this demand in congressional and other federal level pressures, the Kentucky extension service is embarking on a new program for eastern Kentucky. This program is partially supported by a grant from the Kellogg Foundation for 10 specialists to serve the 10-county area. Even in this program, six of the specialists are agriculturists and only four are specialists in what might be called human development: counseling and guidance and community development. Moreover, the program has run into interdepartmental jealousy and competition necessitating formation of the State University Committee to form policy and guide the program.

A major obstacle to working in this area is extreme localism and familism. Agents in the area have difficulty making use of local formal organizations since relatively few exist. A primary task of an agent is therefore to teach the idea of formal organization. Similarly, the school system has until recently been so localistically oriented that it is difficult to use it as a vehicle for change. The smallest schools, which are in the areas having the greatest need for guidance counselors, are those least able to afford them.

II. DISCUSSION

Additional examples, problems, and policy recommendations are listed below by topic or policy under two major headings.

A. Policy Objectives, including: 1. The Primacy of Human Goals, 2. The Needs of Migrant and Minority Groups, and 3. Depressed Area Programs; and B. Program Procedures, including: 1. Organizational Structure, 2. Educational Reorganization, and 3. Program Costs.

A. Policy Objectives

1. The Primacy of Human Goals. American agricultural policy has been oriented to protecting the family farm, whereas the real objective is to protect and foster the family. The farm comes into the picture as an inherent objective insofar as it fosters family and community well-being.

The importance of this principle is illustrated by the almost opposite types of extension programs needed in eastern Kentucky and most of southwestern Washington. Both areas offer very limited possibilities for agricultural production, and in both areas the population seeks technical agricultural aid from Extension. In neither case would it be wise for Extension to provide much encouragement for fulltime commercial farming. But in southwestern Washington there are numerous industrial employment opportunities which permit people to remain on the land despite their demonstrated (and even self-acknowledged) inefficiency as producers. In this situation, Extension can and should provide technical assistance because it helps the population concerned achieve the essentially noneconomic goals which they seek in part-time farming, without interfering with their aspirations for reasonable income and level of living. On the other hand, for Extension to encourage and facilitate this kind of subsistence farming in eastern Kentucky would provide a major block in achieving a reasonable income and level of living which the people of that region also desire. This is because supplementary employment is not available and seems unlikely to become available. Hence, the limited resources of Extension in such an area should as much as possible be focused on what Brown has called the human development task. In short, policies and programs to aid family and community adjustment must not be phrased in terms of helping people move out or helping people stay but rather must be aimed toward developing their fullest human potential whether this implies migration or not.

Preservation of community life must not be viewed as an end in itself, but rather as a means to human development. In a changing society some communities are bound to decline as others rise. It is important not to attempt to preserve an obsolete community structure if this means, as it often does, thwarting other important needs and aspirations of the population concerned.

One problem in this connection stems from the fact that community sentiments are strong and are directly expressed as felt needs; other needs may not be so immediately perceived and expressed, even though they are of at least equal or greater importance. Consequently, agencies must plan and act not only in terms of felt needs of the population they serve but also in terms of objectively determined needs as indicated by careful research and program discussions.

2. Migrant Worker and Minority Group Needs. Although the major focus has been on relatively stable agricultural population, the migrant labor group is a sizeable one, much in need of assistance. Developments in agricultural technology indicate this will remain a sizeable segment of the farm population. We are therefore denied the easy out of simply ignoring this group until they are technologically obsolete.

Minimum standards of wages and working conditions must be established, not only for the sake of the migrant workers themselves but also as a means of aiding one of the most underprivileged groups of children in American society. The impact on children belonging to a migrant worker family is particularly great in the crucial area of education. Local schools cannot be expected to be able to meet the many difficult problems concerning this group without outside technical and financial aid.

Programs for family and community adjustment must be explicit in formulating objectives and assigning resources to meeting the needs of Negro and Spanish-speaking farm people.

3. Depressed Area Programs. Availability of new nonagricultural employment opportunities (both industrial and governmental) is probably considerably less than the needs of small communities. In such a situation it is wasteful to have thousands of local community "industry committees" compete with each other for the scarce supply of new plants. At the same time, since it is generally less expensive and less disruptive to bring industry into a community than to move people out, efforts in this direction must continue. Isolated local community effort, however, should be coordinated with or replaced by a more rational and effective system involving at least state level, and preferably national and regional level, programs designed to bring industry to these communities. Such state and national programs cannot confine their role to advertising and soliciting new industry but must carry out objective studies of local community needs and resources.

In part, this approach is coming in the Area Development Act which will probably be passed by the next Congress. However, since the needs of small communities for development are less dramatic than those of depressed major industrial areas, there is danger that the small communities' needs and resources will be overlooked in the implementation of such an act. Consequently, a development program for small communities is recommended. Such a program must be adequately supported by research and, as noted above, must be careful not to attempt the impossible task of preserving all small communities.

This does not mean there is no room for local initiative, only that such local initiative can be best employed when coordinated on a state regional or national level, and when carried out with the assistance of non-local specialists.

Two examples of the effective use of local resources assisted by non-local specialists were described. The first of these is the "farm family vacation plan" developed in a low income southern Ohio county with the aid of the Ohio Extension Service. The 11 families in this program grossed over $1,000 each during the summer and also provided other local income. Similarly, but in a more general frame of reference, is the program of the Michigan Extension Service in upper Michigan. In this area, agents have been appointed to provide technical aid to facilitate development of the tourist industry.

B. Program Procedures

1. Organizational Structure. There has been a general questioning of the ability of existing agencies to carry out the kinds of programs needed. The problem is seen as involving not so much the technical adequacy of personnel in the existing agencies, but rather their ability to free themselves from obligations to long-established kinds of programs, in order to devote resources to the new programs. The Agricultural Extension Service seems particularly rigid in this respect despite the flexibility of enabling legislation and numerous statements of good intent and need for a reoriented extension program. There is some indication that the Home Demonstration Branch of Extension can be more readily oriented to programs of family and community development, and efforts in this direction should be intensified.

Creation of a new agency directed to human resource development in rural areas has been suggested. Such an agency should be supported by both state and federal governments and should have a very broad range of functions and a high degree of flexibility including:

1. Funds to grant to regional, state, and local agencies to foster their own development and adjustment programs.

2. Direct administrative responsibility for carrying out area adjustment and development programs where such direct action is required.

3. Responsibility for coordination of the work of existing agencies.

4. Research on general problems of local community adjustment and development.

5. A Service Research Department to provide service research (i.e., community surveys of various sorts) for local development programs.

It is extremely important that such an agency be established with the primary, if not the exclusive, objective of human resource development. If this is not made explicit, there is danger that the more tangible problems of agricultural technology and marketing will pre-empt the time and resources of the agency. The experience of the Iowa Center for Agricultural and Economic Adjustment is instructive in this connection. The Center had been established for 3 years and had held numerous conferences before the first one devoted to human problems in agricultural and economic adjustment was held.

In planning for and carrying out any program of family and community adjustment, it is important to involve as many established agencies and institutions as possible, both at the local and higher levels. The church and school systems particularly are institutions which must be consulted and integrated into action programs to maximize the effectiveness of such programs.

A pervasive organizational problem to be faced in carrying out programs of family and community adjustment is the fact that the institutional structure of the society seems to be predicated on the assumption of an unchanging society. Both people and agencies seem to act on the basis of a geographic and social stability which does not exist. They make the implicit assumption that if a certain meliorative effort is successful, stability will be achieved. Instead, any new agency which is established, or attempts to reorient existing agencies, should be based on the assumption of continuing social and economic change. The search for stability in a contemporary industrial society appears to be illusory and pointless. It should be replaced by an orientation which accepts inevitability of rapid change and searches for ways of using these changes to maximize human welfare and potential.

2. Education Structure. We now have a national or at least a regional labor market. The term "labor shed" has been used. One implication of this high rate of labor mobility is that areas

of labor production or supply are not the same as those of labor demand. This raises an important educational problem since the areas of labor production tend to have an educational system which does not adequately prepare people with the skills and orientations needed for successful adjustment in the labor market into which they will move. Moreover, since these tend to be low income areas with small scale educational units, existing organizational structure of education practically precludes providing many out-migrants with the kind of education and training they need for maximum utilization of their talents.

As a result of the factors listed above, there is need for federal aid to education. In addition to federal funds, the following kinds of organizational changes are important steps, whether carried out under local or higher level initiative:

a. The educational structure needs to be more adequately rationalized into larger scale units. This means not only more consolidation but also more "area schools" to provide an adequate population base for provision of specialized services and education.

b. Educational leaders must be drawn into and utilized in any program of area development.

c. A greatly increased number of guidance personnel must be trained and, above all, placed in small community schools. Both training and provision of guidance personnel for small community schools will very likely require subsidization since, as noted previously in this workshop report, the schools in areas most needing a guidance counselor tend to be those without one.

3. Allocation of Costs. There is general agreement with the viewpoint expressed in Schultz's paper, namely, that there are costs as well as benefits involved in economic progress and that some of the benefits must be used to reimburse those who bear the brunt of the cost factors. Within this framework, the costs of programs for family and community adjustment can be regarded as part of the investment costs for economic progress. Consequently, such programs are viewed as having economic justification as well as inherent worth.

Workshop Session: Chairman, **RAY SOLEM,** Minnesota State Employment Service; Resource Person, **HERBERT PARNES,** Ohio State University; Recorder, **JOHN TURNBULL,** University of Minnesota

Chapter 21

Improving Functioning of Nonfarm Labor Market As Related to Mobility Needs

I. PRESENTATION: Herbert Parnes

THE THESIS I should like to advance is that the problem of encouraging transfers from the farm to the nonfarm labor force is conceptually identical with the problem of minimizing structural unemployment generally. The labor market policies appropriate to stimulating out-migration from agriculture are fundamentally the same as those that would facilitate the re-employment of nonagricultural workers whose jobs have evaporated as the result of technological changes, shifts in consumer demand, geographical migrations of industry, or similar developments.

Despite the basic similarity of the problem in the two cases, there are, to be sure, certain characteristics of agricultural employment that may make solutions somewhat more difficult than for the nonagricultural labor force. In the first place, technological change and demand inelasticities have manifested themselves in agriculture principally in underemployment rather than in total unemployment, which is the more typical manifestation in the nonfarm sector of the economy. In agriculture, unlike other lines of economic activity, a large majority of the working force consists of the self-employed and their families; they are made aware of the market's unfavorable assessment of their productive contributions not through lay-off notices but through returns that are inadequate compared with those obtainable in other employments. Secondly, the psychological and sociological bonds between farmers and their work may well be stronger than those in most other lines of activity. The decline of employment in buggy-whip manufacturing was probably not complicated by sentiments of attachment to it as a "way of life"! As the result of these two differences, economic stimuli to occupational movement are perhaps less sharp and resistances to mobility more pronounced among agricultural workers than among other occupational groups that may become victims of structural changes in the economy.

Nevertheless, the labor market policies that are relevant to encouraging mobility would appear to be the same whether one is concerned with depressed sectors of agriculture or with geographical, industrial, and/or occupational pockets of unemployment among the nonagricultural labor force. In both cases, there is the necessity either of facilitating the geographic movement of workers into areas where jobs are available or of encouraging the creation of jobs in the areas of underemployment or unemployment. Whichever of these approaches is relied upon — and they are obviously not mutually exclusive — there is also the problem of facilitating occupational mobility. Occupational shifts are, of course, inherent in the movement of workers out of agriculture. In the nonfarm sector, whether jobs are brought to workers or workers brought to jobs, there is no assurance that the new jobs will involve the same occupational skills as the old.

The foregoing conceptual framework makes the possible approaches to the problem almost self-evident, and a more or less standardized set of proposals are commonly alluded to in the literature on both farm and nonfarm labor markets.[1] As a basis for discussion, I shall list them with little or no elaboration:

1. Developing and making available more adequate labor market information, both within and among local labor market areas. Labor market information, in this context, refers not only to availability and characteristics of current job opportunities, but also to longer run trends that are likely to affect career opportunities in various lines of work. Information on other aspects of the environment in communities where there are job openings — e.g., housing, school facilities, living costs, etc. — might also be helpful.

[1]See, for example, the various papers in Studies in Unemployment, prepared for the Special Committee on Unemployment Problems, United States Senate, Government Printing Office, Washington, D. C., 1960. For discussions of labor mobility in agriculture, see D. Gale Johnson, "Labor mobility and agricultural adjustment"; C. E. Bishop, "The labor market and the employment service"; and Vernon W. Ruttan, "The potential in rural industrialization and local economic development" in Earl O. Heady, et al. (eds.), Agricultural Adjustment Problems in a Growing Economy, Iowa State University Press, Ames, 1958.

2. Developing more extensive and more effective programs of aptitude testing and vocational counseling so that fewer "mistakes" are made in job choices both by youth entering the labor force and by older workers who wish to change careers.
3. Developing free training and retraining programs to facilitate shifts of workers from declining to expanding lines of work.
4. Providing financial assistance in the form of loans or grants to overcome economic obstacles to geographic relocation.
5. Providing financial assistance for subsistence during periods of training and also during the period of unemployment that may accompany transition into a new job. The latter program already exists, of course, for most of the nonagricultural labor force in the form of unemployment insurance, but neither self-employed farmers nor agricultural wage earners are covered.
6. Encouraging (either through financial inducements or through regulation) location of new industrial facilities in areas of underemployment or unemployment.
7. Discouraging or prohibiting discriminatory hiring practices that create special problems for particular groups of workers, primarily older workers and members of minority racial groups.

Although the foregoing are the usual prescriptions for reducing levels of frictional and structural unemployment, and, for reasons that I have indicated, seem to me to be equally appropriate for encouraging out-migration from agriculture, it must be emphasized that none of them can be effective in the absence of full employment conditions. More adequate job information, for example, is desirable because it should hasten and make more efficient the process of matching up unemployed (or underemployed) workers and jobs that are waiting to be filled. But clearly it cannot do this in the absence of high levels of employment opportunities. The most important single policy prescription for increasing the mobility of agricultural and nonagricultural workers alike is to promote higher levels of employment than we have experienced during most of the post World War II period.

Full employment is important not only for the obvious reason that movement into jobs cannot occur in their absence, but also because, even when individuals do know of jobs, the economic risks of making geographical moves in order to take them are considerably less in a tight labor market than in a loose one. When a worker gives up a job to take a new one, or when an unemployed worker leaves his community to take a job elsewhere, he does so with the knowledge that he will be at the bottom of the seniority roster in the new establishment and the first to be laid off in the event of cutback. In a tight labor market, where other jobs are abundant, this is not nearly so threatening a prospect as it is when jobs are relatively scarce. Even when out of work, an urban worker may prefer to remain unemployed in his own community rather than to gamble on becoming unemployed in a strange one.

Levels of unemployment, alone, do not tell the whole story. The incidence of unemployment is very uneven, being much greater among young workers, those without skills, those with low educational attainments, and nonwhites. These are precisely the groups who have been, and will doubtless continue to be, represented in disproportionately large numbers among those who move from farm to nonfarm work. Finally, to compound the difficulties, certain trends in labor force size and composition during the present decade will, given the levels of unemployment we have had, tend to restrict opportunities for shifts from farm to nonfarm work. One of these is the prospective change in age composition. The proportion of young workers in the urban labor force will increase substantially as the result of the high birth rates of the 1940's and 1950's, reducing the need for young recruits from rural areas. Moreover, skill and educational requirements of nonfarm jobs will increase as unskilled and semiskilled jobs decrease in relative importance and skilled and white collar jobs become a large proportion of the total. Thus, we may expect increasing difficulties in matching qualifications of potential farm migrants with the requirements of existing jobs. These factors suggest higher levels of employment may be required even to maintain past levels of farm to nonfarm migration.

No matter how successful we may be in maintaining full employment, and even if all the programs mentioned were to be implemented, it is virtually certain that there would still be substantial immobilities among the agricultural labor force. The rationale underlying the outlined policy proposals is that differentials in economic reward will produce movement if only labor market frictions and economic barriers to mobility are eliminated or reduced. The fact is that impediments to mobility are not only economic, but psychological and sociological as well. Among urban workers, it is well established that the fear of a "leap into the unknown" and a reluctance to sever ties with friends and associates are powerful restraints on voluntary job changing even within a local labor market area, to say nothing of shifts from one community to another.[2] One would suppose that these factors operate even more strongly in the case of the agricultural labor force, since the shift from farming to urban work involves a plunge into an entirely new cultural environment.[3] We do not know how important the psycho-sociological barriers to mobility are relative to the economic barriers. There is a large, albeit decreasing, reverse flow of workers from nonfarm to farm employment each year.[4] Whether these represent largely persons who had previously moved in the opposite direction, and, if so, whether their return to the farm is dictated primarily by economic or by psychological maladjustment in their urban environments, we cannot be sure.[5] This is a challenging field for research, because answers to these questions would permit us to judge the extent to which the kinds of policies outlined above can be reled upon to increase desired forms of mobility.

II. DISCUSSION

Four major points of view arose from discussion of the Herbert Parnes chapter. These include:

1. That while agriculture can be viewed as a depressed economy, from which labor mobility should be encouraged, it also has a geographic dimension and hence can thus be viewed as a depressed area (or series of areas). This suggests that approaches to solving the problem may involve moving industry in as well as moving people out.
2. That, in line with the above illustration, the "farm problem" has many facets which require specific delineation if an intelligent attack is to be made upon them. Phrased another way, there is a need to break the problem down into its various components if rational solutions are to be devised. For example, different mobility problems are involved for (1) self-employed farmers, (2) unpaid farm family workers, and (3) agricultural wage earners.
3. Alternative solutions to the problem may involve different

[2] See Lloyd G. Reynolds, The Structure of Labor Markets, Harper and Bros., N. Y., 1951, pp. 76-112.

[3] Cf. Varden Fuller, "Opportunities and limitations of employment services and other informational aids," in Problems and Policies of American Agriculture, Iowa State University Press, Ames, 1959, p. 379.

[4] Ibid., p. 380.

[5] One study of farm migrants into Indianapolis found that a substantial minority of the migrants were sufficiently dissatisfied that they were hoping or planning to return to agriculture. E. D. Smith, "Nonfarm employment information for rural people," Jour. Farm Econ., Vol. 38, pp. 813-27.

cost-benefit relations. This in turn may require that society make basic value judgments. For example, if it can be shown that full employment encourages mobility from agriculture (desirable) but also causes upward pressure on prices (undesirable), which approach does society choose? (Or, how much of each?) In addition to judgmental issues, measurement decisions may also be involved, either independently, or as a basis upon which the value judgments need be based. Thus, what are marginal social benefits as against costs of moving people out of agriculture as compared with moving industry in? In some cases it may not be possible to make the measurement.

4. Each of the above three points is oriented to agriculture as the issue in direct focus. But, in turn, agriculture is but one of many problems which have a common base; namely, how does one adjust to change?

Answers to the above questions are not easy to come by. However, some generalizations include the following:

1. Agriculture can be regarded as an economic activity in which underemployment is the rule rather than the exception. Additionally, there are many geographical agricultural pockets in which an industrial labor force could be mobilized readily. If one can assume (probably with safety) that capital is more readily mobile than labor, a case can be made for plant expansion in rural areas. If this were new plant expansion (and hence net) there need not be any costs incurred in other communities where the company operates but where it did not construct new plants, this assuming the new location is in total the most economic. (This is to be distinguished from the case where a plant moves and by leaving creates a depressed area.) The basic and unanswered problem, however, is how to get the plant into a rural area; mere labor surplus is not enough. Yet it is concluded that the decentralization process now going on is desirable socially as well as economically.

2. In addition to investment in plant, as in new areas, it is highly desirable to invest in people. Such investment — as in counseling and training — could go a long way toward helping humans adjust to economic change. This approach may, however, have a variety of inherent difficulties: How can one go into an area already losing population, with a counseling program designed to encourage further out-migration? Yet these obstacles must be met if the problems are to be attacked.

3. Investment in plant and people is basic to solving the problems of agriculture. But various institutional practices may be of considerable help. Thus extension of unemployment

insurance coverage to agriculture might expedite desirable mobility in that it would reduce the security fears of migration. (An interesting — and unwanted — side effect may develop here: the receipt of unemployment insurance might deter an individual from leaving a given community.) Extension of employment service activities in rural areas would be useful, if for no other reason than that of increasing the flow of information upon which job choices are made.

4. In general, "the earlier the better" as regards investment in human resources or the development of institutional arrangements to facilitate mobility. This simply suggests that the earlier the person can be counseled or trained, the better the results: It is wiser to counsel a high school youth than a man of 50. Hence there is considerable logic to the Four-H Career Exploration programs as one case in point.

All the above notwithstanding, several problem areas remain to plague any approach which seeks to solve the problems at hand. These include the following:

1. In some areas we may simply not be able to measure (now or ever) the benefits and costs of various alternative approaches. Hence it may be necessary to make decisions based upon social judgment. For example, in plant movement, it may be utterly impossible to measure the marginal social gain of the area into which the plant moved as compared with the marginal social loss of the area which it left. Here additional research might help little if at all.

2. In other cases it may not now be possible to ascertain forces which are imposing limits upon our ability to solve the problems at hand. Thus, there are socio-psychological impediments (about which we know little) to mobility. Here additional research would help; our inabilities arise not out of the inherent measurement difficulties of the problem but rather out of our lack of knowledge. This we should be able to remedy.

The agricultural problem is multi-dimensioned and hence requires a multi-pronged attack for its solution.

Index

www.ingramcontent.com/pod-product-compliance
Ingram Content Group UK Ltd.
Pitfield, Milton Keynes, MK11 3LW, UK
UKHW020206290926
15470UKWH00001B/34

9 780837 175843